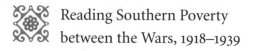 Reading Southern Poverty
between the Wars, 1918–1939

Reading Southern Poverty between the Wars, 1918–1939

EDITED BY RICHARD GODDEN
AND MARTIN CRAWFORD

The University of Georgia Press • Athens and London

© 2006 by The University of Georgia Press

Athens, Georgia 30602

All rights reserved

Set in Minion by Bookcomp, Inc.

Printed and bound by Thomson-Shore

The paper in this book meets the guidelines for
permanence and durability of the Committee on
Production Guidelines for Book Longevity of the
Council on Library Resources.

Printed in the United States of America

10   09   08   07   06   C   5   4   3   2   1

Library of Congress Cataloging-in-Publication Data

Reading southern poverty between the wars,
1918–1939 / edited by Richard Godden and
Martin Crawford.

    p. cm.

Includes bibliographical references and index.

ISBN-13: 978-0-8203-2708-2 (cloth : alk. paper)

ISBN-10: 0-8203-2708-5 (cloth : alk. paper)

1. Poverty—Southern States—History—20th century.

2. Southern States—Economic conditions—1918–

3. Poverty in literature.   I. Godden, Richard,

1946–   II. Crawford, Martin, 1948–

HC107.A13R38 2006

305.5'69097509042—dc22   2005036669

British Library Cataloging-in-Publication Data available

CONTENTS

Poetics in a Poor Place

ACKNOWLEDGMENTS

 This volume of essays grew out of a colloquium held in September 2000 under the auspices of the David Bruce Centre for American Studies at Keele University (Keele, Staffordshire, U.K.). We are grateful to all present—paper-givers, moderators, and other participants—in what turned out to be a stimulating and convivial meeting. The colloquium brought together specialists in the study of southern history and literature; conversation was easy and its intellectual tread more purposeful than we had a right to expect. The editors also wish to thank Robert Garson, then director of the David Bruce Centre, for his support and organizational acumen, and to express appreciation to the current director, Axel Schäfer, for continuing financial and other assistance. Finally, we are pleased to acknowledge the patience and encouragement shown the project by University of Georgia Press editors, notably Derek Krissoff and Nancy Grayson.

We are proud to dedicate this volume to our friend and colleague Stuart Kidd, who died on 25 September 2005.

RICHARD GODDEN
MARTIN CRAWFORD

INTRODUCTION

 At the start of their study of global hunger, Jean Dreze and Amartya Sen express a truism with force: "Life has been short and hard in much of the world, most of the time. Deprivation of food and other necessities of living has consistently been among the causal antecedents of the brutishness and brevity of human life." They note, however, that during the twentieth century, "the enormous expansion of productive power" had ensured that chronic hunger was a political decision.[1] In the South, between the world wars, that decision stemmed from the imperatives of a structural contrast, evidence of which, although a matter of tendencies, is extensive. Any North/South listing of antitheses, for the interwar years, would include at least urban/rural, high wage/low wage, consumption/subsistence, credit/debt, and free labor/coerced labor. The last is perhaps crucial, being the nub of a systematic contrast in regimes of accumulation. In the North, managed production, consumption, and distribution (or partial Fordism) ensured the cultural pervasiveness of the shop window, itself a function of a general rise in postwar wages. Contemplating the department store window, the worker whose national average wage increased by 14 percent between 1922 and 1929 could not have known but might have guessed that the financial growth of corporations in the same period averaged 286 percent. In effect, northern capital learned the equation, "Pay them more, sell them more, prosper more," with an emphasis on the last two injunctions.[2] Consequently, in a modification of Leuchtenburg's claim, "ten years after the war conspicuous consumption had become a [northern] mania"—one in which most middle-class wage earners, equipped with credit, could afford to participate, while all the region's workers might window-shop (hence *partial* Fordism).[3] As the Lynds put it of Middletown—their "mid-channel sort of American community"—"more and more of the activities of living are coming to be strained through the bars of the dollar sign."[4]

In the South, a region having a high percentage of agricultural labor (much of it given over to what are euphemistically called "cash crops"), the dollar sign was an uncommon filter, since most rural workers worked in or close to debt. Stuck at the foot of a one-runged agricultural ladder, the southern laboring class, unlike their northern counterparts, did not, in the early 1920s, become consumers equipped with wage packets. From the end of Reconstruction (1877) to the New Deal (1933) and the onset of war (1941), sharecroppers and tenants were a far more important labor source in the production of southern staples than were waged workers. In 1909 more than 70 percent of plantation land was operated by tenants and croppers, though even that figure probably underestimates the role of tenants and croppers in cotton production.

A survey from 1920 has more than 80 percent of cotton land farmed under some form of tenant agreement.[5] In the 1930s commentators described tenants as "virtual slaves" held "in thrall," subjected to "almost complete dependence" and "incapable of ever achieving but a modicum of self-direction."[6] They were wrong: black or white, those who farmed on shares were not slaves, but neither were they "free." Dependency, grounded in debt, rather than autonomy, guaranteed by a wage, defined the social relations through which they were required to live their lives, at least until the New Deal pushed labor from the South and increased the bargaining power of those who stayed.

In effect, to deploy Gavin Wright's crucial distinction, the South, until well into the 1930s, existed as "a low-wage region in a high-wage country"—a regional enclave in which a premodern regime of accumulation (at least from the point of view of labor mechanisms) existed as an extractive opportunity, or interior colony, for northern capital.[7]

The simplification is deliberate in order to make the comparative point that structural disparity between North and South should be understood as a primary source of southern poverty. The economists Dreze and Sen detail particular "elementary concepts" through which the construction of poverty may be understood. These involve "boom famine" or poverty surrounded by affluence, the vulnerability of those who "possess no means of production excepting their own labor power," "environmental degradation [as it] poses a grave threat to the livelihood of the rural population," and the often disastrous role of government in effecting the employment options of the poor.[8]

Dreze and Sen offer an appropriate framework through which southern immiseration can be detailed. Both regionally and locally, conditions of rural economic destitution were manifest. This process began well before the end of World War I, but the 1920s saw a dramatic fall in personal incomes in the South, from 62 percent of the national average at the beginning of the decade to 55 percent at its end.[9] Since the figure masks an expansion of the urban economy, the concomitant seriousness of conditions within farm society is plain. Hunger was by no means equitably distributed throughout the region; nonetheless, as the nation boomed during the 1920s, it is fair to say that the South hungered. Statistics for hunger and consequent demographic change can be made to tell many stories. For example, African Americans moved north as the Great Migration continued; whites increasingly sought work opportunities in the new economies of the Southwest. Both drifts of population evidenced a shift from the rural/farm to the urban/industrial sectors. This economic migration reflected worsening conditions in the older economies of the South, economies primarily dependent upon agricultural staples.

Workers who stayed in the declining economies exemplify what Dreze and Sen see as hunger within plenty. The condition of such workers was particularly tenuous, given that not only did they "possess no means of production excepting their own labor power" but, given prevalent conditions of tenancy within the agricultural sector, their labor power did not readily yield a living wage, nor could it easily be transferred to alternative forms of employment. Even outside the plantation belt, the inadequacies of labor power were all too visible. Appalachian farms, for example, had reached the limits of self-sufficiency prior to 1919, but the Depression era also saw a significant loss in off-farm employment—in mines, mills, and lumber—on which farm families had depended in large numbers for secondary and sometimes primary income.[10]

With rural employment generally at low or no wage in a nation of increasing wages, as Gavin Wright indicates, the dominant employer in the South, the planter-landlord, necessarily adopted coercive measures to inhibit labor loss. As an Arkansas sharecropper put it in 1939, "De landlord is landlord, de policeman is landlord, de shurf is landlord, everybody landlord, en we ain't got nothin'."[11] Moreover, the laborer had nothing in an increasingly degraded environment, not least because his labor lord, having taken long-term profits from cheap labor, saw no value in investing his accumulations in technological innovation. Soil impoverishment, deforestation, and erosion were simply the visual symptoms of a structural underinvestment that made it virtually impossible for the rural poor, black and white, low country and upcountry, to do anything but get poorer or quit.

Given that between the wars it remained in northern interests to retain the South as a resource, both in terms of raw materials and potentially in terms of labor, relations between the region and the federal government were at best preservative of the status quo. On the face of it, our claim looks contrary: we appear to ignore the manifest and sustained governmental intervention undertaken during the New Deal. Despite many programs, it remains the case, however, that, in the words of Dreze and Sen, "inflexible governmental policies undermin[ed] the power of particular sections of the population to command food." Reflecting on the 1930s experience in the South, the historian Jack Temple Kirby notes that the New Deal agricultural and welfare programs "brought both succor and suffering."[12] In 1933 the Agricultural Adjustment Act sought to stabilize farm incomes by raising commodity prices; in practice, the measure financed the plowing under of crops and resulted in large-scale eviction of tenants, which rapidly led to the demise of sharecropping as the characteristic form of agricultural employment in the plantation belt. In effect, federal modernization undertaken in ignorance of or indifference to local power relations enabled the dispossession and impoverishment of a class.

Long term, New Deal interventions enabled the modernization of southern agriculture: federally prompted inflows of capital financed the enforced outmigration of rural labor. The landowning class shifted its pattern of dependency from traditional labor to northern capital, while the tenantry, increasingly landless and welfare-dependent, waited on the wartime pull of northern employment needs to renew its great migration.[13] By the end of the period we examine, the southern rural economy had been transformed. With capital in place in the immediate postwar years, the landowning class could finally invest in the chemicals and machinery that would oust the mule and the man behind it. Whereas the undoubted technological and managerial transformations that resulted from the Great War drove Fordist innovation in the industrialized North, nothing remotely equivalent occurred in the South. Arguably, the southern owning class simply persisted in its long counterrevolutionary pursuit of profit by means of cheap coerced labor, a pursuit begun under slavery. At the close of World War II, on the other hand, the protracted and deferred modernization, which is central to the period examined in this book, entered its final stage.

But introductions should not give the game away, and neither will this one. Comprehensiveness is not our aim here: for example, the complex politics of leftist cultural production might be focused through an account of the American Communist Party's involvement with the Southern Tenant Farmer's Union, ably documented by Donald H. Grubbs. Alternatively, we might have pursued unionism to elaborate James Cobb's concern for the failure of the region's industrial workers to engage in militant action to redress the sectional wage imbalance.[14] Other chapters might have been solicited, but our interest was in drawing readers into new ways of thinking about the representation of southern poverty by setting side by side contributions from the disciplines of literature, history, and cultural history. For example, in one of the chapters on poverty management, Vivien M. L. Miller tells us how the cotton field might effectively be understood as an extension of the region's penal institution. Similarly, in their preoccupation with intrusive surveillance, two chapters on Farm Security Administration (FSA) photography demonstrate that even an ameliorative federal response to the poor involved elements of policing and thus coercion. The diverse institutional practices through which labor was controlled should necessarily be understood as informing the cultural representation of the laborer. Thus, cross-disciplinarity helps readers recognize opportunities through which particular social and historical practices, as they intersect, may be brought into relation.

OUR INTRODUCTORY PURPOSE has been to provide a structure within which the following essays can be read. Structure can be understood in two ways: as a comparativist sketch of the region's unique economic specificity, and as a principle for organizing this book. The first part, Photograph and Punish, departs from the visual imaging of the poor, not least because popular perception of southern immiseration, then and now, relies on a set of very familiar images. Those images, as we have argued, are devices for the cultural and political management of poverty, the subject of the second part. They are also elements in the way in which poverty is recollected, as discussed in the third grouping. Poetics, as it occurs in the title of the fourth part, Poetics in a Poor Place, indicates how narrative strategies for writing poverty take their form from tensions between contending historical impulses, which might generically be constructed as modernization and its resistance.

The essays chosen and their arrangement as chapters in this book seek to make visible what most strove not to see between the wars. Blindness to chronic and persistent poverty (a cultural facet of what Preze and Sen describe as the "elementary concepts" through which poverty is made) involves veneration for particular terms and mistrust of others. Among the terms that hide hunger are "land," "farm," and "family"; among the terms that draw the poor from hiding are "city," "mobility," and "money." Ted Ownby's overview explores the shared assumption of writers on the left and right that the region had "farm people, not poor people." As American culture gave itself over to the viewpoint of exchange and the generalization of commodity consumption, it became increasingly difficult to hold to such a belief. Stuart Kidd, taking issue with prevailing interpretations of the FSA project, explores image production rather than consumption and maps how photographic subjects unheroically resisted appropriation within the New Deal's "tangled administrative web." The work of the FSA as addressed by Siobhan Davis, in imaging the rural poor for northern consumption, contributed to the visualization of a tenant class as manageable Americana grounded in nineteenth-century values of pioneer individualism rather than the twentieth-century realities of economic oppression.

The contradictory existence of a low-wage region in a high-wage nation requires not only that poverty be visually constructed with care but also that it be managed attentively. Throughout the period between the world wars, what most emphatically distinguishes the South from the North remains its reliance on coercive patterns of labor. In the second part, Poverty Management, Vivien M. L. Miller's work makes clear the link between coercion on the soil and coercion by the state: the chain gang and the prison farm are simply salutary and corrective images of a systemic dependence on bound labor. Even in institutions that might be thought to represent the modern, the factories in the fields, the economic need to maintain a subsistence wage system meant that workers and crucially their children, despite sporadic resistance, remained bound rather than free. Clive Webb and Andrew Warnes describe how white educational and black nutritional deprivation equally ensured the continuity of dependency on both sides of the racial line.

The changed conditions in the postwar South, particularly the release of black labor and its migration northward, altered political trajectories and modified structures of feeling. Where previously memory recalled the farm, the family, and the land—and forgot the poor—the emergent demands of modernization threw up new objects to be remembered (Poverty Remembered). John C. Inscoe, in focusing on finally acknowledgeable class distinctions, reveals how memory goes where the economy has already gone, enabling the genre of southern white middle-class autobiography to serve the cause of racial liberalism. Similarly, James C. Giesen's account of the creation of "Nate Shaw," suggests that All God's Dangers is best understood not as an account of cropping under coercion but as a contribution to the civil rights canon.

In Poetics in a Poor Place, the final four chapters discuss specific literary texts that are perhaps best understood as generated by the kinds of economic and social imperatives that the previous chapters have clarified. In his account of Grace Lumpkin, Richard Gray addresses the force of upcountry religion as a cultural residue that modifies an emergent class consciousness among the Gastonia strikers: a linked archaic emphasis guarantees that the agrarian inclination among southern scholars keeps Lumpkin's To Make My Bread out of the southern canon. Arguably, Peter Nicolaisen's concern for the presence of Spenglerian glorification of the soil in the work of Elizabeth Madox Roberts and Ellen Glasgow might be traced to the historical demand that agricultural workers stay in their place, a place that is ideologically comforting if it is conceived as inseparable from the body, spirit, and value of the worker. In contradistinction to Gray and Nicolaisen, John T. Matthews looks at land from the perspective of money. He contends that the federal programs associated with the New Deal represent "powerfully disruptive forces of capitalist modernization in an impoverished pre-modern region." For Matthews, the desires of Erskine Caldwell's rural degenerates are specifically and traceably created by the unreal conditions established by the Agricultural Adjustment program. Finally, those conditions ensure that blacks will no longer be securely in place and, as Robert Brinkmeyer suggests, with blacks increasingly out of place, the southern place changes. To celebrate immobility and with it "land," "farm," and "family," is tacitly to celebrate segregation. To explore mobility and its related terms "money" and "city" is to discover new social forms, forms that require new modes of representation.

NOTES

1. Jean Dreze and Amartya Sen, *Hunger and Public Action* (Oxford: Clarendon Press, 1997), 3.

2. C. Frederick, *Selling Mrs. Consumer* (1929), quoted in Stuart Ewen, *Captains of Consciousness: Advertising and the Social Roots of the Consumer* (New York: McGraw-Hill, 1976), 22.

3. William E. Leuchtenburg, *The Perils of Prosperity* (Chicago: Univ. of Chicago Press, 1958), 200. We have substituted "northern" for "national." See Ted Ownby, *American Dreams in Mississippi: Consumers, Poverty and Culture, 1830–1998* (Chapel Hill: Univ. of North Carolina Press, 1999), for the limited penetration of the consumption imperative in the South in the period.

4. Robert Lynd and Helen Lynd, *Middletown* (New York: Harcourt & Brace, 1929), 80–81.

5. Jay Mandle, *Not Slave, Not Free: the African American Experience Since the Civil War* (Durham: Duke Univ. Press, 1992), particularly 33–43.

6. See respectively: Norman Thomas in a letter to Senator Robert F. Wagner, quoted in Vera Rony, "The Organizing of Black and White Farm Workers in the South," ed. Thomas R. Frazier, *The Underside of American History: Other Readings*, vol. 2, *Since 1865* (New York: Harcourt & Brace, 1971), 165; Charles S. Johnson, Edward R. Embree, and W. W. Alexander, *The Collapse of Cotton Tenancy: Summary of Field Studies and Statistical Surveys 1933–35* (Freeport NY: Books for Libraries Press, 1972 [1935]), 22; Charles S. Johnson, *Shadow of the Plantation* (Chicago: Univ. of Chicago Press, 1966 [1934]), 4; Harold Hoffsommer, "The AAA and the Cropper," based on 1934 interviews, and quoted in Johnson et al., *The Collapse of Cotton Tenancy*, 58.

7. Gavin Wright, *Old South, New South: Revolutions in the Southern Economy since the Civil War* (New York: Basic, 1986), 12.

8. Dreze and Sen, *Hunger and Public Action*, 5–9.

9. Dewey W. Grantham, *The South in Modern America; A Region at Odds* (New York: Harper Collins, 1994), 5.

10. John A. Williams, *Appalachia: A History* (Chapel Hill: Univ. of North Carolina Press, 2002), 315.

11. Quoted by Jack Temple Kirby, *Rural Worlds Lost: The American South, 1920–1960* (Baton Rouge: Louisiana State Univ. Press, 1987), 239.

12. Dreze and Sen, *Hunger and Public Action*, 6; Kirby, *Rural Worlds Lost*, 56.

13. Clyde Woods offers figures for levels of capitalization in Mississippi: "As a result of the AAA and other related programs, bank deposits, farm values, and farm incomes all doubled. Between 1933 and 1939, the federal government's direct expenditure in Mississippi totalled $450 million, while an additional $260 million entered state banks through ensured loans." *Arrested Development: Race, Power, and Blues in the Mississippi Delta*

(London: Verso, 1998), 143. The labor historian Jay Mandle notes, "America's entry into World War II marks the principal point of discontinuity in the black experience in the United States. Mandle, *The Roots of Black Poverty* (Durham: Duke Univ. Press, 1978), 84.

14. Donald H. Grubbs, *Cry from the Cotton: The Southern Tenant Farmers' Union and the New Deal* (Chapel Hill: Univ. of North Carolina Press, 1971); James C. Cobb, *Industrialization and Southern Society, 1877–1984* (Lexington: Univ. of Kentucky Press, 1984), 161.

Three Agrarianisms and the Idea of a South without Poverty

TED OWNBY

 Until the 1930s, most white southerners who wrote about social and economic life continued the pre–Civil War tradition of writing as if poverty did not exist. The two primary social ideals of the antebellum South—upper-class paternalism and yeoman independence—came close to denying the existence of poverty in the South. Plantation owners and their political and literary spokesmen repeatedly contrasted the poverty and insecurity of the northeastern and English working class to the relative material comforts and basic security of the South's bottom rung, who were slaves but were not poor. Those speaking on behalf of planters claimed that paternalism took care of the sick, the children, and the old, and that slavery allowed no unemployment and no fear of labor strikes, unions, radicalism, and revolution. And, they continued, since people on the bottom rung were enslaved and not poor, the South had few worries about urban theft, violence, and prostitution. The yeoman ideal held that poor whites, as travel writers and abolitionists called them, were not actually poor; they were merely independent and leisurely people who survived easily enough on hogs and chicken, fish and game, corn and potatoes. In much nineteenth-century writing, especially fiction, so-called poor whites were comic figures, but they were rarely limited in their resources or material lives.

There was no room for poverty in either the paternalist or the yeoman ideal. According to both, the South did not have poor people: it had farming people, and farming people could never truly be poor. A third theme, less prominent than the other two, suggested that southerners cared about the people in their communities and would act quietly to make sure no one went hungry.

In the 1920s and 1930s, most white southern writers of nonfiction were still repeating or reinterpreting these ideas. Conservative writers largely repeated them; writers on the left reinterpreted them, attributing the problem not to poverty or other economic factors but to something cultural. There were important

1

exceptions, but most white writers in the South were surprised in 1938 when Franklin Roosevelt, in his introduction to the *Report on Economic Conditions in the South*, called the region the nation's Number One economic problem.[1] A few southern writers, especially those who helped write the report, agreed with the president. But the majority of writers adhered to the popular assumption that farming people were not truly poor.

TO ENGAGE IN regional comparisons that risk gross simplification, American ideology outside the South envisioned the escape from poverty as a central theme. Poverty was always there to be overcome; Americans used the existence of poverty to show their individual strength in overcoming it. According to nineteenth-century ideals in the northern United States, cheap land, political freedom, state-supported free schools, and plenty of rewards for hard work were counted as reasons that most poverty should be only temporary. And it meant that people who remained impoverished beyond a few years as young adults must deserve their failure—they were lazy or ignorant or intemperate. In regional debates in the mid-1800s, political and moral leaders in the Northeast and Midwest made the frequent comparison that their poor had the freedom to rise above poverty through their own efforts, while the poorest people in the South, both slave and free, had neither incentive nor opportunity to do the same.

Outside the South, poverty policy underwent a dramatic change in the early and mid-1800s, in the historian Christine Stansell's words, "from meliorism to active reform." The practice of "outdoor relief," as it was called—giving money to local poor people who went about their lives as they chose—gave way to indoor relief, building poorhouses whose operators attempted to reform the characters of poor people. Antipoverty policy, especially in northeastern cities, developed a strongly moralistic side. Beginning in the 1840s, upper and middle-class men and, in the 1870s upper- and middle-class women, started aggressive policies of visiting the poor to set examples and teaching lessons of hard work, frugality, cleanliness, and sobriety.[2]

From the late 1800s into the 1930s, American poverty policy, especially outside the South, became more scientific and also more muddled. State governments, beginning with Massachusetts and New York, started the first welfare and unemployment bureaus and began to work, though unevenly, toward professionalization. By the turn of the twentieth century, early professional social scientists often argued that poverty was systemic, requiring both large-scale planning to address broad causes and individual casework to deal with poor individuals. Their language was less moralistic but also less certain about the solutions. Scholars have long criticized the relief and antipoverty programs of the New Deal as haphazard and even contradictory. Compared with other industrializing nations of the age, U.S. policies toward the elderly, and health and unemployment insurance seem at best limited and scattered and at worst uncaring and dominated by business.[3]

In the South, white men and women with power did not discuss poverty and how to escape it as moral issues and popular crusades. Southern state, county, and town governments did not design policies to uplift the poor through institutional reforms. Also, white southern intellectuals in the 1800s and early 1900s rarely celebrated an ideology of self-help as a moral achievement. Instead, they upheld some combination of those agrarian principles of paternalism, farmer independence, and rural community. In general, they avoided the topic of poverty, except occasionally to blame the policies of Radical Reconstruction. Until the 1930s, no white southerner wrote a regional version of Upton Sinclair's *The Jungle* (1906) or Jacob Riis's *How the Other Half Lives* (1890).

Until the mid-1930s, official policies of local and most state governments did little to address issues of poverty. Local governments ran poorhouses, but the limited information historians have about them suggests that southern poorhouses operated sporadically and with limited funds, usually combining the physically and mentally ill with people temporarily out of work. Significantly, they were often called not poorhouses or almshouses but "poor farms."[4] One study in the early 1920s found that Mississippi had forty-five poorhouses and poor farms, serving about five hundred people in the entire state.[5] The seventy almshouses in Georgia in 1920 served about a thousand people, most of them in cities.[6] The South's largest group of poor people in the late 1800s and early 1900s, traveling agricultural workers, received little help, especially because employers wanted them as a pool of poorly paid labor and also because state laws throughout the United States required people to live in an area for at least a year before they could receive aid.[7]

Southern states were the last in the country to form government departments to address issues of poverty. North Carolina was the exception, forming a board of charities during Reconstruction in 1869, reshaping it into a welfare department in 1917 and adding responsibilities through the 1920s and 1930s. Other states formed welfare departments in the late 1910s and 1920s, and several waited until the 1930s.[8] On some of the most important movements for relief, the South was notably slow to act. For example, in the early 1930s, every state in the country had programs to assist children without working parents—every state except Arkansas, Georgia, South Carolina, Mississippi, and also New Mexico. And when southern states started Aid to Dependent Children programs, their payments remained dramatically lower than in the rest of the country.[9]

These new agencies did little beyond distributing money mandated by New

Deal programs. Alabama, Tennessee, Louisiana, and Mississippi were among the last states to set up public welfare departments in the late 1930s. Their job was to give federal government money to people in three categories: elderly people who did not live with their families, dependent children, and the so-called needy blind. Some did a little more, overseeing foster homes and adoption agencies and administering New Deal jobs and Social Security programs. But they rarely gave money directly to local governments for so-called general relief, that is, poorhouses or direct contributions to individuals.

Southern state governments wrote about antipoverty efforts as if they were extremely limited, often doing only what the federal government required to receive its money.[10] For example, the reports of Louisiana's Department of Public Welfare were full of personal narratives describing the ways old, sick, and blind people came to need assistance and very often of their reluctance to ask for and accept that assistance. Mississippi's Public Welfare Department distributed surplus food to poor children in schools, but its reports often stated that poor people should not expect food as a right. Food distribution, the reports stressed, was supposed to help farmers, not the children of farmers. The tone of the reports, with only a few exceptions, emphasized the limits of what welfare agencies were trying to accomplish. Note that while state agencies were giving out millions of federal government dollars, they claimed that poverty was not a serious problem in their states.[11]

It seems fair to generalize that, until the mid-1930s, state governments worked according to those antebellum traditions that held that the South really had no problems with poverty as long as people could grow their own food. In Alabama, a report on children's homes in the state said the buildings and educational programs were not well developed, but their excellent gardens, probably their greatest "source of pride," made up for many deficiencies.[12] Even North Carolina, where the state welfare department had more employees and organization and arguably more of a social consciousness than elsewhere in the South, revealed an agrarian perspective on relief for the poor. State regulations required "every pauper . . . to plant a garden" and mandated community gardens and canning programs to be worked by and for people on relief.[13]

The clearest expressions of what southern people with power assumed about poverty or its absence lay in the actions and language of state departments of agriculture, especially their agricultural extension and home demonstration services. Starting in the early twentieth century, the nearly constant message of agricultural and home demonstration reports said that farming people were better off than anybody else because they could grow food and make things at home. Their slogans were "Live at Home" or "Stay at Home." In Alabama, the relief administration created in 1932 to deal with problems of the depression saw its job as fortifying such goals. Trumpeting that "Alabama families now have probably more food preserved than at any time in the history of the State," the Alabama Relief Administration said encouraging people to can food was "a particularly valuable contribution to the State's 'live-at-home' program."[14] The primary effort of agriculture departments, extension services and, often, relief administrations, was to slow the migration of the family members of farm owners to urban centers, although they were not too concerned about out-migration by farm laborers. Like agricultural reformers for generations, agricultural extension workers called for people to produce more food and clothing at home and not be lured by store-bought merchandise. The reports of these agencies resembled sermons about the general good of making things at home. They added one new emphasis, urging that with men out pursuing commercial agriculture, women had become the center of agrarian life, with special practical and moral responsibilities to uphold the principles of self-sufficiency through chicken yards, vegetable gardens, and homemade clothing.[15]

Farm laborers, sharecroppers, and tenants seldom appeared in the reports of state agriculture departments. When they did, state employees encouraged them to remain on the margins of the cash economy by growing more food and sewing more clothing. The clearest example of the agrarian nature of state policies toward African American workers lay in the official policy of the Negro Extension Service in Mississippi in the late 1920s and 1930s: "Take What You Have, and Make Do." Deep South agricultural extension service workers encouraged African American women to sew clothing from sacks, at one point organizing a parade of sack-wearing black women to the Mississippi state capitol building. That idea fit into the tradition of agrarian paternalism that said lower-class people were better off secure in their class positions than with ambitions for anything better, including more and better material comforts.[16]

One of the clearest illustrations of governments' assumption that farm work was best for potentially poor people lay in their creation of prison farms and prison plantations to deal with lawbreakers. Rationales for those farms and plantations stressed that people should work to feed themselves and suggested that the ability to farm was all people needed when they left prison.[17]

For decades, scholars have noted that the reforms that constituted southern progressivism were, by national standards, limited in scope. Southern progressivism tended to concentrate on urban life and a few specific issues: education, prohibition, child labor, health, and voting reforms that limited the numbers of voters. By the standards of much of the country, southern state governments in the early twentieth century did not do much. When southern progressive reformers addressed issues of rural life, they concentrated on agricultural high schools and farm and home demonstration work. Such reforms had the goal of keeping farm owners and their children content to be on the farm. In general, southern state governments practiced what we call a "policy of state agrarianism," in which people with power assumed that rural people could more or less take care of themselves.

TURNING FROM THE government reports to more systematic efforts to explain, defend, or criticize southern society, it is striking that until the late 1930s, southerners with power or close to those in power usually talked and wrote about farming, not tenancy and not sharecropping. Compared to the sophistication and popularity of proslavery arguments in the late antebellum period, one has to look hard to find arguments for the benefits of tenant farming in the early 1900s.[18] Although writers addressed issues of pellagra, child labor, chain gangs, lynching, racial segregation, and disfranchisement, both in criticism and defense of the South, they rarely addressed tenancy and poverty until the mid-1930s.

The clearest restatement of traditional definitions of a South without poverty came in the 1930 agrarian anthology, *I'll Take My Stand: The South and the Agrarian Tradition*, published in 1930. Some recent scholars have argued persuasively that we should not treat the twelve authors, known as Vanderbilt Agrarians because they were all connected with Vanderbilt University, as having set the agenda of southern intellectual life.[19] But we should see the Vanderbilt Agrarians as important figures because their language and concerns were similar to those of people with power. Their statement of conservative agrarianism showed the range of assumptions white southerners made about the virtues of rural life.

The authors of *I'll Take My Stand* assumed—assumed more than argued—that there was no poverty in the American South. The region had farm people, not poor people, and farm people could always feed themselves. The concept of poverty on the farm, they suggested, was not a meaningful term. Writing in the late 1920s, before the documentary fervor to publicize the extent and nature of sharecropping and industrial poverty, the Agrarians did not address issues of low incomes. In *I'll Take My Stand*, the word "poverty" appears only four times: twice in descriptions of economic conditions immediately after the Civil War, once in a description of tenant farmers, and once in a reference to the "poverty of the contemporary spirit."[20]

The historian in the group, Frank Owsley, became the leading proponent of a group of scholars who tried to disprove the idea that "poor whites" made up a significant part of the antebellum South. Angered by stereotypes rooted in the antebellum period, Owsley stressed that whites outside the planter class were not poor—they were self-sufficient yeomen "with centuries of country and farm lore and folk memory." Their "thoughts, words, ideas, concepts, life itself, grew from the soil."[21] Owsley and his Vanderbilt graduate students spent years in census reports and local land records arguing that prior to the Civil War most white southerners were not poor but were, in the titles of their works, "plain folk," "farmers," or "yeomen."[22] Those farming plain folk, according to Owsley, upheld two significant British traditions that flourished in the antebellum South. They were largely self-sufficient, and proud of it. Second, supportive community lives blurred the lines of work and play, as lively house raisings, musical corn-shuckings, and the pleasures of hunting and fishing disguised productive work as enjoyment.

The Vanderbilt Agrarians' approach to the economics of twentieth-century farm life lay in the tradition of farm language inherited from the nineteenth century. People were better off producing food and clothing at home, supported by their families and communities. If they had bad years, it was probably because they had been lured by the possibilities of farming for profits that could buy consumer goods. People who wanted more than they had went into debt, always a danger for farming people. The twelve Vanderbilt writers made a variety of agrarian arguments. John Crowe Ransom stressed the virtues of personal independence, offering a Jeffersonian image of lonely farmers resisting greed, consumer goods, and debt. Donald Davidson praised the virtues of rural community, believing the antebellum culture Owsley described lived on throughout much of the South. The elitist argument that industrial and not agricultural societies had poverty and its consequences was a key element for Lyle Lanier in "A Critique of the Philosophy of Progress." An industrial economy, Lanier wrote, led to periodic unemployment and growing anger of working people toward each other and toward people in power. "Hungry and maladjusted men, women, and children, in numbers that bid fair to increase, is one of the promises of industrialism for the future. . . . The logical outcome of these conditions is growing internal dissension and, eventually, revolution."[23] In Lanier's Hobbesian view, movement back to the farm, perhaps with the help of government policies, was the only way to avoid revolution.

Only one Vanderbilt Agrarian wrote directly about tenancy and sharecropping, thereby confronting the issue of rural poverty. In "The Briar Patch," Robert Penn Warren began by minimizing the material deprivation of slavery, in favor of its security. Slaves, he wrote, only had "the bare necessities, but their coming was certain." Warren wrote that some of the warm and human relations he saw in slavery continued in a different form under sharecropping, in which plantation owners saw their workers as whole human beings and not merely as workers. He used the language of traditional paternalism, describing life for farm workers as offering "a slow way" with "certain compensations."[24]

Warren worried particularly about interracial violence caused by competition when African Americans left the farm. African Americans, he said, would not benefit from industrialization, because employers used them only as strike breakers; their presence in or near factories only exacerbated resentment by the lower-class whites and contributed to those Hobbesian fears Lyle Lanier described.

More important for Warren was a point that lay in a long tradition of southern thinking: "In the past the Southern negro has always been a creature of the small town and farm. That is where he still chiefly belongs, by temperament and capacity; there he has less the character of a 'problem' and more the status of a human being who is likely to find in agricultural and domestic pursuits the happiness that his good nature and easy ways incline him to as an ordinary function of his being." Warren suggested that African Americans had moved from one agrarian ideal to another—from secure recipients of paternalism to secure, independent farmers. As slaves, he said, they had been content to be taken care of, and now in the 1920s, they had achieved "a certain degree of independence on the land," and Warren predicted they would achieve more independence in the future. He hoped the typical African American could make what he called "a decent living" and could find "his garden and his cotton patch pleasant enough to make him decline the offers of industrialism."[25]

In the nineteenth-century South, the leading proponent of the moral and material gospel of individualistic economic effort had been Booker T. Washington. For him, thrift, cleanliness, sobriety, and hard work all led up—up from slavery and up from poverty. But in *I'll Take My Stand*, Warren used Washington's ideas to argue that African Americans should be and could be content with what they had. Warren's argument sounds much like the doctrine of the Negro Extension Service: Take What You Have and Make Do.

The most aggressive pro-sharecropping argument came eleven years later with the publication of *Lanterns on the Levee: The Recollections of a Planter's Son* by Mississippian William Alexander Percy. Percy did not write his autobiography as a defense of sharecropping; in fact, he wrote that people he knew did not even know the word. He wrote instead as "a planter's son," and his book offered a defense of a social system that, according to Percy, offered noble ideals even as it was in decline. Percy was even harsher than the Vanderbilt writers in condemning the allure of mass culture and consumer goods, perhaps because he interpreted African American out-migration as coming in part from their hunger for new pleasures. Percy did not deny the existence of poverty in the South, but he said poverty should not exist on plantations run according to paternalistic principles. In the tradition of conservative thinking, he stressed the security he believed workers had on his family's Trail Lake plantation in the Mississippi Delta. "I watch the limber-jointed, oily-black, well-fed, decently clothed peasants on Trail Lake and feel sorry for the telephone girls, the clerks in chain stores, the office help, the unskilled laborers everywhere—not only for their poor and fixed wage but for their slave routine, their joyless habits of work, and their insecurity."[26] The "well-fed" African Americans became truly poor, he wrote, when they went off to Chicago dreaming of more money and more ways to spend it. Percy took some pride in describing the ways he and the declining number of other properly paternalistic plantation owners saved workers with problems with jail, alcohol, and bad times that came when they chose to leave the plantations.

CONSERVATIVE WRITERS DENIED the existence of poverty in the name of greater agrarian virtues, whether they dwelled on independence, community, or paternalism. It is more unexpected that a number of writers on the left had a difficult time viewing poverty as a central problem. Writers H. C. Nixon, W. J. Cash, and James Agee, all of whom criticized southern social life and economic conditions, did not concentrate on poverty as defined by limited resources, low incomes, or the inability to afford material comforts and pleasures. They mentioned poverty, but when they wrote about economic problems, they used traditional categories of southern thinking, addressing issues of farming independence and rural community far more than poverty. All three argued that farming people in an earlier day had something valuable that American society—including the South—in the 1930s and 1940s was missing. In that sense, they represent a third type of agrarianism—they were agrarians on the left.

The clearest example of a left-wing agrarian was H. C. Nixon. An unusual contributor to *I'll Take My Stand*, Nixon maintained friendships with several of the Vanderbilt writers even while he moved farther to the left in his stances on public policy. In his two most important books, *Forty Acres and Steel Mules* and *Possum Trot, Rural Community, South*—about his hometown in Alabama— he asked what was wrong with rural life, how to fix it, and how he envisioned connections between rural past and future.

The books are poorly developed. They bounce from policy suggestions to poetic descriptions of the beauties of rural community life, only occasionally connecting the two. Nixon recognized this, offering the folksy justification that one book "serves all things on the table at once, as is the long-standing dining custom in Possum Trot, and in corn-bread language, the reader is honestly urged to 'help yourself' to whatever you like best."[27] This approach shows

Nixon's aesthetic side. Although he was writing to convince readers of the need for new agricultural policies, he was also writing to celebrate the special virtues farm life once had and could have again.

Two points distanced Nixon from his friends among the Vanderbilt Agrarians. First, he wrote about poverty as a serious problem. Numerous blacks and whites in the Deep South not only had tiny homes, scarce furniture, and poor water, they also had poor diets and bad health.[28] The diet and health problems would have surprised and troubled all of the conservative agrarians, not just Will Percy, who was writing at the same time about the same people. The nineteenth-century belief that rural people could not be poor as long as they could grow vegetables was simply untrue. The second characteristic that divided Nixon from most of the Vanderbilt writers was that he was far more confident that government action could solve farmers' problems.

Nixon's agrarianism was liberal in his untroubled optimism about the possibilities of government programs for rural people and his goal of eliminating tenancy. He wanted to ban absentee landowning, and he supported government credit for tenants trying to buy land. Often he seemed a direct descendant of the populists, with their willingness to use government and their reliance on community institutions to fight for the right to own farms.

The most traditionally agrarian side of Nixon's thinking was his fascination with the rural community. H. C. Nixon, like the other Vanderbilt Agrarians, thought urban life had seduced small farming people away from their interests in one another. He worried that people, especially men, in small towns and rural areas identified themselves more with people in large towns than with their neighbors. He shared with extension service writers the notion that women were closest to the heart of southern agrarian virtue. He wrote that while his own father and all his male relatives grew more interested in goods and opportunities in the growing Alabama towns of Anniston and Jacksonville, his mother "continued to be preoccupied with children and grandchildren, with chickens and eggs and milch cows, with gardening and cooking, with rural gossip and healing the sick. She alone of the Nixon household of ten remained entirely rural."[29]

Nixon mixed aesthetics and community concerns with typical agrarian suggestions to get back to the land, diversify agriculture, and regain independence. He began one chapter, "What Could Be," in *Possum Trot* with no surprises: "Possum Trot could produce more milk and drink it. It could produce more food and eat it. It could provide more shelter and use it." Then, the surprise: "It could provide more beauty and see it." Cooperating to terrace land, reinvigorating local schools and churches, and building an intercommunity council to represent Possum Trot among other towns and villages were all ways to reinspire and rebuild a face-to-face community outside the economic hope-lessness and also the self-denigration of rural life in the 1930s. Nixon hoped to retire in neighborly Possum Trot to do four things: "Cultivate the soil. Cultivate the neighbors. Cultivate the neighborhood. Cultivate neighborly relations with the larger region." Nixon supported New Deal plans for resettling rural people into communities that incorporated everything from open-range hog farming to banjo picking, all under the benign guidance of government employees. Even when Nixon split with the more conservative Vanderbilt writers, he maintained an agrarian ideal not too far from that of Donald Davidson. Overcoming ten-ancy and rural poverty was just a small step toward the larger goal of restoring rural community life.[30]

The second author on the left to deal with poverty through old categories was W. J. Cash, in *The Mind of the South*. Cash would have been irritated to be de-scribed as an agrarian. He saw nothing attractive about farming itself, whether a life close to the soil or a life sustained by rural family and community.

Like H. C. Nixon, Cash mentioned the growing poverty of tenant farmers and the limited incomes of cotton mill workers. But, like Nixon, small incomes and limited resources did not strike him as poor people's greatest problems. Cash's indictment of cotton mill life was largely a denunciation of how it denied so many white southerners their birthrights of dreamy leisure and extravagant play. To understand what was going wrong in the early 1900s, one must return to Cash's interpretation of the antebellum South. With his typically hyperbolic language, he analyzed how the combination of slavery and available land domi-nated the thinking of antebellum white southerners. The ordinary farming free man had "freedom from labor beyond the wildest dream of the European peas-ant and the New England farmer," and beyond that, he would never have "the haunting specter of want. He would never actually go hungry; for the posses-sion of some sort of land and hence some sort of subsistence, you will recall, was almost universal."[31] In the rare moments when southerners lacked food, Cash said, their communities would not allow them to go hungry. Thus, Cash understood that free people in the South did not think in terms of poverty, and he said they were right.

Even more crucial were the consequences of having food and independence without having to work hard. Without having to struggle with the land or to struggle with rich people or poor people, the free southern man became "one of the most complete romantics and one of the most complete hedonists ever recorded." He "sat much on fences, dreaming." He grew comfortable "with mak-ing love, with dancing, with extravagant play." His "dominant mood" was "one of well-nigh drunken reverie." "To lie on his back for days and weeks, storing power as the air he breathed stores power under the sun of August, and then to explode, as that air explodes in a thunderstorm, in a violent outburst of emotion—in such fashion would he make life not only tolerable but infinitely sweet."[32]

These few outlandish phrases do not necessarily define Cash's perspective on farm life. Cash worked dialectically, always building arguments with counter-arguments.[33] Along with freedom and romanticism came the unchecked egos, violence, anti-intellectualism, and white supremacist thinking that damaged all people in the South. Still, it is impossible to read those lines about the infinite sweetness of life without believing that Cash wished he could have tasted that sweetness, enjoyed that well-nigh drunken reverie, and had some of those violent outbursts of emotion.

Cash interpreted tenancy and especially cotton mill work as a kind of lost sweetness. When he turned to mill workers, he started with their wages, but he quickly stressed, "It was not only that Southern wages were bad." Compared to generations who preceded them, their hours were longer, their work more tedious. "Here was a complete end for these people of that old wide leisure which the common male, at least, had commonly enjoyed in the South." Working indoors and working too hard led to unhealthy people who were defined solely by their work. He was horrified by physical conditions: "a dead-white skin, a sunken chest, and stooping shoulders . . . chinless faces, microcephalic foreheads, rabbit teeth, goggling dead-fish eyes, rickety limbs, and stunted bodies abounded."[34] For Cash, this represented a great decline from the healthy and well-fed farm people who never had to work very hard and sat on fences, dreaming.

Cash believed, as many historians today believe, that industrialism—what Cash called "Progress" with an ironically capitalized *P*—did not merely allow but actually enhanced some essential continuities from the farming South. Continuities included low-wage labor, an economic system resting on and reinforcing ideas of white supremacy, and a general lack of class consciousness and class conflict. Cash feared that economic change kept alive the worst of southern social life and killed off the best. The best parts were economic independence and the aesthetic possibilities it allowed. Like the Vanderbilt Agrarians, he did not see consumer spending as much compensation. Cotton mill workers, he said, now had the chance for store-bought tobacco, candy, and soft drinks, and some seem to have found those things satisfying. Candy and soft drinks were sweet, but Cash had in mind a deeper, more romantic, reverie-filled sweetness, so the brief pleasures of consumer goods represented a significant decline from something better.[35]

Cash was more critical than H. C. Nixon, and far more complex. But, like Nixon, he interpreted what was wrong with the modern South according to traditional categories, even if Cash's interpretations were more idiosyncratic.[36]

W. J. Cash might seem the epitome of southern idiosyncrasy if not for James Agee and Walker Evans's *Let Us Now Praise Famous Men*, published the same year as Cash's *Mind of the South* (1941). Agee and Evans went to Alabama in 1935 to document the nature of sharecropping for a piece for *Fortune* magazine. The immediate background was the effort by the Farm Security Administration to depict poor Americans sympathetically so a national audience would be compelled to help them. Evans's sixty-three photographs and Agee's feverish prose went far deeper than merely documenting the existence of poverty. Instead, they ended up attempting to portray the depth and beauty of the lives of rural poor people. Agee, at least, ended up believing those people probably had something a more comfortable and respectable America lacked. In that belief, the native of eastern Tennessee joined Cash and Nixon as agrarians on the left.

Unlike Cash and Nixon, Agee did not call on a vision of southern history to help him understand the sharecroppers he met and described. Like Cash, he was not a conventional agrarian. If the Gudger, Woods, and Ricketts families had ever known about agrarian traditions of independence, community, and leisure, they had forgotten them. Independence was out of the question. The phrase Agee imagines for the sharecroppers most often is, "How was it we were caught?"[37] The families worked not to feed themselves but to grow cotton that went to merchants and creditors.

Agee and Evans also saw nothing admirable about the place of the Gudger, Woods, and Ricketts families within their communities. Local people made fun of the families through the lens of the same stereotypes of ignorance, isolation, filth, and sexual degeneracy that had long been common in literary stereotypes of poor whites. None of the families seemed to have the extended circle of family and friends so important to agrarian ideals.

Leisure was almost nonexistent. Agee began an important section titled "Work" with an attempt to describe the "complete awefulness" of the labor of sharecropping. He tried three times, first with a desperate air of pity: "the ends of this work are absorbed entirely into the work itself, and in what little remains, nearly all is obliterated." In his second effort, he emphasized the family as a working organism: "The family exists for work. It exists to keep itself alive. It is a cooperative economic unit." This section, which comes closest to humanizing the work lives of sharecroppers, described the yearly rhythms "as a heroic dance" with all the dancers knowing their parts.[38] But the parts end up enslaving the dancers, as the children who grow up working leave the home only to start the dance again with their own children. Finally, Agee portrayed the families' work more broadly with a detailed description of the cotton season. Cotton controlled the families; they did not control their work or their time.

But Evans and especially Agee strove to look beyond victimization. Agee bounced dramatically and breathlessly between the extremely painful and the surprisingly beautiful. One of Agee's persistent fears was that he was just another romanticizing journalist intrigued by rural people whose idiosyncrasies made them different from himself and his fascinated readers. More an outsider intruding in sharecroppers' homes than an insider who shared their background, Agee feared, perhaps above all, that he was using them as local color as writers and journalists and anthropologists had so long used poor people—holding them up to say, "behold, the bizarre world of the rural folk." Inspired by this fear, Agee put great energy into describing the positive features of the sharecropping families.

More than any other writer who addressed southern social life during the Great Depression, Agee wrote about beauty. He found especially beautiful the goods that people made themselves—hats made of corn husks, dresses made from feed sacks. Agee was amazed by the beauty in sharecroppers' homes. He loved their simple home decorations—what he called "altars"—that suggested a reverence for the most basic of all things to worship: survival. With his passion for overstatement, he tried to summarize his emotional response to their homes.

> Here I must say, a little anyhow: what I can hardly hope to bear out in the record: that a house of simple people which stands empty and silent in the vast Southern country morning sunlight, and everything which on this morning in eternal space it by chance contains, all thus left open and defenseless to a reverent and cold-laboring spy, shines quietly forth such grandeur, such sorrowful holiness of its exactitudes in existence, as no human consciousness shall ever rightly perceive, far less impart to another: that there can be more beauty and more deep wonder in the standings and spacings of mute furnishings on a bare floor between the squaring bourns of walls than in any music ever made.[39]

Agee's interest in the material lives poor people constructed outside store-bought, brand-name goods parallels the interests of all the writers discussed here. In their own ways, all feared or condemned consumer culture. Worrying about the moral consequences of capitalism and consumer culture is certainly not unique to the southern intellectual tradition. All sorts of intellectual movements in the twentieth century involved political radicals and cultural critics on both the left and the right who condemned consumer culture for its smugly amoral, politically distracting greed.[40] But Agee did not simply praise the families for their ingenuity in surviving or for retaining part of their traditional independence. To Agee, the sharecropping families he and Walker Evans documented were important not because they upheld admirable principles or represented a social type. Rather, they were important because, whether as subjects of photographs or as creators of intriguing home decorations, they made the world more beautiful.

It is helpful to see James Agee as the South's beat poet, predating by a few years most of the other beats. But as *the South's* beat poet, he looked for his great adventures not on the road but in sharecropping households in the rural South, not far from the place he grew up in eastern Tennessee. To him, families tied together by necessity, creating beauty where they could, sometimes even if they did not see it themselves, pursuing the basics of existence, knowing the immediacy of physical experience, and inheriting an uncomplicated approach to sexuality, provided as deep and powerful an encounter as he could imagine.[41]

IN 1958, C. VANN WOODWARD listed a "quite un-American experience with poverty" along with racism and military defeat as the defining points of southern distinctiveness. It would have been surprising for a white writer to make such a point a generation earlier, when so many white southerners were surprised and angered to hear the president describe their region as the nation's number one economic problem. It was later in the twentieth century that southern nonfiction writers began to portray poverty as central to regional identity. And it was later that so many began to embrace poverty—or, for many, memories of poverty—as a defining source of strength and endurance. For conservatives, that consciousness of poverty allows government programs based on the idea that any economic development is better than none.[42] For liberals, that consciousness encourages both government antipoverty programs and respect for the creativity and spirit of poor people. But that consciousness of regional poverty often seems so pervasive that we may assume southerners have always imagined themselves to be poor.

The Great Depression and especially the New Deal were turning points in white southerners' understandings of regional identity. The New Deal brought about a dramatic increase in outsiders' comments about the southern economy, a growing bureaucracy to deal with economic and welfare issues, and extraordinary levels of federal funding. In the South, some responded with anger and defensiveness, while others responded with great hopefulness. Take, for instance, the report of the Georgia Department of Public Welfare in 1938. According to department employees writing the report, the reorganization of the department in 1937 represented a monumental turning point. "Georgia for the first time took an active interest in the welfare of its citizens and divorced itself from a philosophy of government which had ignored suffering, destitution, and poverty." The report continued, "The depression brought the startling realization that the State was wholly without any adequate means of meeting destitution of any great number of citizens."[43] The department started closing local almshouses (replacing them with Social Security payments), stated that surplus commodities they were distributing were intended not only to help farmers but also to feed the poor, and used the term *federal funds* with great energy and excitement. From that perspective, recognizing the existence of poverty was part of a new point of view that would turn the force of government toward studying poverty and trying to end it.

There were, increasingly in the later 1930s and 1940s, southern writers who more squarely addressed the issue of poverty. Most obviously, a small but growing group of reformers emphasized the notions of developing, planning and economic balance as the keys to changing the southern economy. The economists and academics behind the *Report on Economic Conditions in the South* argued that the region needed more industrial jobs, higher industrial wages, higher agricultural wages, greater agricultural diversity, far less concentration on cotton, and a wider range of education and vocational training. Frank Porter Graham went from his work on the report to leading the first Southern Conference for Human Welfare, which upheld the document as a blueprint for regional change.[44]

The most prolific writer and teacher to emphasize that the South was underdeveloped—a less offensive, more sociological term than "poor"—was Howard Odum, who taught at the University of North Carolina. Beginning in the 1930s, Odum's writing started with the idea that the South needed to develop its various forms of capital more fully and efficiently. Odum's works were long, dry compilations of statistics, descriptions, and comparisons designed to show that the southern economy would benefit from fuller integration into the world's economic system.[45] Odum, unlike agrarians left or right, had no agrarian longing for the old rural community, or for agricultural independence, or for premodern leisure. In a 1940 address titled "The South at Its Best," he defined the region's best as "a growing South, a developing South, utilizing, developing, and conserving all of its resources in a balanced economy of, for, and by the people and of, for, and by all of the institutions."[46] Such a definition had no room for any use—whether creative or merely nostalgic—of memory and tradition.

Another group of southern writers believed southern poverty existed. Sociological and economic studies by Arthur Raper and Charles S. Johnson and Katharine Du Pre Lumpkin and Richard Wright—Wright's *Twelve Million Black Voices*—did not use agrarian assumptions, language, or categories.[47] All of those, significantly, dealt largely with African Americans. While some of those authors came too close to culture-of-poverty thinking for today's reader, all pointed to structural problems in the region's economic, political, and social systems, rather than seeing poverty as a secondary problem within a broader failure of the South to live up to its best traditions. Likewise, a small but growing number of agricultural radicals like Howard Kester wrote about and protested for dramatic economic change in the South. Kester, who helped form the Fellowship of Southern Churchmen in the mid-1930s before going to work with the Southern Tenant Farmers Union (STFU), wrote *Revolt Among the Sharecroppers* in 1936. Both the Fellowship of Southern Churchmen and the STFU labored to improve conditions for southern farming people, and both, significantly, never upheld old traditions of southern farm life as models on which to base reforms. Kester and other radicals knew agricultural poverty existed, and they worked to address it.[48]

But for writers like W. J. Cash, Herman Nixon, and James Agee, as for writers like Robert Penn Warren, Donald Davidson, Frank Owsley, and Will Percy, as for most people writing and working in southern governments, the South was not a land of poverty. To them the South was—or at least it had been and should continue to be—a land of farming people. And if there were problems, they found fault not in the poverty of farming people but in the fact that too many people were losing access to the special virtues farming people should possess.

NOTES

1. National Emergency Council, *Report on Economic Conditions of the South* (Washington DC: U.S. Government Printing Office, 1938).

2. Christine Stansell, *City of Women: Sex and Class in New York, 1789–1860* (Urbana: Univ. of Illinois Press, 1987), 34. On ideology and antipoverty practices in the northern United States in the 1800s, see Amy Dru Stanley, *From Bondage to Contract: Wage Labor, Marriage, and the Market in the Age of Slave Emancipation* (New York: Cambridge Univ. Press, 1998); Walter I. Trattner, *From Poor Law to Welfare State: A History of Social Welfare in America*, 6th ed. (New York: Free Press, 1999); Paul D. Boyer, *Urban Masses and Moral Order in America, 1820–1920* (Cambridge: Harvard Univ. Press, 1978); Alexander Keyssar, *Out of Work: The First Century of Unemployment in Massachusetts* (New York: Cambridge Univ. Press, 1986); Eric Foner, *Free Soil, Free Labor, Free Men: The Ideology of the Republican Party before the Civil War* (New York: Oxford Univ. Press, 1970); Michael Katz, *In the Shadow of the Poorhouse: A Social History of Welfare in America* (New York: Basic, 1986).

3. On the comparatively limited nature of U.S. welfare efforts, see Theda Skocpol, *Protecting Soldiers and Mothers: The Political Origins of Social Policy in the United States* (Cambridge: Belknap Press of Harvard Univ. Press, 1992); Edward D. Berkowitz and Kim McQuaid, *Creating the Welfare State: The Political Economy of Twentieth-Century Reform* (New York: Praeger, 1980).

4. See James H. Tuten, "Regulating the Poor in Alabama: The Jefferson County Poor Farm, 1885–1945," in Elna C. Green, ed., *Before the New Deal: Social Welfare in the South, 1830–1930* (Athens: Univ. of Georgia Press, 1999), 40–60; Roy M. Brown, *Public Poor Relief in North Carolina* (Chapel Hill: Univ. of North Carolina Press, 1928); Elizabeth Wisner, *Social Welfare in the South from Colonial Times to World War I* (Baton Rouge: Louisiana State Univ. Press, 1970); Pete Daniel, *Breaking the Land: The Transformation*

of Cotton, Tobacco, and Rice Cultures since 1880 (Urbana: Univ. of Illinois Press, 1985), 66–67; J. Wayne Flynt, *Dixie's Forgotten People: The South's Poor Whites* (Bloomington: Indiana Univ. Press, 1979), 37.

Funding of local relief was always limited. In 1922, North Carolina counties spent a total of about $14,600 per month on relief. In 1938, Tennessee's counties spent about $13,000 a month. In the early 1940s, Mississippi county governments spent about $4,500 a month on general relief. See Brown, *Public Poor Relief in North Carolina*, 133; Tennessee Department of Institutions and Public Welfare, *Report on Public Assistance and Direct Relief*, 1938, 155; Mississippi State Department of Public Welfare, *Public Welfare in Mississippi* 3 (1–3). Alabama's public welfare reports consistently mentioned that it gave out less money than most American states. Alabama, Department of Public Welfare, *Statistics*, monthly reports in the late 1930s.

5. Nathaniel Batson Bond, "The Treatment of the Dependent, Defective and Delinquent Classes in Mississippi," Ph.D. dissertation, Tulane University, 1924, 40–44.

6. Georgia Department of Public Welfare, *Georgia's Fight against Dependency and Delinquency*, 1921, 92–93. The number of almshouses in Georgia declined to fifty-eight by 1929, and dropped to thirty-three by 1937. See Georgia Department of Public Welfare, *Report*, 1929–1931, 23; Georgia Department of Public Welfare, *Report*, 1937–1938, 124.

7. See Cindy Hahamovitch, *The Fruits of Their Labor: Atlantic Coast Farmworkers and the Making of Migrant Poverty, 1870–1945* (Chapel Hill: Univ. of North Carolina Press, 1997), 128; Josephine Chapin Brown, *Public Relief, 1929–1939* (New York: Henry Holt, 1940), 18–19; George Brown Tindall, *The Emergence of the New South, 1913–1945* (Baton Rouge: Louisiana State Univ. Press, 1967), 480–82.

8. Tindall, *Emergence of the New South, 1913–1945*, 283–84; Brown, *Public Relief*, 23–24; Trattner, *From Poor Law to Welfare State*, 87–88, 223–26; Howard W. Odum and D. W. Willard, *Systems of Public Welfare* (Chapel Hill: Univ. of North Carolina Press, 1925), 173–74; Virginia Ashcraft, *Public Care: A History of Public Welfare Legislation in Tennessee* (Knoxville: University of Tennessee Record 50:6, 1947), esp. p. 12; Arthur W. James, *Virginia's Social Awakening: The Contribution of Dr. Mastin and the Board of Charities and Corrections* (Richmond: Garrett & Massie, 1939), 10–18.

9. On the importance of assistance to mothers in American social policy, see Skocpol, *Protecting Soldiers and Mothers*; Robyn Muncy, *Creating a Female Dominion in American Reform, 1890–1935* (New York: Oxford Univ. Press, 1991). On the South, see Skocpol, 456–65; Brown, *Public Relief*, 27–31; Trattner, *From Poor Law to Welfare State*, 225; Ashcraft, *Public Care*, 25–26.

10. On the substantial amounts of money the federal government was distributing through state governments for relief, social security, and jobs programs, see Roger Biles, *The South and the New Deal* (Lexington: Univ. Press of Kentucky, 1994); Bruce J. Schulman, *From Cotton Belt to Sunbelt: Federal Policy, Economic Development, and the Transformation of the South, 1938–1980* (Durham: Duke Univ. Press, 1994); James C. Cobb and Michael V. Namorato, eds., *The New Deal and the South* (Jackson: Univ. Press of Mississippi, 1984); Tindall, *Emergence of the New South*.

11. Mississippi State Department of Public Welfare, *Report*, 1936–1937; *Report*, 1937–1939; Louisiana Department of Public Welfare, *Report*, 1942–1943; *Report*, 1943–1944.

12. Lee Bidgood, "Child-caring Institutions and Home Finding," in Edward N. Clopper, ed., *Child Welfare in Alabama* (New York: National Child Labor Committee, 1918), 181. The author, a professor at the University of Alabama, said most children's homes tried to raise all of their food.

13. North Carolina State Board of Charities and Public Welfare, *Report*, 1930–1932, 55.

14. Alabama Relief Administration, *Two Years of Federal Relief in Alabama* (Wetumpka AL: Wetumpka Printing, 1935), 4.

15. Scholarship on home extension work in the South begins with Lu Ann Jones, "Revisioning the Countryside: Southern Women, Rural Reform, and the Farm Economy in the Twentieth Century," Ph.D. dissertation, University of North Carolina, 1996; Melissa Walker, *All We Knew Was to Farm: Rural Women in the Upcountry South* (Baltimore: Johns Hopkins Univ. Press, 2000); Lynne A. Rieff, " 'Go Ahead and Do All You Can': Southern Progressives and Alabama Home Demonstration Clubs, 1914–1940," in Virginia Bernhard et al., eds., *Hidden Histories of Women in the New South* (Columbia: Univ. of Missouri Press, 1994), 134–49; Janet Hutchison, "Better Homes and Gullah," *Agricultural History* 67 (spring 1993): 102–18.

16. Ted Ownby, *American Dreams in Mississippi: Consumers, Poverty, and Culture, 1830–1998* (Chapel Hill: Univ. of North Carolina Press, 1999), 104–8.

17. See David M. Oshinsky, *"Worse Than Slavery:" Parchman Farm and the Ordeal of Jim Crow Justice* (New York: Free Press, 1996); William Banks Taylor, *Down on Parchman Farm: The Great Prison in the Mississippi Delta* (Columbus: Ohio State Univ. Press, 1999); Alex Lichtenstein, *Twice the Work of Free Labor: The Political Economy of Convict Labor in the New South* (New York: Verso, 1996); Matthew J. Mancini, *One Dies, Get Another: Convict Leasing in the American South, 1866–1928* (Columbia: Univ. of South Carolina Press, 1996).

18. Most people would be disappointed by the book that seems to be the most energetic effort, *Studies in the Southern Race Problem* (New York: Doubleday, Stone & Co., 1908).

19. See, for example, Michael Kreyling, *Inventing Southern Literature* (Jackson: Univ. Press of Mississippi, 1998); Patricia Yaeger, *Dirt and Desire: Reconstructing Southern Women's Writing, 1930–1990* (Chicago: Univ. of Chicago Press, 2000).

20. Robert Penn Warren, "The Briar Patch," 249; "Introduction: A Statement of Principles," in *I'll Take My Stand: The South and the Agrarian Tradition, by Twelve Southerners*, ed. Louis D. Rubin Jr. (Baton Rouge: Louisiana State Univ. Press, 1977 [1930]), xliii.

21. Frank Lawrence Owsley, "The Irrepressible Conflict," in *I'll Take My Stand*, 69. Owsley developed the argument that the body of white southerners was not poor but plain in his *Plain Folk of the Old South* (Baton Rouge: Louisiana State Univ. Press, 1982 [1949]).

22. See Frank Lawrence Owsley and Harriet C. Owsley, "The Economic Basis of Society in the Late Ante-Bellum South," *Journal of Southern History* 6 (Feb. 1940): 24–45; Blanche Henry Clark, *The Tennessee Yeomen, 1840–1860* (Nashville: Vanderbilt Univ.

Press, 1942); Herbert Weaver, *Mississippi Farmers, 1850–1860* (Nashville: Vanderbilt Univ. Press, 1945).

23. Lyle H. Lanier, "A Critique of the Philosophy of Progress," in *I'll Take My Stand*, 150.

24. Warren, "The Briar Patch," in *I'll Take My Stand*, 247, 262.

25. Ibid., 260–61, 262, 263.

26. William Alexander Percy, *Lanterns on the Levee: The Recollections of a Planter's Son* (Baton Rouge: Louisiana State Univ. Press, 1941), 280.

27. H. C. Nixon, *Possum Trot, Rural Community, South* (Norman: Univ. of Oklahoma Press, 1941), vii.

28. H. C. Nixon, *Forty Acres and Steel Mules* (Chapel Hill: Univ. of North Carolina Press, 1938), 22–24; H. C. Nixon, "Social Security for Southern Farmers," *Southern Policy Papers*, no. 2 (Chapel Hill: Univ. of North Carolina Press, 1936), 1.

29. Nixon, *Possum Trot*, 56.

30. Ibid., 75, 82. For scholarship on Nixon, see Sarah N. Shouse, *Hillbilly Realist: Herman Clarence Nixon of Possum Trot* (University: Univ. of Alabama Press, 1986); Paul K. Conkin, *The Southern Agrarians* (Knoxville: Univ. of Tennessee Press, 1988).

31. W. J. Cash, *The Mind of the South* (New York: Alfred A. Knopf, 1941), 49.

32. Ibid., 52, 48.

33. See Michael J. O'Brien, *The Idea of the American South, 1920–1941* (Baltimore: Johns Hopkins Univ. Press, 1979), 213–16.

34. Cash, *Mind of the South*, 203, 204.

35. Ibid., 212.

36. For scholarship on Cash, see Bruce Clayton, *W. J. Cash, A Life* (Baton Rouge: Louisiana State Univ. Press, 1991); O'Brien, *Idea of the American South*; Richard H. King, *A Southern Renaissance: The Cultural Awakening of the American South, 1930–1955* (New York: Oxford Univ. Press, 1980); Charles W. Eagles, ed., *The Mind of the South: Fifty Years Later* (Jackson: Univ. Press of Mississippi, 1992); Paul D. Escott, ed., *W. J. Cash and the Minds of the South* (Baton Rouge: Louisiana State Univ. Press, 1992).

37. James Agee and Walker Evans, *Let Us Now Praise Famous Men* (New York: Houghton Mifflin, 1988 [1941]), 91.

38. Ibid., 320, 323.

39. Ibid., 134.

40. See Richard H. Pells, *Radical Visions and American Dreams: Culture and Social Thought in the Depression Years* (Urbana: Univ. of Illinois Press, 1998 [1973]). Pells discusses Agee on 246–51. See also Ownby, *American Dreams in Mississippi*, 130–48.

41. For scholarship on Agee, see Alan Spiegel, *James Agee and the Legend of Himself: A Critical Study* (Columbia: Univ. of Missouri Press, 1998); Mark A. Doty, *Tell Me Who I Am: James Agee's Search for Selfhood* (Baton Rouge: Louisiana State Univ. Press, 1981); Michael Lofaro, ed., *James Agee: Reconsiderations* (Knoxville: Univ. of Tennessee Press, 1982); Alfred T. Barson, *A Way of Seeing: A Critical Study of James Agee* (Amherst: Univ. of Massachusetts Press, 1972).

42. C. Vann Woodward, "The Search for Southern Identity," in *The Burden of Southern History*, rev. ed. (Baton Rouge: Louisiana State Univ. Press, 1968), 17; about Roosevelt, see Schulman, *From Cotton Belt to Sunbelt*, 50–54; on conservative thinking, see James C. Cobb, *The Selling of the South: The Southern Crusade for Industrial Development, 1936–1980*, 2nd ed. (Urbana: Univ. of Illinois Press, 1993).

43. Georgia Department of Public Welfare, *Report*, 1937–1938, 6, 11.

44. National Emergency Council, *Report on Economic Conditions of the South*; David L. Carton and Peter A. Coclanis, eds., *Confronting Southern Poverty in the Great Depression, "The Report on Economic Conditions in the South," with Related Documents* (Boston: Bedford Books of St. Martin's Press, 1996); Paul E. Mertz, *The New Deal and Southern Rural Poverty* (Baton Rouge: Louisiana State Univ. Press, 1978); Schulman, *From Cotton Belt to Sunbelt*; Linda A. Reed, *Simple Decency and Common Sense: The Southern Conference Movement, 1938–1963* (Bloomington: Indiana Univ. Press, 1991); John Egerton, *Speak Now Before the Day: The Generation Before the Civil Rights Movement in the South* (New York: Knopf, 1994).

45. Howard W. Odum, *Southern Regions of the United States* (Chapel Hill: Univ. of North Carolina Press, 1936); Howard W. Odum and Harry Estill Moore, *American Regionalism: A Cultural-Historical Approach to National Integration* (New York: H. Holt, 1938). On Odum's work, see O'Brien, *The Idea of the American South*, 31–93; King, *A Southern Renaissance*, 39–71.

46. Howard Odum, "The South at Its Best," an address to the American Association of University Women, Hotel Tutwiler, Birmingham, Ala., 4 April 1940, box 11, folder 632, Howard Washington Odum Papers, Southern Historical Collection, University of North Carolina, Chapel Hill.

47. See, for example, Charles Spurgeon Johnson, *Shadow of the Plantation* (Chicago: Univ. of Chicago Press, 1934); Arthur F. Raper, *Preface to Peasantry: A Tale of Two Black Belt Counties* (Chapel Hill: Univ. of North Carolina Press, 1936); Raper, with Ira DeA. Reid, *Sharecroppers All* (Chapel Hill: Univ. of North Carolina Press, 1941); Katharine Du Pre Lumpkin, *The South in Progress* (New York: International, 1940); Richard Wright, *Twelve Million Black Voices: A Folk History of the Negro in the United States* (New York: Viking, 1941).

48. Howard Kester, with an introduction by Alex Lichtenstein, *Revolt Among the Sharecroppers* (Knoxville: Univ. of Tennessee Press, 1997 [1936]); Robert Francis Martin, *Howard Kester and the Struggle for Social Justice in the South* (Charlottesville: Univ. Press of Virginia, 1991); Anthony P. Dunbar, *Against the Grain: Southern Radicals and Prophets, 1929–1959* (Charlottesville: Univ. Press of Virginia, 1981).

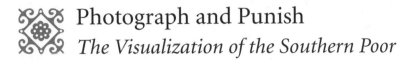

Photograph and Punish
The Visualization of the Southern Poor

Dissonant Encounters

FSA Photographers and the

Southern Underclass, 1935–1943

STUART KIDD

In 1938 *Look* magazine reported on the visit of forty-seven students from the senior class of New York's Lincoln High School to the rural South. The trip, funded by the Sloan Foundation, included visits to monumental New Deal projects in the region such as the Resettlement Administration's Greenbelt model town in Maryland and the Tennessee Valley Authority's Norris Dam in Tennessee. However, the purpose of the trip was not merely to admire the New Deal's achievements. The students were acquainted with the lives of those southerners for whom the New Deal's initiatives were intended, and to that end they "rubbed shoulders with sharecroppers" and "chatted" with a chain gang. They also helped renovate a Georgia sharecropper's cabin. Its appreciative owners "gasped" as their home was transformed and, for their part, the New York adolescents "found Georgia farm life much to their liking." Not only did they repair the cabin, they also strung fences, plowed with teams, and "ate heartily of hominy grits and eggs." The presentation of this condescending intrusion into poor people's lives in this manner suggests the degree to which the southern tenant farmer had become culturally established during "the depression decade." By inverting the conventional hillbilly-in-the-city narrative, the photo-story constructed a parable that could be read either as an affirmation of New Deal collectivism or as an example of back-to-the-land utopianism. By 1938, the "sharecropper narrative" had become amenable to generic experimentation.[1]

For a brief period during the 1930s, the southern underclass received an unprecedented amount of exposure in media that sought both sensational copy to illustrate the ravages of the Great Depression and affirmative imagery to reassure a nation threatened by social dislocation and on the precipice of global war. As such, the southern tenants' cultural status was ambiguous or contradictory. On the one hand, the rural poor represented "the nation's No. 1 economic problem" and the low incomes, poor housing, soil depletion, inadequate educational provision, and ill health in the South, which the rehabilitation programs of the Resettlement Administration (RA) and its successor, the Farm Security Administration (FSA), aimed to eradicate. However, the southern tenant also served as an icon of New Deal populism and symbolized more positive values. As a cultural symbol, "the common man/woman" embodied qualities of nobility, stoicism, and simplicity that resonated profoundly in a time of economic collapse. The southern underclass was a prominent component of the so-called cult of the people, which registered the New Deal's liberal politics, New Dealers' efforts to "democratize" American culture, and that also signified a national yearning for stability and harmony in a turbulent era.[2]

The photographs of the FSA contributed to the development of this ambiguous cultural imagery.[3] Directed by Roy E. Stryker, twenty photographers took more than 13,000 photographs of the South and its people between 1935 and 1942. The principal aim of the project was to cultivate public support for the economic and social programs of FSA's parent agencies, which needed to establish both the need for economic assistance and the worthiness of the needy and to do so by having stories and photographs published that highlighted poverty in the South. The inherent representational tensions involved in promoting the economic rehabilitation and cultural recuperation of the southern tenant were compounded by other aspects of the project's work. Whether blighted or beatific, the dramatization of the southern tenant was a product of the relentless, even indiscriminate, pursuit of publicity by information officers. The resulting photos were also inevitably refracted through the creative sensibilities of the photographers.

As a national icon, the southern tenant was the creation of the nexus between mass communication and New Deal publicity. Stryker and the FSA's regional officers were avid for publicity to promote their programs and to justify their operation. They colluded with newspaper and periodicals editors eager for dramatic copy, supplying images that highlighted the plight of the South's underprivileged. The Historical Section's photographs appeared under sensational banner headlines like "Poverty's Pioneers," "Uncensored Views of Sharecroppers' Misery," and "Is This America?" Such photographs established the popular image of the barefoot South and educated the national public to the need for remedial programs. During its early years, in particular, Stryker's Historical Section seemed to take a perverse pride in distributing images of "the more seamy side" of American life, and the group derived pleasure from the reaction of the "skittish" to them.[4] More positive studies of grateful farmers holding aid packages of seed, or of farmers, too poor to buy a mule, hauling their own plow with the assistance of the women of their families in the FSA archive were acquired from the Red Cross and the Wide World Press Agency. The Historical Section's photographers based the people's case on its humanity as much as upon material deprivation. Effective public relations required the reversal of a set of negative stereotypes about the South's rural poor that had become entrenched within American culture, and only a slight shift of emphasis was required to transform rural deprivation into rustic charm. Residents of isolated communities in Virginia's Blue Ridge, photographed by Arthur Rothstein before their evacuation to make way for Shenandoah National Park (fig. 1), served the See America First campaign to promote national tourism. Rothstein's photographs prompted the *Washington Post* to reflect that "Millions of Americans go abroad every year to see the 'quaint sights and people,' little realizing, apparently, that right in their own back yard the sights and people are 100% quaint as well as 100% American." When the *Washington Daily News* reviewed Walker Evans's *American Photographs*, which contained many images from the Hale County, Alabama, assignment with James Agee, the featured headline read, "This Our Native Land: America, the Beautiful."[5]

A symbiotic relationship developed between the Historical Section's operation and the creative input of its photographers, most of whom lived and worked in the metropolitan centers of the East and West Coasts. For them the American heartland, and the South in particular, was terra incognita. Traveling the country as government employees was revelatory, and the photographers' backgrounds did not prepare them for the levels of poverty and oppression they encountered. Recalling his first brush with "the nationwide problem" of tenancy, Russell Lee reflected that he was "shaken" and "angered," responses shared by colleagues who became motivated by a liberal idealism and commitment that gave point and purpose to their work. "There were many wrongs in our country that needed righting," Jack Delano reflected, "and I for one believed that my photographs would help to right them."[6] Photographers identified with the circumstances of their subjects partly due to their own struggles while on assignment. Southern landlords were often hostile to outsiders who wished to photograph their land and labor, and Carl Mydans recalled experiencing "frequent harassment and threat." Dorothea Lange was unwilling to make an extensive tour of the South during 1937 unless Stryker allowed her husband, economist Paul Taylor, to accompany her. She wrote: "I shall be travelling into areas which are disturbed with heavy valuable equipment making negatives of subjects that obviously will reveal what is wrong. I shall at times be unwelcome" (fig. 2).[7] The photographers' fleeting sense of personal jeopardy encouraged an affinity with subjects for whom such jeopardy was often chronic. Yet they were often inspired

Figure 1. "Fennel Corbin who is being resettled on new land." Virginia, October 1935. Photograph by Arthur Rothstein. Library of Congress Prints and Photographs Division, LC-USF33-002187-M4.

Figure 2. "Laborers in Memphis—'You can't live the commonest way on six bits a day. Not alone nor no way . . . The people here in the morning are hungry, raggedy, but they don't make no hungry march." Memphis, June 1938. Photograph by Dorothea Lange. Library of Congress Prints and Photographs Division, LC-USF34-018198-E.

less by indignation about their subjects' circumstances than by their subjects' capacity to transcend their circumstances. The photographers were intrigued by the local communities and the premodern cultures of the American hinterland, and they admired the exceptional qualities they detected in the people. Arthur Rothstein was impressed by their individualism, their "inability to conform," and their determination to be "the master of their own fate." Ben Shahn recalled finding people "a constant pleasure" during the 1930s, especially "the poor[,] who were rich in spirit" and who maintained "a transcendent indifference to their lot in life." Even Walker Evans, who tended to be less sentimental in his relations with subjects, was attracted by what he perceived as a purity of lineage and an embalmed heritage in white southern communities. "I saw old America again," he said of Allie Mae Burroughs. "That sharecropper's wife is a classic portrait of a real, old pioneering, American woman of English stock, and pure, too."[8] The photographers perceived in their subjects' faces not only suffering but wisdom and a serene reflectiveness, qualities that, David Peeler reflects, had a vicarious resonance for the fundamentalist strand of the progressive imagination, wistful for simplicity, silence, and a firm sense of place.[9]

Professional considerations also informed photographers' opinions of their lower-class subjects. In a letter to Stryker from Kentucky of June 1940, Marion Post Wolcott established an inverse relationship between the quality of subjects and their social standing:

> In fact, I've decided in general that it's a helluva lot easier to stick to photographing migrants, sharecroppers, tenants, "niggers," clients—and the rest of those extremely poverty stricken people who are depressed, despondent, beaten, given-up. Most of them don't object too strenuously or too long to a photographer or picture. They believe it may help them, or they may get something out of it—a little money, or better houses, or a government loan. . . . But these more prosperous farmers, and middle "classes"—they will have none of it, unless they look right, well dressed, powdered,—and unless they know who you are and what it's for.[10]

Her reflections are reminiscent of James Agee's distinct lack of interest in Frank Tengle during the *Let Us Now Praise Famous Men* project because of his dissembling manner and his efforts to convey a good impression to visitors.

The idealization and objectification of southern subjects, contradictory points of view that alternate in the photographers' contemporaneous descriptions and subsequent recollections, reveal more about the photographers themselves than about those they photographed. Rarely did they question their relations with the southern underclass and the preconceptions that underpinned them. Most seemed to have felt that the benign nature of the New Deal's rural uplift programs coupled with their own sincerity of purpose were adequate justifications for their work. Initially obscured by the photographers' craft, vocation, and political idealism, the southern rural poor does not fully emerge in the analyses of historians of photography who have focused upon broader processes of which the photographs are a part: the nature of the New Deal order; the development of the documentary movement; representation and authorship; the visual semiotics of race and gender, and the contrivances or manipulations of both image making and reproduction. The subjects of FSA photographs exist vicariously within scholarship, lending their images to publicize or illustrate larger issues. At most, it is claimed that documentary photography provided an inclusive medium that enabled groups previously ignored by reform movements to communicate with the American public. This capacity of photography to empower the subject was registered by William Stott in his groundbreaking work, *Documentary Expression and Thirties America.* According to Stott, the "documentary movement" of the 1930s highlighted lower-class sections of the population hitherto obscured, conferred on them an aesthetic respectability, and established their moral worthiness. It also invested the common people with "voices" as well as identities.[11] Through the vehicle of the documentary they were able to project their interests as much as their characters.

However, often the "voice" belonged to a ventriloquist, so to speak. As visual documents, the photographs themselves provide highly mediated insights into the lived experiences of the underclass and, necessarily, encourage intuitive or counterfactual readings of them. It is necessary to reconstruct the processes by which the photographs were taken and to recover from the photographers' correspondence and from the testimony of subjects themselves echoes of a "voice" that is seldom projected visually. If the unprivileged of the FSA photographs could really "speak," what would they say?

For the southern tenant, his or her co-option by the photographic project began at the very point the Historical Section's images were created: in the photographers' contacts with their southern subjects. FSA photographers were not free spirits whose encounters with their subjects were unpremeditated and serendipitous. When on assignment they were expected to register at FSA regional offices and to seek the guidance and advice of local officers. Often the photographers worked directly for the regional offices, and when they did not, considerations of protocol and convenience required a preliminary visit to the regional office before commencing an assignment. With photographers working to shooting scripts provided by Stryker and under instructions to maximize their output, the experience and local knowledge of administrators were invaluable in identifying potential subjects. Many of them were drawn from the agency's own client records, which identified them as "types" and virtually ensured the cooperation of the subject.

Regional offices did more than provide leads for the photographers; often they also made the introductions. Photographers frequently complained that they were chaperoned by FSA field officers to the homes of subjects, occasionally accompanied by landlords.[12] Those iconic images of women photographed on the porches of their homes were products of encounters riven with tensions of social class, regional geography, and gender. For the southern woman standing apprehensively on the stoop of her cabin, her husband working in the fields, and confronted by her landlord, an FSA rehabilitation supervisor, and a New York photographer, aesthetics or politics were not immediate concerns. Colie Smith, a child in 1941 when Jack Delano photographed his family in Carroll County, Georgia, remembers the arrival of the "fancy people" in "more cars than we'd seen at one time," the unwelcome presence of "strangers in the house," and the restrictions imposed upon children during the photographer's visit. His sister, Corine, also recalled the FSA's impact on her family: "It didn't seem that we were poor. We always had hard times. We didn't know it until someone come along and told us so."[13] Such encounters reveal a tension in the relationship between the individual and the liberal state and its functionaries that is not revealed by the historian's traditional analytical tools—electoral statistics, relief rolls, opinion polls, and their like.

In fact, "the people" often proved unwilling specimens and reluctant icons. Russell Lee and Marion Post Wolcott frequently encountered "overtones of resentment" and "antagonism" and felt themselves required to justify their intentions in order to reassure anxious subjects. During their assignment for *Fortune* in Hale County, apparently two hundred prospective case studies refused Agee and Evans before they chanced upon three farmers outside the courthouse in Greensboro. Agee described their first encounter with the Tengle family in terms of the farm family's panic at an intrusion by strangers. While the children fled behind bushes, ridiculing the visiting party "like young wild animals," Tengle's wife gave her husband a reproachful look "wild with fury and shame and fear." Agee respected Mrs. Tengle's reluctance "to stand there on the porch. . . . In the average sorrow of your working dirt and get your picture made." She seemed to appreciate the abuse implied by the expectation that she and her family would pose "naked in front of the cold absorption of the camera in all your shame and pitiableness to be pried into and laughed at." Agee sensed that, unlike the men, she recognized the camera's significance as a "weapon" and "a stealer of images and souls." Jack Delano also emphasized the self-consciousness of subjects when he explained why many poor southerners were reluctant to be photographed. He compared the reactions of country people in Puerto Rico and the South and suggested that centuries of domination by ruling classes or castes had instilled such a sense of inferiority that "they could not conceive of themselves being portrayed" in a manner they associated with celebrities and movie stars. So embarrassed was one pregnant woman Marion Post Wolcott tried to photograph in Kentucky that she fell while attempting to escape from the portrait and the photographer was mobbed by her family.[14]

William Stott claimed that the Historical Section's photographers searched for "the look" that conveyed fortitude in the face of adversity and grace despite the pain of the subjects' circumstances.[15] Walker Evans's 1936 portrait of Floyd Burroughs in Hale County, Alabama, registers the formula exactly (fig. 3). Underpinning Evans's fiction is a deliberate tension between what the camera reveals and what the subject appears to deny. Deprived of any context by the close-up format, Burroughs's socioeconomic identity becomes secondary to his humanity. He becomes an enigmatic presence, possessing a depth of character that resists visual appropriation. The brilliance of Evans's craft is that in his sitter's expression he produced an open text capable of multiple interpretation. By distilling Burroughs's preoccupation, his subject could be described variously as vulnerable, resigned, or proud.

However, Evans's representations of Burroughs elsewhere in the Hale County series would suggest that "the look" is less the artifice of the photographer than of the subject himself. Throughout the series, Burroughs is generally detached and distanced even when accompanied by members of his own family or the children of his neighbor, Frank Tengle (fig. 4). In only one of the photographs, of Burroughs leaning against a porch post, does he appear to be communicating with the children who accompany him. Where he does not directly confront the camera, the object of his own gaze is unidentified.[16] If Burroughs possesses "the look" then it is, surely, assumed for the camera and, as such, is as much his own construct as it is that of Evans. Burroughs's determination not to be caught off guard is visually translated into a self-contained figure, independent of social or environmental context, and existing in a sort of hermetic serenity. Evans's aesthetic achievement was to naturalize Burroughs' artifice and to convert a pose of mannered reserve into a symbol of either the dignity of poverty or of transcendental innocence. FSA subject photography required an intimacy between strangers, and the photographers brought to their work both an innocence and an insouciance that often achieved dramatic visual expression in images that register both the photographer's intrigue and the subject's apprehension.

Working in the South appears to have had a liberating effect on Stryker's photographers. Photographers armed with government credentials and accompanied by FSA supervisors or local landlords did not allow themselves to be stopped by consideration of privacy or property. The photographers were not above behaving like Gauguins with Leicas and fanciful notions of the rural South as an innocent, premodern culture seemed to make the restraint and re-

Figure 3. "Floyd Burroughs, cotton sharecropper." Hale County, Alabama, Summer 1936. Photograph by Walker Evans. Library of Congress Prints and Photographs Division, LC-USF342-008138-A.

Figure 4. "Floyd Burroughs and Tengle children." Hale County, Alabama, Summer 1936. Photograph by Walker Evans. Library of Congress Prints and Photographs Division, LC-USF33-031306-M2.

serve of metropolitan etiquette unnecessary. Furthermore, the photographers felt that their liberal sympathies and their progressive mission justified the unwanted intrusions into the lives of poor people. Of all the photographers, Jack Delano was the most sensitive to the tensions of class, region, and race that were conjured in the encounters of Stryker's team with the South's rural poor. Delano recorded incidents in his log or recalled them in oral testimony as if to purge his conscience. Although he was a progressive liberal in race relations, he was aware of the uncomfortable dynamics generated by his contacts with African Americans. "We ran into a kind of deference on the part of the blacks we approached," he reflected. "We stood in front of the house and asked if we might come in—they said yes, but you felt that it was a 'no' because they were afraid to say no . . . it was an intrusion and we felt it was always an invasion."[17]

During 1940 and 1941 Jack Delano ignored the wishes of his African American subjects in his determination to obtain dramatic images. While covering the subject of migratory labor in Elizabeth City, North Carolina, he stole into railroad boxcars at 2 a.m., accompanied by two boys carrying flash equipment, to take pictures of sleeping packing house workers although he had learned that the use of flash alarmed the workers. However, Delano discovered that African American subjects could be more assertively uncooperative and even hostile. In 1940, while on assignment with the Institute for Research in Social Science of the University of North Carolina, and accompanied by Howard W. Odum's assistant, Harriet L. Herring, he provoked the distrust of a black family near Swepsonville. Delano encountered a woman hoeing in her garden and asked permission to take photographs. The situation was typical for the Historical Section's photographers, with the woman and children at home and the man away at work. Her initial, confused response, so often visually registered by photographers in the expressions of poor farm women, was also familiar. She gave a flustered answer: "Just took my shoes off," an embarrassed apology for being barefoot, which Herring interpreted as evidence that she was "rattlebrained." While she appeared to consent to being photographed, once Delano began to take shots of her children she became "suspicious" and summoned her husband from a nearby filling station. Confronted by a "well-built" but ill-disposed mechanic who "spoke courteously enough, but with a distinct challenge in his voice," Herring thought it sensible for the pair to withdraw. In fact, she had already gleaned enough information from the woman's responses to her questions to explain the friction. Not only had "white folks" stopped unexpectedly, but also, the children, one of whom was mentally retarded, were not all of the same parentage. In another instance, near the hamlet of Graham, Delano and Herring met with "a rather gruff reception" when they tried to enter an old corrugated metal garage where a family was living. According to Herring, the father declined "with some spirit," offering the excuse that the home was untidy and insisting that his children be photographed outside.[18]

Beyond an insensitivity to their subjects' personal circumstances, the photographers also sometimes lacked an informed appreciation of their broader, social context. This was particularly the case with new appointments to the Historical Section during their initiation into fieldwork. Eager to impress Stryker with interesting copy and sometimes, perhaps, an inflated sense of the social importance of their work, they tended to ignore the lived realities of their subjects. No photographer produced more images of southern African Americans for Stryker than New Yorker Marion Post Wolcott, who contributed about one-third of the Historical Section's stock of prints featuring southern blacks. However, during her first extended assignment in the South, late in 1938, her lack of experience of rural southerners was evident in her reports to Stryker.

During the Christmas period, Wolcott was working in the Gullah communities of South Carolina's coastal lowlands and bewailing her progress because the cold weather kept farmers indoors. However, she noted the residents' "very suspicious" and "quite unfriendly" attitudes. None would allow her to photograph inside their houses, some would not even permit photographs of the outsides of their homes, and in one community she was chased away. Residents seemed "awed" by her car and disturbed by her willingness to drive the roads alone. Wolcott attributed their hostility to her tanned complexion, bright clothes, and a bandana headscarf, which created the impression that she was a gypsy. However, although she amended her attire for subsequent visits, the reaction was the same. "I tried every different line I could think of," she advised Stryker. "And carried small bribes and food along with me." Impertinence and naïveté are improbably combined in Wolcott's actions and reflections. In fact, her reluctant subjects advised her in no uncertain terms why she was an unwelcome presence in their community and why they would not cooperate in her work.

Residents who did communicate with her claimed they resented strangers because they "played dirty tricks" on them or brought "bad luck." When informed that they were afraid of theft, Wolcott was aghast: "Several said [they] got things 'tookin from them,' but what? They haven't got anything!" Such a literal interpretation of the locals' comments indicates an ignorance of the history of the small farmer in the South and an innocence of the region's race relations. She was also surprised by the explanation offered for the groups of neighbors and relatives who gathered around her parked car when she was on assignment. "Whenever a strange car or person comes by and stops 'too long' they came around to see if their friends need any help," she wrote. "That's the onliest way we could git along," she was told. This simple expression of the communal solidarity of oppressed groups was lost on Wolcott. One prospective subject summed up the community's lack of interest in the documentary exercise and gave more than a hint about the nature of its shared culture: "We don't ask for nuthin' and times is hard but as long as we're not abothered none we're satisfied." When Wolcott left the pine woods tracks for the rural roads, she encountered a more astute and less defensive rural folk who had a "commercial" approach to the relationship between photographer and subject. "They . . . immediately asked for money, and no nickels or dimes, or food either—*real* money," the indignant and bewildered photographer reflected. "And then they'd just stand up in front like stiffs and not move until you 'snapped it and left.' " Wolcott was not to discover any idealized version of a primitive folk in South Carolina's swamplands that was amenable to visual appropriation by a young, progressive, New York woman carrying expensive equipment in an automobile.[19]

Stryker's team probed and pried into the health and religion of their subjects, perhaps the most intimate aspects of their lives. Prompted by headquarters' eagerness for material on health to capitalize on the National Economic Council's *Report on the South*, photographers sought images of the South's health problems, especially hookworm, pellagra, and malaria. However, they were not always easy to obtain, as Russell Lee discovered in Texas when public sensitivity caused him to abandon an assignment in San Augustine. In fact, the photographic file contains relatively few images that explicitly identify southern subjects as victims of disease. Partly this is due to Stryker's concern to avoid replication of the Public Health Service's work, but it was also caused by the diseased's refusal to cooperate.[20] Photographers were also aware that the taking of photographs in churches was a sensitive issue. When Dorothea Lange worked near Gordonton in Person County, North Carolina, she found that the "well-fed looking" farmers who willingly posed before her camera were reluctant to allow her to take photographs of preaching Sunday inside Wheeley's church, the Baptist church and focus of local pride. Although Lange persisted, she was obliged to yield after the pastor insisted that the congregation would object. However, in Georgia during 1941, Jack Delano ignored the silent protests of the congregation of a small, African American church and positioned flash bulbs next to the dais during a service. "I came out of that place just shaking," Delano's wife, Irene, recalled, "and so was Jack." The Delanos argued that the use to which their pictures were put justified their means of obtaining them.[21]

Suspicions of the photographers did not abate as the world crisis deepened in the 1940s and availability of defense work lured small farmers to the towns. Stryker assigned his photographers to document the preparedness movement in the development of defense industries and the construction of military encampments throughout the South. However, occasionally, the photographers' missions were interpreted by defense workers as part of an effort to enforce the military draft, to send underage workers back to school, or to return labor to the plantations. George C. Stoney, an information officer–cum–occasional photographer for the FSA's region 5 (Alabama, Florida, Georgia, and South Carolina), reported the concerns of one reluctant subject in Alabama during 1941 that " 'the government might be trying to get all us farmers back on the land by spring.' " Popular reactions to the escalation of World War II, especially after the Fall of France, also influenced the photographers' reception. Their documentary activities began to be associated with espionage and although popular anxieties were not restricted to the South, they were, undoubtedly, more pronounced in isolated rural areas, where wartime nervousness heightened customary suspicions of inquisitive strangers. "It's hard to get away with just 'taking pictures' any more," wrote Wolcott. "Everyone is so hysterically war and fifth column minded. You'd be amazed. So suspicious!" She reported that Cajun children in Louisiana, fearing that she was a spy, had fled from her, state troopers had apprehended and interrogated her, and on one occasion, she was arrested by a Kentucky sheriff.[22] A by-product of wartime preparedness was the eviction of farmers to make way for army camps and other defense developments, and occasionally the distress and aggression of the evicted was directed at the photographers. Jack Delano arrived at Hazlehurst Farms in Georgia to discover that rapid evictions and delayed compensation in the Hinesville–Camp Stewart area had resulted in a suicide, a protest meeting attended by five hundred farmers, and a general animus that was expressed toward the photographer himself as a government employee.[23]

The issue of lower-class agency is crucial to an appreciation of the FSA photographic project's engagement with the southern rural poor, and the examination should not be confined to representations in celluloid. Certainly, some of the most identifiable images—which were recycled in the contemporary newspaper and magazine press, valorized by prestigious exhibitions, and are still available in coffee-table books and large-format postcards—emphasize their subjects being rather than their doing. Although they provide scholars with an inexhaustible source for close textual analysis, they misrepresent the entire body of the Historical Section's work and fail to acknowledge Stryker's anthropological curiosity. The photographs reveal that FSA subjects did churn butter, plow fields, sell tobacco at auction, and repair barns. However, the agency that was available to them as participants in the photographic process is less apparent. Certainly, the issue is not clear-cut because the political activists of the Southern Tenant Farmers Union—who cannot be characterized as lacking agency— enthusiastically sought the FSA's cooperation, introduced the Historical Section's photographers to its members at its cooperative in the Delta, and were rewarded, subsequently, by the FSA's support of the Missouri roadside demonstrations of 1939.[24] To Stryker's credit, he encouraged the collaboration, but the association was one of mutual advantage. Elsewhere, southern subjects did not have as much latitude to negotiate the terms of their cooperation and they had no control over the ways in which their images would be utilized.

In the Historical Section's personalization of poverty, Gladys Reed, wife of Alvis Reed of Winslow Township, Washington County, Arkansas, achieved nearly the iconographic stature of Dorothea Lange's "Migrant Madonna" (see fig. 1 in chapter 3). While hers did not become a household name because her identity was never revealed by captions, Mrs. Reed did become a familiar face (fig. 5). Photographed by Arthur Rothstein on his first assignment for the Resettlement Administration (RA) in August 1935, Mrs. Reed and her children appeared in the next eighteen months in the *New York Times* (see figs. 2–4 on pp. 52 and 55), the *Huntington Advertizer*, the *Boston Sunday Post* and in March 1937 illustrated an article in the fledgling *Look* magazine, whose banner headline read, "Humanity Hits Bottom. . . . in the Deep South." The Reed family was portrayed as an archetype of the tragic southern underclass. *Look*'s caption drew particular attention to the three featured children and reflected: "Sharecropper children are often hungry. Undersized, scrawny, with large heads, misshapen bones, they are easy prey to disease." Archibald MacLeish also used an image of the Reeds to different effect in his illustrated poem of 1938, *Land of the Free.* They exemplified the "stubborn inward livingness" of an American folk that had begun to question the currency of the national ideal of liberty as enshrined in the Declaration of Independence. The vulnerability and confusion projected by Mrs. Reed's image provided an apposite visual foil for MacLeish's patronizing "soundtrack":

> Maybe the proposition is self-evident
> Or maybe it isn't
> Maybe we just thought so.[25]

However, the circumstances of the photo shoot suggest that Mrs. Reed's concerns were more immediate and prosaic. Rothstein visited the Reed home during a month of record-high temperatures in the Fayetteville area. He was accompanied by John Caufield, an RA information adviser, and a local county supervisor. The Reeds had been identified as potential subjects because the family had become clients of the agency during the previous month. While his companions engaged the woman in conversation about "home economics problems," Rothstein photographed Mrs. Reed and her children in the doorway of their timber-board home.[26] In three images she appears with three children who crowd beside her on a wooden plank floor. Her shoes are cracked and her

Figure 5. "Wife and child of a sharecropper." Washington County,
Arkansas, August 1935. Photograph by Arthur Rothstein. Library of
Congress Prints and Photographs Division, LC-USF33-002022-M4.

plaid cotton dress is frayed. A fourth image, taken in profile, with only one child in the frame, explains the tight fit of her dress: she is pregnant (see fig. 5). Understandably, in the circumstances, Mrs. Reed's poses are gauche and her expressions are self-conscious and confused. Her gestures are protective and self-conscious. In two photographs she anchors one arm to the door frame for support while the other is folded across her breasts, its hand clumsily clutching the dress fabric beneath her armpit.[27]

In December 1938, the *Saturday Evening Post* used an image of the Reeds for the sole illustration of an article by Samuel Lubell and Walter Everett, "Rehearsal for State Medicine." The *Post* used the most unflattering image of Rothstein's series. Mrs. Reed is caught off guard and in midspeech; she looks both garrulous and inane. Its caption was a general quote by the FSA supervisor for Chicot County, Arkansas, embedded in the article, and not intended to apply to the Reeds in particular: "'They don't know how to use a doctor; they've never had one'; An Arkansas Sharecropper's Family."[28] In September 1939 the Reeds issued a libel suit against the Curtis Publishing Company, the proprietor of the *Saturday Evening Post*, on the grounds that they were not sharecroppers and had not been when the picture was taken. They were tenants.

The Reeds' action caused a flurry of activity in the Farm Security Administration headquarters, and all legal aspects were transferred to lawyers in the U.S. Department of Agriculture. Of particular concern was the administration's own liability, since the *Post* had drawn accurately upon Rothstein's file caption to identify the anonymous subjects as "sharecroppers." Neither Rothstein nor Caufield could shed light on how they obtained the information about the subject's status. Indeed, they could not even recall the woman's name. Rothstein and Caufield were obliged to defend the use of the term in a loose sense as a generic and widely accepted designation. Rothstein explained that he had used "sharecropper" as a general "descriptive phrase" that neither intended nor implied libel. More surprisingly, Caufield, a regional information adviser based in Dallas, supported Rothstein's usage although he was aware of the hierarchy of tenancy arrangements in the South. He advised the *Post*'s lawyers of the distinction between sharecroppers who were furnished by landlords and "third-and-fourth" tenants who provided their own equipment and retained a higher proportion of their produce. Nevertheless, he insisted that the two should have the same designation. "The term 'sharecropper' is used correctly for any farmer who is paid by a share of the crop instead of cash," Caufield wrote. "Strictly speaking all of the people we visited were sharecroppers."[29] The regional officer's sophism contrasts to James Agee's awareness of how rank and status were used to gauge personal worth where material deprivation was widespread. In *Let Us Now Praise Famous Men* he described the "full horror" of Frank Tengle, who farmed on "thirds and fourths," at the prospect of "sinking to the half-crop level where nothing is owned."[30] By obscuring this point, Rothstein and Caufield evaded the grounds upon which the Reeds sought legal redress. The Reeds claimed that their status within their own community had been misrepresented: the *Post*'s libel was not to depict them as poor, but to depict them as *so* poor.

The case of the Reeds has relevance for the Historical Section's modus operandi during its early years. The ideological and actuarial aspects of documentary photography were interrelated. Casual note-taking and brief captions in which the subjects remained anonymous register the extent to which the photographers prioritized the visual aspects of their documentation. They are also symptomatic of the photographers' conviction that effective publicity required symbolic rather than biographical representation. Rothstein made no effort to glean his subjects' precise identities and status and to include the detail in his caption. In contrast, he identified another woman of Washington County as "the wife of a resettlement administration client."[31] The fact that he did not accord the same status to Mrs. Reed suggests both the Historical Section's need for images that could be generically defined as "sharecroppers" and Rothstein's judgment that the Reed family approximated the ideal more closely. In 1942 he used an image of the Reeds to illustrate an essay on photographic technique and described its making in these terms: "I wanted to show their poverty, their sad expressions, their worried faces, their apathetic gestures," he recalled. "These were apparent to even a casual observer. There were such pictures to be taken all around me."[32]

In their correspondence with the attorneys of the *Saturday Evening Post*, Stryker and Rothstein explained that it was not the Historical Section's practice to secure releases from photo subjects. Securing the written permission of the folk in the viewfinder to authorize the developing, retention, and circulation of their images would have impaired the photographers' efficiency. Whatever the merits of this position, the Reed's legal action reminds us that the photographers' subjects considered themselves to be "persons" rather than "people," and individuals rather than American stereotypes.

A final aspect of the Reeds' case sheds light on a significant aspect of the photographic project that is customarily ignored by cultural historians: the bureaucratic politics of the production and reproduction of the Historical Section's images. Stryker's unit never exercised sole responsibility for the production and dissemination of the agency's visual information. In effect, the FSA's Information Division was a tangled administrative web containing its own centralized services in Washington and information offices in each of its twelve regions. Lines of authority and areas of responsibility were not always clearly demarcated, and there were tensions between center and periphery stemming from institutional insecurity, bureaucratic ambition, and divergent notions of operational effectiveness. Each party was interested in justifying its own work, in increasing its autonomy, and in directing FSA information in ways that would reflect most favorably on its own contributions. From the inception of the project, rivalry plagued the Historical Section and southern regional information offices over control of visual information.[33] It is ironic, therefore, that the controversy over the Reeds was provoked by a regional information office providing the *Saturday Evening Post* with a copy of a photograph by one of Stryker's photographers that was drawn from the Historical Section's own central archive.

Samuel Lubell obtained the print of the Reeds from regional headquarters in Little Rock. Originally, he requested photographs of FSA clients in Chicot County he had interviewed, but the request was denied on the grounds of client confidentiality. Neither were residents and officials of another project in the same region prepared to provide Lubell with photographs that illustrated its medical program, fearing the "harm" that might result for "localizing" a story about such a sensitive aspect of the FSA's work. Instead, Oscar E. Jones, the regional information adviser, personally secured copy from the Historical Section's central files although he was aware it did not precisely match the requirements of the *Post* author. Ironically, while the FSA's regional officers had sought to avoid controversy by "generalizing" the images they provided Lubell, they provoked it by particularizing them in their selection of a portrait of the Reeds. It is also notable that, while regional officers solicitously protected the interests of their immediate clients by preserving their anonymity, they seem to have had few scruples about releasing the photograph of the Reeds to illustrate an article whose concerns had no apparent relevance to them.[34]

The Reed case reflects the expediency that characterized the FSA's information effort at both the center and periphery of its communications network. Inadequate documentary practice and inappropriate placement of copy were casualties of a public relations strategy that too readily acted on the assumption that ends justified the means. Not a judgment on the progressive character of the agency, this is more a reflection on its capacity to realize such character fully in its visual publicity. The Reed dispute exposes the central dilemma of the FSA's information program in microcosm because two parties to the legal action were clients of the FSA. The plaintiffs typified the poor, southern farmers for whom the agency's economic and social programs were intended; Curtis Publishing represented the media establishment whose cooperation was considered crucial to the FSA's political fortunes. The Reed case illustrates how the FSA and its components were obliged to maintain a fine balance between organizational effectiveness and institutional integrity. There was always a tension between the agency's mission on behalf the South's underprivileged and the necessity of having to work through the established media to achieve a high visibility for its programs and clients. As a result, the Reeds, like other icons of the Historical Section, occupied a limbo between the agency's progressive ideals and the expedient ways in which it sought to achieve them.

The fact that the Reeds' action never reached court does not diminish its significance as a commentary on the FSA photographic project and the constituency it professed to champion. The Reeds' unsolicited cultural prominence during the 1930s was occasioned by a diverse coalition of interests that was central to cultural production and communications in the New Deal state, each element of which had a distinctive agenda. Creative intellectuals, administrators, bureaucrats, academics, editors, and journalists all contributed to the transmogrification of the Reeds into cultural symbols. But, beyond this, the Reeds' legal action invests an FSA subject with agency more tangible than a look, a voice, one that is not contained in *and by* visual texts, and that does not require mediation of privileged others to ensure its significance. The case caused apprehension both in Philadelphia and Washington. It also prompted Stryker to encourage his photographers to develop rigorous documentation practices, whose hallmarks were to be full and detailed captions, in-depth picture stories, and the thorough contextualization of subjects. However, Stryker's objectives were never fully realized.

Despite the acclaim that the FSA photographs received from contemporaries, as late as 1941 members of the agency's Information Division were not convinced that its publicity had been effective in educating the public to the experience and identities of the small farmer. The division was so concerned about the proliferation of stereotypes of the tenant poor that it devoted an agenda item to the topic at its personnel conference of January of that year. It was claimed that relentless media coverage had simplistically classified small farmers into "wards of government," "problem children," or "sterling examples of American manhood." Roy Stryker's response was to lay down clear guidelines for his photographers' work with the agency's clients—in a memorandum issued five years after the Historical Section began its work. "Keep in mind that the purpose is to show that the residents are leading normal, settled lives," Stryker advised. This involved depicting them not only as working clients or members involved in their community, but as people who ate, slept, laughed, raised children, gossiped, read books, and washed clothes. In particular, Stryker encouraged his photographers to represent the homesteaders as "responsible, hard working, family loving, settled citizens."[35]

Apodictic interpretations of the relationship between cultural expression and the social process have long fallen out of fashion. Cultural historians who favor auteurism tend to confine the Reeds and their like to celluloid and gauge their significance with reference to the creative canon. Historicists have tended to regard the southern underclass as either the beneficiary of progressive, New Deal publicity, or as victims of appropriation by the hegemonic cultural dynamic of the liberal state. Ostensibly occupying center stage, the subject has become marginalized by agents who invent, redeem, or manipulate him or her and subordinated by discourses whose conceptual underpinnings require that the subject become a sort of palimpsest. That Gladys Reed was still alive in 1999 would be as irrelevant to a working cultural historian as her specific identity was to Arthur Rothstein in 1935. The arbiters of culture have long consigned actuality or lived experience to the trash can of reductivism. However, the Reeds' legal action and those more mundane instances of conflict between the photographic project and its subjects unlock perspectives on FSA photography that have been neglected. "The people" did not need to be endowed with a "voice" by dint of favor; neither were they dependent on a point of view that was not their own. Interaction and dialogue did exist between the project and its southern subjects, but it was not always visually expressed. It stemmed from the lived realities of the southern underclass and involved subjects using their limited agency to resist co-option by a network of forces that included the creative intelligentsia, the liberal state, the mass media, and the documentary movement. The dissent was unheroic, parochial, disturbing in some respects in its implied attitudes to liberalism and progressive change, and, perhaps, it was ultimately futile. The residents of Winslow Township—"Top of the Ozarks" as it used to refer to itself—who had lived alongside the Reeds for decades were astonished to learn that they had sued the *Saturday Evening Post.* "Someone must have put 'em up to it," one claimed to me in 1999. The sentiment is familiar, inflecting as it does an attitude about class relationships that six decades appear not to have corroded.

NOTES

Abbreviations

AAA   Archives of American Art, Smithsonian Institution
FSA-OWI Farm Security Administration–Office of War Information, Library of Congress
LC   Library of Congress
NA   National Archives
OHP   Oral History Program, Archives of American Art
RG   Record Group

1. *Look* 2 (June 1938): 54–55.
2. Warren I. Susman, *Culture as History: The Transformation of American Society in the Twentieth Century* (New York: Oxford Univ. Press, 1984), 212; Alan Lawson, "The

Cultural Legacy of the New Deal," in Harvard Sitkoff, ed., *Fifty Years Later: The New Deal Evaluated* (New York: Knopf, 1985), 169; Cara A. Finnegan, *Picturing Poverty: Print Culture and FSA Photographs* (Washington: Smithsonian Institution Press, 2003).

3. The most comprehensive studies of the FSA photographic project are F. Jack Hurley, *Portrait of a Decade: Roy Stryker and the Development of Documentary Photography in the Thirties* (Baton Rouge: Louisiana State Univ. Press, 1972); James C. Curtis, *Mind's Eye, Mind's Truth: FSA Photography Reconsidered* (Philadelphia: Temple Univ. Press, 1989); Nicholas Natanson, *The Black Image in the New Deal: The Politics of FSA Photography* (Knoxville: Univ. of Tennessee Press, 1992).

4. Interview of Theodor Jung conducted by Richard K. Doud, microfilm 625, OHP.

5. *Washington Post*, 4 March 1936; *Washington Daily News*, 1 Dec. 1938.

6. Lee to Stryker, 4 Jan. 1960, microfilm NDA8, 654, Stryker Papers, AAA; Delano quoted in Greg Day, ed., "Folklife and Photography: Bringing the FSA Home. Recollections of the FSA by Jack Delano," *Southern Exposure* 5, nos. 2–3 (1977): 124–25.

7. Mydans quoted in Hank O'Neal, *A Vision Shared: A Classic Portrait of America and its People, 1935–1943* (New York: St. Martin's, 1976), 116; Lange to Stryker, 27 April 1937, microfilm NDA30, 665, Stryker Papers, AAA.

8. Richard Doud, "Interview: Arthur Rothstein Talks with Richard Doud," *Archives of American Art Journal* 17 (1977): 23; Shahn quoted in Bernarda Bryson Shahn, *Ben Shahn* (New York: Harry N. Abrams, n.d.), 134; Evans quoted in Carol Lynn Yellin, ed., *Images of the South: Visits with Eudora Welty and Walker Evans. Southern Folklore Reports*, no. 1 (Memphis: Center for Southern Folklore, 1977), 34.

9. David P. Peeler, *Hope Among Us Yet: Social Criticism and Social Solace in Depression America* (Athens: Univ. of Georgia Press, 1987).

10. Post to Stryker, 28 and 29 July 1940, microfilm NDA30, 323–24, Stryker Papers, AAA.

11. William Stott, *Documentary Expression and Thirties America* (New York: Oxford Univ. Press), 267–89.

12. Stuart Kidd, *Farm Security Administration Photography, the Rural South, and the Dynamics of Image-Making, 1935–1943* (Lewiston NY: Edwin Mellen Press, 2004), 27–61.

13. Quoted in Denise Montgomery, Louis Schmier, and David Williams, "The Other Depression: A Farm Security Administration Family in Carroll County, 1941," *Georgia History Quarterly* 77 (winter 1993): 812–14.

14. Lee quoted in Archie Robertson, "They Have Seen Your Faces," unpublished manuscript (ca. 1943), microfilm NDA4, 88, Stryker Papers, AAA; interview of Marion Post Wolcott conducted by Richard Doud, 18 Jan. 1965, microfilm 1150, OHP; James Agee and Walker Evans, *Let Us Now Praise Famous Men*, (Boston: Houghton Mifflin, 1969), 362–64; Dale Maharidge and Michael Williamson, *And Their Children After Them* (New York: Pantheon Books, 1989), 20; Delano quoted in Day, "Folklife and Photography," 124; Post to Stryker, 28 and 29 July 1940, microfilm NDA30, 323–24, Stryker Papers, AAA.

15. Stott, *Documentary Expression*, 60–61, 267–89.

16. The Library of Congress catalog number of the portrait of Burroughs is LC-USF342–008138-A, and the entire series is published in Walker Evans, *Photographs for the Farm Security Administration, 1935–1938* (New York: Da Capo, 1973).

17. Delano quoted in Louis Schmier and Denise Montgomery, "The Other Depression:

The Black in Georgia through an FSA Photographer's Lens," *Georgia History Quarterly* 78 (spring 1994): 136.

18. Delano to Stryker, June 1940, microfilm NDA25, 995–96, Stryker Papers, AAA; H[arriet] L. H[erring]—Delano, May 28, 1940–4, Subject: Negroes working garden; 3, Subject: Garage used for dwelling, microfilm reels 18, 119, 118, FSA-OWI Written Records.

19. Post to Stryker, January 1939, microfilm NDA30, 43–46, 57–65, Stryker Papers, AAA; Wolcott–Doud interview, microfilm 1150–51, OHP.

20. Memo. From Rosskam to Stryker re: "Gaps in Files," n.d., ca. 1939, microfilm NDA8, 909, Stryker Papers, AAA; "Mississippi," Reports from Jean Lee, January 1939, microfilm reel 18, 836–37, FSA-OWI Written Records; Russell Lee to Stryker, 19 April 1939, microfilm NDA31, 509, Stryker Papers, AAA.

21. General Caption Nos. 23 and 24, microfilm reels 18, 55, 61, FSA-OWI Written Records; interview with Jack and Irene Delano conducted by Richard K. Doud, 12 June 1965, microfilm 573–74, OHP.

22. George C. Stoney, "Childersburg Still Squats," microfilm reels 14, 97, 99, FSA-OWI Written Records; Post to Stryker, 28 and 29 July, 9 Sept. 1940, NDA30, 324–25; 367–68. Suspicions of subversives were not confined to the South. In 1941 John Collier was detained as a spy by local police in Chatham, N.Y., until his credentials were checked. Collier to Stryker, 10 Oct. 1941, microfilm NDA25, 823–827, Stryker Papers, AAA.

23. Delano to Stryker, 20 March and 5 May 1941, microfilm NDA25, 870, 874; 1088, 1118, Stryker Papers, AAA.

24. Kidd, *Farm Security Administration Photography*, 168–70; 208–9.

25. *New York Times*, 15 Dec. 1935; *Huntington Advertizer*, 1 May 1936; *Boston Sunday Post*, 14 Feb. 1937; *Look* 1 (March 1937), 19; Archibald MacLeish, *Land of the Free—U.S.A.* (London: Boriswood Limited, 1938), 14; 89.

26. Rothstein to Stryker, 14 Aug. 1935, NDA25, 1496, Stryker Papers, AAA; Rothstein to Philip M. Strubing, 9 Oct. 1939, Records of the Farmers Home Administration, box 136, RG 96, series 2 (Cincinnati Office, 1935–42), NA; Arthur Rothstein, "Direction in the Picture Story," *Complete Photographer* 4 (10 April 1942): 1356–57.

27. The references to the images are LC-USF33–002021-M1, -002021-M2, -002021-M3, -002022-M4.

28. Samuel Lubell and Walter Everett, "Rehearsal for State Medicine," *Saturday Evening Post* 211 (17 Dec. 1938), 23.

29. V. O. Collins to T. Roy Reid, 3 Nov. 1939, microfilm reels 7, 81, FSA-OWI Written Records; Rothstein to Strubing, 9 Oct. 1939; John H. Caufield to Strubing, 27 Oct. 1939, box 136, RG 96, series 2, NA.

30. Agee and Evans, *Famous Men*, 108.

31. LC-USF33–002019-M3.

32. Rothstein, "Direction in the Picture Story," 1356–57.

33. The connections between the Reed case and the FSA's administrative system are discussed in more detail in Kidd, *Farm Security Administration Photography*, 138–48.

34. Oscar E. Jones to John Fischer, 17 Oct. 1938, Strubing to Mastin G. White, 23 Oct. 1939, George Wolf to Jones, 25 Oct. 1938, and Jones to Wolf, n.d., microfilm reels 7, 61,

64, 82, FSA-OWI Written Records; Samuel Lubell to Wolf, 9 June 1939, and T. Roy Reid to William Alexander, 3 Nov. 1939, box 136, RG 96, series 2, NA.

35. John Fischer to George Wolf, and attachment, "Suggestions for Public Relations Committee, New Orleans Conference," box 26, RG 96, series 2, NA; "Suggestions for Community Photographs," n.d., microfilm NDA8, 944–45, Stryker Papers, AAA.

Not Readily Visualized by Industrial Workers and Urban Dwellers

Published Images of Rural Women from the FSA Collection, 1935–1937

SIOBHAN DAVIS

"Look in her eyes!" exclaimed a headline in the *Midweek Pictorial* on October 17, 1936. Dominating the newspaper page is a photograph: an anonymous mother, her two children, and a baby asleep in the crook of her arm. Cupping a hand to her face, she looks beyond the photographer with an expression combining both despair and inner strength. Projecting a tension between vulnerability and purpose, the photograph by Dorothea Lange simultaneously invites the viewer to witness the obvious degradation of the subject while offering reassurance about the power of the human spirit. The mixed emotions evoked by the photograph, turning on confusion between identification and otherness, are key to the image's power. By projecting such a dynamic combination of victimization and strength, along with an undeniable aesthetic appeal, this photograph has come to represent the spirit of a people in the depths of hardship and struggle.

Known widely as "Migrant Mother," this photograph dominates, and to some degree subsumes, the image of women in the Farm Security Administration file. Widely published and exhibited as an outstanding portrait, the essence of an assignment, and perhaps "the picture of Farm Security," it raises questions about how images from the collection were used to depict women and their lives.[1] For instance, has the continued reproduction of one photograph with its powerful iconicity served to overshadow an institutionally approved representation of women's roles during the 1930s?

In this chapter I address the image of poor rural white women presented in photographs from the FSA Office of War Information collection taken from 1935

Figure 1. "Destitute peapickers in California; a 32 year old mother of seven children." February 1936. Photograph by Dorothea Lange. Unlike other FSA cardboard mounts, this one does not give the location, which is Nipomo, California. Library of Congress Prints and Photographs Division, LC-USF34-009058-C.

to 1937 under the auspices of the Resettlement Administration (RA). Using an article published in the *New York Times Magazine* and the Resettlement Administration *First Annual Report* from the same period, I consider how such images were presented within visual narratives that neglected the experiential and regional diversity of those imaged.

Headed by Rexford G. Tugwell, the RA was an independent agency from April 30, 1935, to January 1, 1937, when it was absorbed into the U.S. Department of Agriculture and eventually renamed the Farm Security Administration (FSA). Tugwell established the Information Division as one of the twelve coordinate divisions designed to support the four main areas of the RA. The historian F. Jack Hurley points out that Tugwell was aware of how unpopular many of the agency's projects were, and suggests that he created the Information Division to present the "positive programs and accomplishments to the country."[2] Along with Editorial, Special Publications, Radio, and Documentary Film sections, the Information Division contained a Historical Section, headed by Roy E. Stryker. In comparison to the specificity of the other section titles, the context for the term *historical* is ambiguous.

Stryker's early job description details an ambitious project involving the direction of a group of professionals, utilizing a variety of recording methods, to document RA programs comprehensively.[3] Toward the end of a convoluted account of tasks, a single statement concisely indicates the purpose of the section: to prepare "in *one unified form of expression*, a complete representation of the aims, objectives, achievements and interpretations of the Resettlement

Administration."[4] The one unified form was soon recognized as the documentary photographic image, reflecting a cultural impulse of the period.[5] By the 1930s developments in radio, film, and photographic technology had played a role in the creation of a "culture of sight and sound."[6] James Agee wrote in *Let Us Now Praise Famous Men* that "the camera seems to me, next to unassisted and weaponless consciousness, the central instrument of our time."[7] While he then denounces its "misuse," Agee's initial statement encapsulates a contemporary belief in informed documentary practice.

Stryker brought with him to the Historical Section a knowledge of picture editing, acquired while working at Columbia University, and for the Agricultural Adjustment Administration, but he knew little of the practicalities of photography. Input on aesthetic style, ideas, methods, and equipment would come from the group of young professional photographers employed by the agency. Thanks to the interactions of this group, the section moved from an indiscriminate photographic response to the production of informed image sequences.[8] While defining what to photograph, the section had also to consider how to place the images effectively in the public sphere.

The controversial nature of some of the programs, amalgamated to form the RA, drew critical attention from the press and created a situation aggravated by Tugwell's less-than-amicable relationship with reporters. Whether Tugwell's tactlessness toward journalists was "a reaction to an antagonistic press, or . . . the enmity of the press a response to his arrogant conduct," RA projects were often declared "Tugwellian" by alienated reporters. A November 1935 article in the *New York Times* condemned the complex organizational structure employed in the administration of the RA. Under the headline "Tugwell has staff of 12,089 to create 5,012 relief jobs," three reading lines reiterated administrative excess and its cost.[9] The article proclaims the ineptness of the agency's contribution to the work relief program: noting a shortfall on job targets, it argues that the Works Progress Administration would have to take up the RA's slack. The concentration, in the article's opening paragraph, on the amount of relief work created by the administration, illustrates a common trait in press reports of RA activities. The bulk of work undertaken by the agency, through the Rural Rehabilitation Division, did not involve the creation of work relief; rather, the agency was responsible for coordination of loans, grants, debt adjustment, education, and technical advice to the rural poor. The *Times* article misses the structural point, instead emphasizing comparative numbers and costs: "[the] administrative force numbers more than twice as many persons as the relief workers hired to date, and . . . the amount paid to this directing is about five times as great as the sum paid to relief workers." By juxtaposing these statistics with those of the Works Progress Administration and the Public Works Administration (the main responsibility of both agencies was to create work relief), the article is able to portray the RA as wasteful and ineffective.

Although some newspapers sought to correct the "facts" presented by the *New York Times* article, and despite an ongoing correspondence between Tugwell and the *Times*, the damage was considerable.[10] It is well caught by a letter to the president from the administrator of the Information Division: The news stories and editorials based on the original *New York Times* story "have appeared in newspapers all over the country. An analysis of the clippings at hand shows that editorial comment far exceeded news articles, and in most cases used the misleading TIMES figures as a basis for attack on the Administration. Also, that the editorial comment on the Administrator's reply was almost unanimously unfavorable in the clippings which were received."[11] The letter notes the article's wide dispersal and the quantity of editorial responses. The number of clippings received—115, with many from the Northeast and Midatlantic—does "not definitive[ly]" correlate with how many papers picked up the story, but it gives a general idea of the number. Such wide syndication of the *Times* article, misrepresenting the activities of the RA, indicates a key question for the agency: how were Tugwell and his administration to counter a negative press, and to revisualize the rural poor for the "urban dweller?"

In an apology to Tugwell, the *Times* offered to print an article by the administrator.[12] Tugwell responded with the illustrated "Problems—and Goal—of Rural Relief," which was published December 15, 1935 (fig. 2).[13] The reading line beneath the headline states, "The aim, says Tugwell, is soundly to rebuild rural life, protector of our individualism." Emphasis is on restoration rather than change, with "rural relief" positioned as the means of achieving that goal. The dashes punctuating the headline text create three distinct subject areas: problems, goal, and rural relief, a triad mirrored by the three photographs below the headline. The proximity of the images to the headline creates a caption–image relationship between headline and photographs. It is reasonable to assume that the RA supplied multiple images from which the *Times* editors made their final selection for publication. It is likely, therefore, that the magazine, not Tugwell, directed the arrangement and choice of the photographs used in the article.

The first portrait appears directly below the word *Problems*. A woman is photographed with three children in the doorway of a building. The image has been cropped to the frame of the bare wood door, centering the viewer's attention on the subjects (compare fig. 3). The woman's body, arm extended, leaning against an upright of the doorway, constitutes an internal frame, enclosing and protecting her children. In effect, she bars the entrance to the house. The sense of protection is further signified by her right arm, which crosses over her body in a self-protective manner. Her right elbow is bent to form an arrow, pointing

PROBLEMS—AND GOAL—OF RURAL RELIEF

The Aim, Says Tugwell, Is Soundly to Rebuild Rural Life, Protector of Our Individualism

By Farbmann and Lange, Courtesy Resettlement Administration.
Resettled—New Homes, Good Land and "Character Loans" Open New Farms for Families Like Those Shown Here.

By R. G. TUGWELL,
Administrator,
Resettlement Administration

THE problem of taking people off relief rolls has two distinctly different aspects, one is the urban, the other the rural. On June 1, 1935, there were approximately 3,100,000 relief cases on the Federal rolls which were classed as urban. They consisted of people who live in towns and cities of more than 2,500 population—day laborers, semi-skilled and factory workers, white collar employees, and others.

At the same time there were about 1,400,000 relief cases classed as rural. They include many classes of people: farmers, miners, lumber workers, some industrial employees—all relief cases in towns or cities of less than 2,500 population. More than 414,000 of these rural cases are farm families who, although living on the land, are unable to support themselves.

Taking rural families off relief is quite a different thing from providing work relief in the city. In the first place, rural families, especially those on farms, are scattered over a much larger area, which makes the development of works projects far more difficult than in cities where masses of relief workers are available.

Secondly, to put a farmer to work on the road or in building a schoolhouse in his county seat is only a stop-gap that bears no relation to his real trouble. The industrial workers will be re-employed when business creates more employment. The farmer is probably on relief either because he has not sufficient tools or equipment with which to get under way or because his land is unproductive. His objective is to return to profitable farming. Temporary relief work is of little help in this.

BECAUSE of these marked differences, the job of decreasing rural relief rolls was placed in the hands of an organization established for that primary purpose, the Resettlement Administration. The program of the Resettlement Administration was drawn up on three basic principles:

First, that a large proportion of the farm relief rolls could be reduced by extending farmers small loans sufficient to enable them to purchase capital goods with which to conduct their own operations, provided that adequate instruction and technical advice were given them;

Second, that many of our rural relief cases represented a chronic rather than an emergency situation, which could be solved only by helping these people to move to better land where they could have

a reasonable chance to farm successfully, or engage in other rural activities such as forestry or ranching;

Third, that there were a number of jobs, closely associated with farm rehabilitation and resettlement, which could provide employment for persons on relief in a way similar to the program conducted by the Public Works Administration and the Works Progress Administration, although in rural and suburban areas.

Several of these activities had already been undertaken by a number of different Federal agencies, and when the Resettlement Administration was formed approximately 18,000 people were transferred to its payroll by virtue of the shifting of these other bureaus to the new organization.

The first job of the Resettlement Administration was to put this tremendous, uncoordinated staff into efficient shape. One of the first acts was to cut the administrative payroll by about one-third. Other changes were made from time to time to weld together a strong but sufficiently decentralized organization equipped to handle the detailed and widespread work assigned to it.

From the point of view of the immediate need, the rural rehabilitation program was the most important activity assigned to the Resettlement Administration. "Rural rehabilitation" is the term given to the program of extending loans to farmers who can thus be helped to get off relief rolls, or to avoid going on relief.

Because of the rock-bottom agricultural prices which prevailed during the early years of the depression many farmers were deprived of their last financial resources, and were even bereft of their work animals and machinery. Others had been faced with destitution because of the severity of drought in good agricultural areas rarely visited with such extreme affliction. They were as helpless as men with their hands cut off, yet had, in their own farmlands, the basis upon which to become once more independent American families.

Small loans are given to those farmers who are adjudged good risks. The loans are secured by mortgages and liens, but more than anything else they approach what has been traditionally called the "character loan"—that type of credit which has played so important a part in

the upbuilding of individualized American farming. During recent years the "character loan" has been almost unknown so far as commercial banks are concerned. The government is being forced to supply that opportunity for the small individual which private finance no longer provides.

Rural rehabilitation is not only the most pressing but also the largest job of the Resettlement Administration. More than 350,000 families are having such help extended to them—which means that more than 1,500,800 people are being helped. During November, the first of an additional 175,000 families were placed on the rural rehabilitation rolls. More than $82,000,000 is now outstanding in loans of twenty to several hundred dollars.

THE goal of rural rehabilitation is not temporary relief but permanent independence for the families receiving this help. Therefore, it cannot be carried out in the same way as hiring and supervising relief workers. The task of the county rehabilitation agent, who, with the help of a committee of local farmers, recommends individuals for loans, is a large one.

In the first place, he must cover a tremendous territory. Some of the Western counties are as large as some of the Eastern States. Yet he must know each family intimately, understand the real cause of their present distress, and help them plan to improve their condition. He must be tactful enough to make suggestions on how the family budget should be drawn up, and how much member of the family can contribute to its support.

If the county rehabilitation agent, who is often a man with Extension Service training, finds a family trying to make the best living it can on a small plot of fair land, he usually counsels them first of all to "live at home." When the largest cash income that can be reasonably expected from good management of their acreage is just enough to provide clothing, necessary food purchases, and a modicum of comfort, he urges them to bend their efforts first of all to supply their own immediate needs.

Instead of the usual meager supply of canned goods, empty cellars are now filled with home-grown foods to be transferred to the mouths of hungry children during the Winter. For many of the farmers born and bred in a one-crop system of farming, this raising of vegetables means a new technique to be carefully nurtured by the county rehabilitation agent. The extension service is giving excellent cooperation in helping to teach these farmers more ways of providing for their needs.

The task is a *Continued on Page 22)*

By Evans, Courtesy Resettlement Administration.
Three of the Houses in the Resettlement Project at Reedsville.

Figure 2. "Problems—and Goal—of Rural Relief," *New York Times Magazine,* Sunday, 15 December 1935, 3. Copyright © 1935 the New York Times Company. Reprinted by permission.

down toward the abdomen, and emphasizing her heavily pregnant condition. She does not confront the camera directly but looks off to the side, her knitted brow expressive of tension and concern. The position of the word *Problems* above the image raises the question: what makes this woman and her children problems?

The article text stresses the difference between urban and rural relief, emphasizing the ineffectiveness of temporary aid in alleviating farmers' problems. Tugwell explains that taking families off direct relief, in favor of work relief projects, is less feasible in a rural environment, where dispersed housing renders the gathering and transportation of a workforce impractical. When read in conjunction with the text, the first image suggests that divided families are the result of poor agricultural conditions. The absence of a husband-father in the photograph implies that the woman has been left to cope alone: her difficult situation magnified by her obviously advanced pregnancy.

The article lists principles basic to the RA. Reducing farm relief rolls by making small loans for agricultural equipment is fundamental. In addition, the agency funds a program offering "adequate instruction and technical advice" to ensure effective use of its aid. The fact that the emphasis on restored production, via correct instruction, is effectively headed by an image of family reproduction (minus the reproductive head), tacitly suggests that the "problems" of productivity on the land apply to the reproduction of the rural population. An evocation of the land-woman analogy, through the image-text placement, suggests that lifestyle problems might also be addressed through "adequate instruction and technical advice." *Problems*, therefore, can be read both in terms of worsening agricultural conditions and—to the urban viewer—of a growing and impoverished rural population.

The first of the three top images does not carry the caption assigned to the original by photographer Arthur Rothstein: "Washington County, Ark. Aug. 1935. The wife and children of a sharecropper." Though not particularly detailed (and indeed, as we learned in chapter 2, containing errors), the caption provides a context for the image. The woman is married; her husband is apparently a sharecropper, a role differing from that of the generic farmer mentioned throughout the piece. Sharecropping, as part of a tenant-based cash crop system, developed its own socioeconomic problems and patterns of behavior, separate from those of other agricultural practices. As a means of male employment, it had acute consequences for all aspects of the sharecropper's family life. Margaret Jarman Hagood suggests that "although the lives of most women are somewhat effected by the occupations of their husbands, there is probably no group where the influence is more profound than in the case of tenant farm women."[14] She details how such women share directly in their husbands' occupation as field-workers, whose workday is governed by the needs of the cash crop. As such, this woman's experiences differed radically from those of other rural women connected with agricultural practices outside the South. With the image artistically cropped and missing the original caption, the subjects become anonymous examples of rural poverty—visual "types" that fail to convey the specific problems of southern sharecropping families.

Viewing the original sequence of photographs of the woman and children, however, allows us to assess the selection of the image for the *New York Times* article.[15] The sequence consists of eight photographs, beginning with three exposures—including the selected image—taken at the doorway of the house; all show more surrounding detail than the published version. A broom, handle down, leans against the planked wall to the right of the frame in the published image (fig. 3).[16] A second handle leans against the other side of the door frame, and a bucket stands on the step below the door. These household implements indicate a certain level of cleanliness and pride; in addition, domestic implements suggest female labor other than childbearing. One image, taken outside the house, indicates that Rothstein was not alone with his subjects (fig. 4): the left side reveals a man standing facing the woman.[17] His attire is not characteristic of what a sharecropper would have been likely to wear. In fact, this is an RA employee accompanying Rothstein, suggesting that the family was already known to the government agency. The woman's changing facial expressions as she is photographed in the doorway suggest she is in conversation; initiated and directed by the photographer, conversation allows him to manipulate the facial expression of the subject.[18] Three subsequent photographs, taken inside the house, show the woman tending to a baby, indicating that there are already four children in the family. No single image includes all the children. Seen as a whole, the sequence prompts tentative conclusions regarding the selection and cropping of the published photograph. While there is nothing to suggest that the RA supplied the newspaper with the whole sequence, we can speculate about both the choice of image, and the manner in which the *Times* then chose to crop and present the photograph. My reading indicates that the image was chosen for the woman's facial expression, the number of children, and her obvious pregnancy. The cropping and placement of the image removes extraneous details, focusing attention on the subjects and their relationship to the apparent heading, "problems."

In the portrait, positioned under the word *Relief* at the far right of the article, a man seated in the foreground is reaching out to a small child, who clasps the man's finger tightly (see fig. 5). Behind the man stands a woman with a baby in her arms. She looks down at the small child, as does the man, whose gaze is reciprocated by the child. The shared gazes of the family, suggesting that they

Figure 3. (*left*) Sharecropper's wife. Washington County, Arkansas, August 1935. Photograph by Arthur Rothstein. Library of Congress Prints and Photographs Division, LC-USF33-002021-M1.

Figure 4. (*below*) Sharecropper's wife. Washington County, Arkansas, August 1935. Photograph by Arthur Rothstein. Library of Congress Prints and Photographs Division, LC-USF33-002021-M3.

Figure 5. Detail from "Texas tenant farmer in Marysville Migrant camp during the peach season." Marysville, California, June 1935. Photograph by Dorothea Lange. Library of Congress Prints and Photographs Division, LC-USF34-009066-E.

are unaware of Dorothea Lange's presence, creates the image of a self-contained unit. Unlike the incomplete family imaged under "problems," the "relief" photograph presents a conventional family group—a little down on their luck, but united. Perhaps "Rural Relief" has enabled this family to stay together, keeping the father at home. Alternatively, as a conventionally recognizable unit, this family constitutes the type of people deserving of government assistance. The image of the united family addresses the anxieties of small town communities, expressed in urban newspapers, concerning the type of rehabilitation or resettlement client. In keeping with the first photograph, this image is cropped closely to frame the subjects, decontextualizing the family. The viewer is aware via the headline of the rural background of the subjects; however, the absence of a caption serves to typify those imaged.

The caption of another photograph from the original sequence offers additional information (fig. 6): "California fruit tramp and his family in a migrant camp. The mother is twenty two years old."[19] In this image, two more children are shown, both appearing to be older than the child in the printed photograph. The structure behind the family is revealed as a large trailer or boxcar. Various elements of the image indicate mobility: a license plate next to the man; the silhouette of a wheel in the background and, in the left middle foreground, what appears to be a large tire. The white triangle, left of the mother in the published image, is in fact a large tent, behind which is another temporary shelter. When the tents are read with the trailer, and the framing of the subjects between the two wheels, the image projects the transient nature of the family's existence.

Although the photograph published in the *New York Times* suggests a rural farm family, their reality is quite different. As a migrant family, they would not have been entitled to the relief discussed in the article. The column of text directly below the image elaborates on the work of county rehabilitation agents in assessing clients for "character loans." "Those eligible for such financial aid were situated on the land: If the county rehabilitation agent . . . finds a family trying to make the best living it can on a small plot of fair land . . . he urges them to bend their efforts first of all to supply their own immediate needs . . . farm families are being made independent in this manner with an average loan of $600."[20] As published, the image appears to represent the ideal type of family who justify government intervention. The photograph of a young husband and wife with two children depicts unity and evokes that "individualism," which— with a little financial assistance and technical instruction—will reclaim a self-sufficient agrarian lifestyle. Such an ideological scenario ill fits a California fruit tramp.

The article's top center, circular image shows a man and woman working in a garden (see fig. 7). Behind them are a well-maintained white house and a growing crop. The image appears below the word *Goal*. Below the photograph is the caption: "Resettled—new homes, good land and 'character loans' open new paths for families like those shown here," which refers to all three images. The center image represents the "resettled" family. Appearing within the circular frame, the subjects are enclosed in their own sphere both in terms of layout and metaphorically, through the restoration of a self-sufficient rural life. The circumference of the circle cuts into but does not merge with the two rectangular images, leaving a slight gap between pictures. Cutting away sections of the side photographs indicates connection to, yet displacement by, the center image. The space between the photographs implies that transition from the margin is not direct: the gap might be read as indicating the small but significant degree of intervention needed, if the two families left and right are to achieve the self-sufficiency of the center photograph.

The fourth image in the article is positioned page bottom, center (see fig. 8). The photograph shows three new houses, with plowed land in the foreground,

Figure 6. "California fruit tramp and his family in a migrant camp. The mother is twenty two years old." Marysville, California, June 1935. Photograph by Dorothea Lange. Library of Congress Prints and Photographs Division, LC-USF34-002534-E.

Figure 7. Untitled photograph of settlers on McComb Homesteads. Pike County, Mississippi, August 1935. Photograph by Arthur Rothstein. Library of Congress Prints and Photographs Division, LC-USF33-002039-M2.

Figure 8. Untitled photograph from the Arthurdale Project. Reedsville, West Virginia, 1935. Photograph by Walker Evans. Library of Congress Prints and Photographs Division, LC-USF342-000841-A.

and a road lined with telegraph poles. Captioned, "Three of the houses in the Resettlement Project at Reedsville," this image is located by the "rebuilt rural life" of the subheading. The image concludes the visual narrative by anchoring the bottom of the page. Despite the furrowed land and crop lines, the proximity of the houses to one another and to the road is more suggestive of suburban than rural.[21] The presence of telegraph poles—representing communication—suggests the technology and information considered, by the article, as essential to rebuilding rural life. The row of houses, and the crop lines and furrows, lead the viewer's eye to the center of the image, occupied by the furthest house. Starkly contrasted against a dark background of trees, the house resembles an arrow pointing upward. Directed out of the image, and up between two columns of text, the viewer's eye is led back to the photograph above, whose circular shape is thereby rendered focal. The circle provides a viewpoint from within which the resettlement project may be telescopically seen as rebuilding the essential individualism of rural life, so that it can continue within a modernized agricultural environment.

The final image appears on the article's second page and is captioned,

"Children of an Arkansas farmer who has been 'resettled'" (fig. 9; see also fig. 10). The happy countenance of the older girl projects a sense of freedom. Both children are facing toward the right of the image, with looks fixed beyond the frame of the photograph. Impressionistically, they gaze toward a future from an open, bright setting, in marked contrast to the enclosed environment framing the first image (fig. 2, top left).[22] Use of a single photograph of children at the end of the article emphasizes the importance of RA projects to help ensure the productivity of the next generation.

Significantly, in the "problems" and "relief" images, children are positioned closest to the center photograph, tacitly suggesting that the "new paths" mentioned in the caption are of primary benefit to the young. The article closes with "Resettlement's goal is to lay the basis of a sound and permanent reconstruction of rural life, the parent and protector of American individualism." Unlike the article's reading line, which indicates that "rural life" itself is the "protector of individualism," the closing statement suggests that such a role is fulfilled (long-term) by the RA. In effect, resettlement becomes "parenting." In its parental role, the RA may justly intervene in the dysfunctional rural family to reconstruct the rural life of the young. Emphasis on the child, as motive for government intervention, challenges negative perceptions about an undeserving underclass. If the situation of the woman, presented in the first photograph, is read as illustrative of the human "problem," her children are set within a visual sequencing that casts them as that which renders federal assistance necessary and desirable.

Suppressing the original captions decontextualizes the photographs and visually amalgamates the southern sharecropper and the Californian migrant worker, to produce a generic—less problematic—narrative of rural poverty. Published only seven months after the RA was established, the article stresses the aims of the administration, the difficulties faced by the rural population, and the programmatic nature of relief. The visual narrative present in the before and after ordering of photographs, reinforces the assertions of the text, placing particular emphasis on the results of rural relief. However, while the text emphasizes rural rehabilitation, the positive images of the sequence all carry the word *resettlement* in their captions (rehabilitation and resettlement constituted two distinct programs within the RA). Perhaps, and implicitly, the images address the underlying concerns of the urban reader, offering visual reassurance over the more controversial resettlement projects. The ambiguous problems of the first image, and the deserving family of the second, pander to ingrained ideas of agrarian individualism and of the American family. The round photograph reinforces such ideals as in line with RA purposes, while the fourth suggests that traditional values may contribute to a new technologically modified environment. The construction of the visual narrative is aided by three key editorial

THE PROBLEMS OF RURAL RELIEF

The Aim, Says Tugwell, Is to Rebuild Farm Life

(Continued from Page 3)

large one, requiring a large and well-trained force of field workers who can keep in close touch with families scattered over several miles of country, and representing all types of farmers. Yet farm families are being made independent in this manner with an average loan of $600.

Often, however, in fact too often, farmers are on relief because their land is too poor to make farming successful under the best of management. One head of a family, who had lost everything but his sense of humor, wrote, "This land is so bad that you can't raise Cain with it with a bottle of cider." Loans will not help people so situated, unless they are able to relocate on land that will prevent taxes with the means of making a living.

Resettlement attacks what might be called the chronic rural-relief problem. The present situation, in which families are trying to live on land that will not support them, is costing the taxpayers money.

It costs them money in direct relief, and in indirect forms of relief such as loans that cannot be repaid because the borrower has not a chance of making a profit from his land. It costs the taxpayers money because of tax delinquency on the part of those who live on poor land, but who must still be provided with roads and schools by the public treasury.

Less money more wisely spent to give families a chance to make good on better land will do much to help clear up these conditions.

* * *

ABOUT 12,000 families, or 30,000 people, are being helped by the Resettlement Administration. Included in this number are several tenant farmers who are being helped to acquire farms of their own. Resettlement of families, even though carried out in response to the direct appeal of the families concerned, is the most difficult problem of all.

Last session the United States Senate passed the Bankhead-Jones Farm Tenant Home Bill, which would aid tenant farmers in acquiring homes of their own. At the coming session this bill is to be considered by the House of Representatives. If it should be passed the beginnings made by the Resettlement Administration will be of great value in pointing the way toward a sound application of this program on a larger scale.

Resettlement of farmers is closely related to land use. Partly for this reason, the land-use program, previously carried out cooperatively by the Federal Emergency Relief Administration, the Agricultural Adjustment Administration and other Federal agencies, was transferred to the Resettlement Administration.

This division of the Resettlement Administration has optioned more than 10,000,000 acres of land, of which it proposes to buy about 9,000,000 acres. Options have already been accepted on 1,353,000 acres valued at $32,943,000. A large amount of this land has been finally purchased and title work is under way on the balance.

Three important objectives are being realized by the land-use program. About 22,000 families now living on poor land are being given an opportunity to aid and move elsewhere. Half of them will need no further financial aid when

they have received payment for their land.

Secondly, the program is converting to beneficial use between nine and ten million acres of land that is now either being destructively farmed or otherwise subjected to an unprofitable and undesirable use. This land will be greatly increased in value as a result of reforestation, erosion-control work, re-establishment of pasture grasses and recreational development, and will help meet the present requirements for land devoted to these purposes.

Finally, the land-development program alone can provide employment to a daily average of more than 75,000 men in rural communities; and the first contingent are already on the job.

In addition to these projects the land utilization division is carrying out the further study of land-use problems, preliminary results of which were published by the National Resources Board in 1934. The rural program is directed toward permanent reconstruction. If it is to be soundly executed, we must have adequate scientific knowledge about the quality of all our land and its value for farming, forestry, ranching, or other purposes.

We must also find better means of promoting a good use of land by private owners, partly to protect the land itself, and partly to help solve the taxation problems of local communities. This is the work of land-use planning.

* * *

RECENTLY ground was broken in Berwyn Heights, Md., about ten miles from Washington, for the first of four large suburban housing projects which constitute another important feature of the Resettlement Administration's work-relief program. These four projects, for which a total of $31,000,000 has been allocated, will consist of groups of multiple-unit homes, each housing several hundred families who will commute to their work in the city.

Because they are located outside of city limits, it is possible to have these housing projects cover a large area, including adequate space for recreation. Protective "greenbelts" of park land will surround each project to prevent any industrial or unwelcome commercial development from infringing upon the residents' area, and provide an opportunity for gardening to those families who wish to avail themselves of it.

In all these is available to the Resettlement Administration the sum of $375,000,000 with which to carry out its program of con-

struction. The larger part of this amount is finding its way into the hands of individual farmers who are thereby restored to economic independence.

About $80,000,000 is being invested in the purchase and improvement of land resources, for the enrichment of poor rural areas. Families now living on poor land are being given a new chance to make good through development or resettlement plans with $40,000,000 allotted for that purpose. Finally, about 150,000 men — who in turn will help support more than half a million people with their wages—will be employed in areas where relief labor is looking for jobs.

Resettlement does not pretend to inject a temporary stimulus into the economic arteries of depressed rural areas. Unlike our industrial problems, the rural problems are to a large extent chronic. Rural poverty has existed during the past decades right alongside of industrial prosperity. Resettlement's goal is to lay the basis of a sound and permanent reconstruction of rural life, the great protector and defender of American individualism.

THE OPERA NOW REACHES OUT

Radio and the Pictures Widen Its Audience

(Continued from Page 13)

proved and tried stuff. That may mean that new plays are good and new operas bad, or that old plays are not good enough and old operas are good enough to hold their own. Whichever is the case, the way to keep old operas new is to refresh them with new productions and new people in the familiar rôles.

This, in a nutshell, is the recipe which the new general manager of the Metropolitan has for giving zest to his first season in Gatti's shoes. He thinks his new people—many of them Americans—are going to provide agreeable surprises and unexpected discoveries, and that assignment of unaccustomed rôles to the artists already familiar to the Metropolitan public (nearly all of these artists are back) will add to the sense of adventure in attending performances at the Metropolitan under a new régime the first purpose of which is to maintain standards and the method of which is to introduce changes gradually.

The New American Ballet is really the only feature of the new season's set-up which represents a complete change and a clean sweep. And the ballet is one of the arts in which the Metropolitan has sensibly lagged far behind the times.

Observing that he had noted as a happy omen the unparalleled display of ermine and velvet with white shirt-fronts, tails and toppers at the recent National Home Show in Madison Square Garden—one of a series with a beginning coeval with that of the Metropolitan—the general manager, bright-eyed and brisk, gave this parting shot: "The opera on its way to becoming national may be democratic, but it need not be dowdy. The audience is part of the gala spectacle of the show."

Figure 9. "Problems—and Goal—of Rural Relief," *New York Times Magazine*, Sunday, 15 December 1935, 22. Copyright © 1935 the New York Times Company. Reprinted by permission.

Figure 10. "Children of rehabilitation client resettled in the Ozark Mountains." August 1935. Photograph by Arthur Rothstein. Library of Congress Prints and Photographs Division, LC-USF33-002017-M2.

choices: a rejection of the original captions, a removal of geographical detail, and a typifying of the subjects.

This before-and-after arrangement suggests that the selection of photographs provided by the RA privileged the reproduction of particular kinds of subject and image over specific regional difficulties, and at least made possible, if not likely, a progressive temporal narrative. However, the final arrangement and choice would have rested with the magazine editors. The Resettlement Administration *First Annual Report* offers a less mediated route to how the administration used and sequenced photographs supplied by the Historical Section.[23]

Published in 1936, the RA report was well designed and drew heavily on Historical Section photographs. Sidney Baldwin points out that such published materials were not addressed to "the people of small towns, the editors of rural journals, or the political people in county courthouses, but rather to the presumably more literate and sophisticated people in the cities . . . academic audiences, and to the editors of slick national publications."[24] The report presents the aims of the four main divisions of the RA and the roles of the twelve supporting subdivisions. Photographs illustrate projects being undertaken by the administration and emphasize the results of the different programs. Seven images featuring women are used: three in the illustration of the "Rural Rehabilitation" section, two in "Rural Resettlement," one in "Management," and one in "Public Health." The selection of photographs showing women implies an institutional interpretation of their function, which privileges established expectations of women's roles.

The section addressing rural resettlement features four images: a photograph of a father and son on the land; a landscape of houses and fields; and two photographs, on a double page spread, showing a refugee family, and a resettled farmer and his wife. The three-quarter page image of the father and son opens the section and is elaborately captioned, "Resettled. Father and son working on their part-time farm at Granger Homesteads in Iowa, where many miners and their families have been helped to resettle themselves by the Resettlement Administration" (fig. 11).[25] The photograph shows a man holding a cultivator while his son stands nearby. The land around the subjects looks freshly culti- vated and ready for planting new crops. The caption suggests that as a miner the man had been unable to achieve the stability subsequently facilitated by resettle- ment. New land has provided a Jeffersonian restart for the man and his family, supplying fresh means to fruitful labor. The photograph roots the father and son to the land; their shoes disappear into the dark soil, as if drawing sustenance directly from the earth. The man's grip on the cultivator establishes a further connection; his labor and the land are bound in a mutually reciprocal cycle, each enabling the productivity of the other. A new house stands in the background, but only behind the boy. Unlike his father, connected by stance and labor only to the land, the son is suspended between land and home—perspective points a link between boy and building. His position, facing forward and away from the house, however, suggests a movement from home toward father and land, from childhood to manhood. The land can be read as the public male sphere, toward which the boy moves. An absence of women in the photograph rein- forces male landed dominion, tacitly suggesting that a woman's place is in the private domestic space, represented by the house in the background. If the boy's proximity to his father is read through a maturation story, the house becomes the center of child rearing and nurture.

The two-page spread in figure 12 juxtaposes an image of a refugee family with a photograph by Arthur Rothstein of a resettled farmer and his wife.[26] The pho- tograph on the left-hand page is captioned: "No work and no home. Drought refugees from a southwestern state looking for jobs near San Jose Mission, in California." Explicitly stating the final destination of those imaged, the caption is less exact about their origins. The photograph features the front of a battered truck, with one woman standing, her head turned toward the camera. The eyes of the woman are in shadow cast from her sunbonnet. A younger woman sits in the front seat of the truck, a baby on her lap and a small boy standing inside the vehicle. The older woman's dominant position in the image marks her as the matriarch. Men are absent from both the image and the caption. In the cen- ter background of the photograph (visible through the window of the truck) is a sign or billboard with three partial words.[27] The visible letters suggest "Pi- oneer cleaning" and, since the image was taken in California, "Oakland" is a possibility for the last word. The logo constitutes an internal caption that adds dimension to the image.[28] With the photograph cropped to the hem of the older

Figure 11. "Resettled. Father and son working on their part-time farm at Granger Homesteads in Iowa, where many miners and their families have been helped to resettle themselves by the Resettlement Administration." Resettlement Administration, *First Annual Report*, 1936, 32. Photograph by Carl Mydans. Library of Congress Prints and Photographs Division.

woman's skirt or dress, and with a portion of the calves removed, her clothing is rendered archaic and resonant of the nineteenth century. The frilled sunbonnet enhances an archaism that in the full context of the hoarding evokes images of early pioneer women and recasts the truck as a covered wagon.[29] Whatever the mode of transport, the destination is west (left). So inflected, positive connotations associated with the pioneer spirit (strength and individualism), can be read into the image as applicable to its subjects. However, the picture of the pioneer family is incomplete without a male (husband/father) to lead the group. Having reached the "west," this family remains destitute, with "no work" and "no home." The original photograph, shown in figure 13, discloses the presence of a fourth person: a hand and arm rest against the side of the truck.[30] The forearm is not gendered, but the presence of a male subject would change the reading of the image. Having associated men with work in the first photograph, a textual reference to "no work" tacitly suggests a reason for male absence. As with the initial illustration in the *Times* article, a split family is implied. The presence of a man in the photograph could be read as a sign of laziness or unwillingness to seek employment—reinforcing urban anxieties about RA clients, and suggesting qualities that would contradict connotations of pioneer spirit.[31]

Shown with the women and children, the truck is perceived as an inadequate home. Unlike the boy planted on the land (with the security of the home behind him) in figure 11, the small male child stands in the truck, trapped in a means

No work and no home. Drought refugees from a southwestern State looking for jobs near San Jose Mission, in California.

The granting of a low rate of interest alone would not solve this problem. Supervision is as necessary as a low rate of interest, and such is a part of the Resettlement program if the aims of the Resettlement Administration are to be accomplished.

Supervision does not mean discouragement of individualism or of initiative. On the contrary, it will develop more initiative and more individualism than exist at the present time. A farmer who has $300 to $400 gross return does not have much independence. He is subservient to landlords and to merchant creditors. The man whose income under supervision rises to with a low rate of interest, making from $800 to $1,200 a year, will feel that he is in a position to establish his independence.

If the total number of farms, not including labor camps, is divided into the total estimated cost, the average cost figure would be about $8,000 per unit. If the cost of livestock and operating equipment, household furniture, cooperative and community serv-

low buildings, and management were excluded from the cost, the average cost per farm would be approximately $5,353. This compares favorably with the average value of $7,610 for all farms in the United States.

The cost of buildings is the largest single item in the project budgets. A minimum number of farm and out-buildings are provided for. These provide protection for livestock, implements, and products. Designs are based upon analyses of the requirements of the farm. These buildings are added in the beginning, because of the loss which would result from a delay in construction.

The cost of houses varies from $1,000 to $3,000, with an average cost ranging from $1,800 to $2,000. These costs include, in general, the cost of water heating. Houses costing less than $1,000 do not have these facilities. In the very low-cost projects, running water is provided in the kitchen by the use of a hand pump with small pressure tank.

The cost of utility services represents a small per cent of the total unit cost. These services usually cannot be afforded by farmers in the low-income group with which the Resettlement Administration is particularly concerned, without the aid that is made available. Their incomes have not been sufficient to pay for electricity, and, therefore, they have not been considered as potential consumers. Upon becoming Resettlement settlers, on the other hand, they have sufficient income to pay for utility service where rates are reasonable. Where power cannot be provided at reasonable rates, utility service are not provided.

Furniture is included as an item in the majority of cases. This is done because of the fact that most of the farmers in the low-income group do not possess adequate furniture. The furniture is being designed specifically for farm homes by the Special Skills Division.

Livestock and operating equipment are included in the total cost figures. Although this money represents loans to the settlers, it should not be included in the cost of the farm where the farm cost is compared with the cost of farms in general.

The cost of management is included as a part of the purchase price of the farm. This cost ranges from $300 to $400 per client, and covers the entire period. This is low when compared to commercial rates of $50 per year for a less comprehensive service. Success is dependent upon adequate funds for management.

The cost of the development of processing plants for cooperative organizations is added as a cost in the budget for the unit. This item, however, is self-liquidating, and should not be considered as a charge against the farm. It does appear, however, in the total budget and should not be charged against

individual farms, but which does appear in the total budget for projects where villages are being developed as a part of the project plans. The village cost should be self-sufficing, and, in the case of schools, should be considered as a public expenditure.

Taxation

The Land Utilization program will definitely reduce the need for taxes for the support of roads and schools in areas where roads and schools must now be maintained at a high cost. Such savings and where the return in taxation is negligible. This saving must be deducted from any increase in road construction costs in Resettlement areas.

The transferring of families from Land Utilization areas, or from other areas, to Resettlement projects will not increase the number of pupils of school age to be educated out of State funds.

Roads on projects will be improved by the Resettlement Administration with no cost to the State, although now-existing roads from projects to main highways will have to be improved where these roads are now inadequate to serve the newly developed areas. The net effect of the Resettlement program should be a saving in expenditure on roads.

Government land does not pay taxes; but, in order that project lands may bear their share of the tax burden, the Resettlement Administration will pass title on to the land and improvements to a local corporation, and will, at the same time enter into a contract with the corporation whereby the management of the project will remain in the hands of the Resettlement Administration.

Two effects of all new developments are an increase in values, because of increased population, and an increase in total taxation to support local services. The increased values should create sufficient taxable wealth to support the increase in services.

Effect on Local Real Estate Values

Land values in areas where Resettlement projects are located will be increased by the resettlement of families which will be self-supporting in the local communities. The newly settled families will create wealth through efficient production on good land. In many localities, chambers of commerce are actively engaged in attempting to secure Resettlement projects for their areas because of increased wealth and values which will result.

Real estate values are dependent on the volume of business which is carried on within the community. An increase in population on productive land would increase business, and the demand for city services would in turn increase the demand for city property. This increase in demand would result, as it always does, in an increase in local values, particularly those of

town properties. The effect would be entirely positive. There would be nothing that would tend to decrease values. Increased production, better school facilities, improved health conditions, and improved social conditions would all react beneficially on local values.

The Extent to Which Such Projects Have Benefited and Will Benefit Labor

Labor will be benefited in two ways. The construction of buildings and the development of farmlands will give direct employment to approximately 13,500 laborers for a year. The use of building materials will provide indirect employment for laborers in the production of the material itself.

The increased business activity stimulated locally by the establishment of successful farms, will increase

Pride in their work. A young farmer and his wife who have been given the chance to relocate themselves on a Federal resettlement project in Texas.

Figure 12. Two-page spread featuring "No work and no home. Drought Refugees from a southwestern State looking for jobs near San Jose Mission, in California" and "Pride in their work. A young Farmer and his wife who have been given the chance to relocate themselves on a Federal resettlement project in Texas." Resettlement Administration, *First Annual Report*, 1936, 38–39. Photographs by Dorothea Lange and Arthur Rothstein. Library of Congress Prints and Photographs Division.

Figure 13. "Drought refugees from Oklahoma looking for work
in the pea fields." Vicinity of San Jose Mission, California, March
1935. Photograph by Dorothea Lange. Library of Congress
Prints and Photographs Division, LC-USF344-001608-ZB.

of motion without destination and stability. Going west no longer provides an
opportunity to the pioneer family; rather migration leads to segregation and
insecurity. The main text, below the image, addresses the role of supervision in
the resettlement program, underlining that government "supervision [support
and advice] does not mean discouragement of individualism or of initiative."[32]
The assisted will not forsake their traditional ideals; rather, they will be provided with facilities to develop such values. Perhaps the text and image are juxtaposed in order to frame federal assistance as a metaphorical "pioneer cleaning,"
or restoration. The argument would then run that the refugees' individualism
should be developed to fit the purposes of a modern and mechanized agriculture.[33] The image attempts to counter popular and stereotypical assumptions

about RA clients, by presenting those clients through the stencil of values and aims associated with the pioneer.

The caption for the image on the right-hand page in figure 12 reads: "Pride in their work. A young farmer and his wife who have been given the chance to relocate themselves on a Federal resettlement project in Texas."[34] The caption ties the relocated couple to the father and son who were "helped to resettle:" the phrasing of both captions—involving a "chance" offered and assistance shared—suggests an alliance of purpose between the RA and their clients. Cropped closely to the open doorway of a house, the image of the young couple is halved by the doorframe, the woman inside the home, the man outside. The "farmer" and his "wife" are appropriately dressed for their restored roles. The woman wears a fresh white apron, symbolic of her domestic position. Her clean, efficient appearance is enhanced by the framing darkness within the house. The man, in contrast, wears the familiar denim overalls and shirt of the farmer.

Main text subheadings to the left and above the image address concerns associated with the public response to RA projects: taxation, local real estate values, and labor. The image contains features oriented to counter such criticisms. Resettlement has supplied the man with adequate economic resources to provide for his family, and to ensure their higher standard of living. The woman, through the family's improved position, can perform her domestic role efficiently, and as a consumer gain access to a "greater supply of diversified products."[35] In contrast to the family—as yet unaided by the state—on the facing page of the article, the couple in this photograph appear settled. The farmer and his wife, with their divided gender spheres, resemble an urban middle-class economic unit. The loose fit of the woman's clothing, and the crease of the apron across her upper abdomen, hint at pregnancy.[36] The absence of children in the photograph tacitly suggests that the couple have waited until they were settled and could afford a family—care of the RA. In contrast, the women at the truck appear as homeless, lone parents. The visual may connote nineteenth-century pioneer values, but contemporary environmental and economic conditions justify government intervention. Without federal assistance, essential American qualities might be lost, unable to participate productively in a modern environment. The farmer and his wife are both literally and socially "cleaner" than the modern "pioneer" family. If the images of the contrasted families are juxtaposed, as their content and placing allows, any allusive "cleaning" in evidence directly results from the RA's supervisory role. The narrative, built into the sequential relation of the images, implies that resettlement involves more than putting people on new land: the RA offers information and technical assistance which will enable families to retain their values and to adapt to a changing agricultural environment.

The report includes one photograph featuring a lone woman, in the chapter titled "Management" (fig. 14). The section addresses three main areas: the land utilization program, the rehabilitation of rural families on relief, and the facilitation of "better adjustment to the economic system of low income groups . . . where the possibility of attachment to the land gives promise of higher economic standards and of healthier and more wholesome patterns of living."[37] The caption represents the improved pattern of living, as promoted by the Management Section: "Management aids farm women with their problems. A homesteader of Austin Acres, in Minnesota, canning home grown vegetables in her new kitchen." Standing by a modern cooker, in an airy, clean kitchen, the woman is lit by natural light entering the room through large windows. Although the setting appears new and quite modern, her activity as captioned suggests a more traditional, self-sufficient lifestyle. The woman's homely appearance complements her activity and enhances the "traditional" connotations implied by the caption. Clear shadows cast on the tabletop highlight the clean white surface, but the worn paint of the table's legs indicate age. By combining new and old in image and caption, the photograph posits a potential harmony between "traditional" activity and a modern environment. The association of women with the domestic sphere, established in the right-side image in figure 12, is reiterated by the relationship between caption and image, as it binds "women's problems" to a domestic setting.[38]

Those imaged in the report typify "the deserving." As in Rexford Tugwell's *New York Times* article, it addresses public concerns about burdensome and lazy clients. By juxtaposing the migrant family with the young couple (see fig. 12), the report implies the before-and-after scenario familiar from the *Times* article. As such, it confirms the official visual narrative as compatible with that presented by the magazine. Although it is generally accepted that the FSA collection, as a whole, added more upbeat images after 1937, the early published visual narratives of RA activity also arguably foregrounded the positive results of government intervention. The suppression of exact regional information provided a way to both simplify and unify the published visual representation of RA programs.

Unlike the self-contained and transcendent quality of Dorothea Lange's "Migrant Mother," the formulaic images of rural women—reproduced in publications concerning RA activities—participated in a visual storytelling, which reiterated a narrowly defined, but regionally ambiguous, interpretation of women's roles based in the domestic sphere. As such, published RA and FSA images ignored many rural women's activities outside the home, in effect domesticating them. Despite underlining women's continued nurturing function, sequencing implied that continuity was dependent on a male provider. Male restoration, management. It has been recognized from the outset that there must be close cooperation between the Management Division and the developing divisions from the very inception of projects. In the regional offices as well as in Washington, there has been encouraged an attitude of helpful cooperation as opposed to one of jealous concern about divisional authority or prerogatives. In a number of cases, the selection of personnel is made jointly with the other divisions concerned, which has contributed materially to mutual sympathy and understanding.

Communities Under Management

The communities that have been fully completed and turned over to Management total fifteen. Nine other communities still in process of construction, but which are in part inhabited, have been turned over to Management. The full list follows.

Location:

	Region
Alabama:	
Palmer Tract, "Palmerdale" (Birmingham)	V
Jasper Unit A, "Bankhead Farms"	V
Arizona: Phoenix Unit 2, "Phoenix Homesteads"	IX
California:	
San Fernando, "San Fernando Homesteads"	IX
El Monte, "El Monte Homesteads"	IX
Indiana: Decatur, "Decatur Homesteads"	III
Iowa: Granger, "Granger Homesteads"	III
Minnesota: Austin "Austin Acres"	II
Mississippi:	
McComb "McComb Homesteads"	VI
Meridian, "Magnolia Homestead Gardens"	VI
Tupelo, "Tupelo Homesteads"	VI
Hattiesburg, "Hattiesburg Homesteads"	VI

Management aids farm women with their problems. A homesteader of Austin Acres, in Minnesota, canning home grown vegetables in her new kitchen.

Figure 14. "Management aids farm women with their problems. A homesteader of Austin Acres, in Minnesota, canning home grown vegetables in her new kitchen." Resettlement Administration, *First Annual Report*, 1936, 65. Photograph by Paul Carter. Library of Congress Prints and Photographs Division.

resulting from RA intervention, was visually prioritized. Image sequencing presented programs that, through an improved environment, enabled the subjects to perform existing and socially accepted gender roles efficiently. Projecting the recipients of RA assistance through an urban stencil promoted a revisualization of the rural poor palatable to the "urban dweller."[39]

NOTES

Abbreviations

FSA-OWI   Farm Security Administration–Office of War Information, Library of Congress

NACP   National Archives at College Park, Md.

P&P   Prints and Photographs Division, Library of Congress

The title of this chapter is from Rexford G. Tugwell, "Why Resettlement?" *Labor Information Bulletin* 3 (1936): 2.

1. Alan Owen, "Two of the Best: Photographic Portraits that Epitomize their Eras," *Connoisseur* 216 (1986): 60. See also Dorothea Lange, "The Assignment I'll Never Forget," reprinted in Liz Heron and Val Williams, eds., *Illuminations: Women Writing on Photography* (London: I. B. Taurus, 1996), 151–53. Lange explains, "I did not approach the tents and shelters of other stranded pea-pickers. It was not necessary; I knew I had recorded the essence of my assignment."

2. The four main areas of the RA were rural rehabilitation, rural resettlement, suburban resettlement, and land utilization; F. Jack Hurley, *Portrait of a Decade: Roy Stryker and the Development of Documentary Photography in the Thirties* (Baton Rouge: Louisiana State Univ. Press, 1972), 34.

3. The description states: "To direct the activities of investigators, photographers, economists, sociologists and statisticians engaged in the accumulation, selection and compilation of reports of field data, statistics, photographic material, vital statistics, agricultural surveys, maps and sketches necessary to make accurate descriptions of the various introductory, progressive and concluding phases of the Resettlement Administration, particularly with regard to the historical, sociological and economic aspects of the several programs and their accomplishments." Stryker Papers, series 2, part C, U.S. Government 1936–1962, section 1 FSA Administrative Records 1936–1943, reel 6, P&P.

4. Stryker Papers, series 2, part C, reel 6, P&P (emphasis added).

5. The RA was not the only government agency to employ photography to record its programs. A Time Inc. survey, commissioned to assess sources of visual material for a new picture magazine, considered Washington "the center of the photographic field." Though state use of the medium was extensive, it remains the case that government documentary photography, from the 1930s, has come to be predominantly associated with the FSA-OWI collection. Pete Daniel et al., *Official Images: New Deal Photography* (Washington: Smithsonian Institution Press, 1987), viii.

6. Warren I. Susman, "The Thirties," in Stanley Coben and Lorman Ratner, eds., *The Development of an American Culture* (Englewood Cliffs: Prentice-Hall, 1970), 192.

7. James Agee and Walker Evans, *Let Us Now Praise Famous Men* (Boston: Houghton Mifflin, 1988 [1941]), 11.

8. F. Jack Hurley, *Portrait of a Decade: Roy Stryker and the Development of Documentary Photography in the Thirties* (Baton Rouge: Louisiana State Univ. Press, 1972), 37.

9. On alienated reporters see Bernard Sternsher, *Rexford Tugwell and the New Deal* (New Brunswick: Rutgers Univ. Press, 1964), 292; "Tugwell Has Staff of 12,089 to Create 5,012 Relief Jobs," *New York Times*, 17 Nov. 1935, p. 1.

10. "Hitting Below the Belt," *Philadelphia Record*, 27 Nov. 1935, p. 3. Tugwell responded in writing to the article published in the *Times*, and a version of his letter was printed in the newspaper on 20 Nov. 1935. In his letter, Tugwell corrects the figures quoted in the article, actually increasing the number of people involved in the administration. He stresses that the "program is primarily one of rehabilitation rather than . . . direct work relief," going on to address each of the points raised by the article. Included with the letter is a terse summary of the administrative numbers and costs, and an overview of the land utilization, rehabilitation, and community projects not mentioned in the *Times* article. The summary was not published with the letter. Arthur Hays Sulzberger, publisher of the *Times*, replied to Tugwell expressing his "regret at the unfortunate manner in which the material available was presented in the offending story," stating "it was unfair to [the] administration, and as such deeply deplored." However, the reprint of Tugwell's response is foregrounded by an editorial introduction that places the administrative costs of the RA at 10 percent, compared with 1 percent for the Public Works Agency (PWA) and 5 percent for the WPA. Without contextualizing the statistics in terms of the type of work undertaken by the respective agencies, these figures reinforce the claims of the previous article. In a letter to Sulzberger, following this publication, Tugwell points out to the publisher that "we are . . . left in almost as bad a position as before. It is clearly represented that the RA is twice as inefficient as the WPA and ten times as inefficient as the PWA." However, not wishing to alienate Sulzberger further, Tugwell concludes his letter, "we shall be glad to take advantage of your offer to print a piece describing our activities," underlining the importance of publicity for the RA programs. "Tugwell Protests Published Figures," *New York Times*, 20 Nov. 1935, p. 5; Rexford Tugwell to Arthur Hays Sulzberger, 20 Nov. 1935, folder: Public Relations Newspapers and Magazines S, box 30, RG 96, NACP; Arthur Hays Sulzberger to Rexford Tugwell, 21 Nov. 1935 (letter is misdated 1934), and Rexford Tugwell to Arthur Hays Sulzberger, 27 Nov. 1935, folder: Newspaper Clippings S, box 31, RG 96, NACP.

11. Administrator, Division of Information to the President, 23 Dec. 1935, folder: Newspaper and Magazine Clipping N, box 30, RG 96, NACP.

12. Arthur Hays Sulzberger to Rexford Tugwell, 21 Nov. 1935 (letter is misdated 1934), folder: Newspaper Clippings S, box 31, RG 96, NACP.

13. Rexford G. Tugwell, "Problems—and Goal—of Rural Relief," *New York Times Magazine*, 15 Dec. 1935, p. 3.

14. Although the woman featured in the photograph was not in fact a sharecropper's

wife, this was the description assigned to her by the photographer. As such, my analysis of the image—based on its publication in the *Times* article—assumes that the magazine's editors were only supplied with the information available in the original caption. For details on the captioning of this photograph, see chapter 2. Margaret Jarman Hagood, *Mothers of the South: Portraiture of the White Tenant Farm Woman* (Charlottesville: Univ. Press of Virginia, 1996 [1939]), 5.

15. I am considering the sequences of photographs reproduced in digital format and accessed through "America from the Great Depression to World War II: Black and White Photographs from the FSA-OWI, 1935–1945," P&P, American Memory (Library of Congress website, http//memory.loc.gov/ammem/fsowhome.html). The photographs are reproduced in the sequences they were taken, following the initial filing arrangement of the collection. There are twelve frames digitally reproduced in the sequence, however these include copy negatives, and blank frames ("no digital image available"). I have therefore considered the eight usable frames, call numbers: LC-USF33-002021-M1; LC-USF33-002021-M2; LC-USF33-002021-M3; LC-USF33-002022-M1-M2; LC-USF33-002022-M2; LC-USF33-002022-M3; LC-USF33-002022-M4; LC-USF33-002022-M5.

16. Call no. LC-USF33-002021-M1, "The wife and children of a sharecropper," Washington County, Ark., August 1935, FSA/OWI, P&P.

17. Call no. LC-USF33-002021-M3, "Sharecropper's wife Arkansas," Washington County, Ark., August 1935, FSA/OWI, P&P.

18. Jefferson Hunter states that "some photographers were open about technical contrivances," pointing out that, Arthur Rothstein—in "Directions in the Picture Story," in Willard D. Morgan, ed., *The Complete Photographer* (New York: National Educational Alliance, 1941), 1,357–59, "discussed at length how he got the right photographable expression on the face of a southern woman standing at the door of her cabin. She posed graciously for him, but Rothstein wanted 'sad expressions,' 'worried faces,' and 'apathetic gestures,' so he had a friend 'engage the woman in conversation until these appeared, then snapped the shutter.' " Jefferson Hunter, *Image and Word: The Interaction of Twentieth-Century Photographs and Texts* (Cambridge: Harvard Univ. Press, 1987), 97, 101.

19. Call no. LC-USF34-2534E, "California fruit tramp and his family. The mother is twenty two years old," Marysville, Calif., June 1935, FSA-OWI, P&P.

20. Tugwell, "Problems—and Goal—of Rural Relief," 3, 22.

21. The original framing of the photograph shows an expanse of land next to the nearest house which reduces the suburban impression created by the published version. Call no. LC-USF342-000841-A, untitled, P&P.

22. The two subsequent photographs in the sequence: LC-USF33-002017-M3 (untitled) and LC-USF33-002017-M4 (untitled)—both killed—include the presence of an older girl who appears to be laboring, although it is unclear exactly what she is doing. While many accounts of the FSA collection refer to Stryker as responsible for "killing" negatives, Edwin Rosskam highlights the photographer's involvement, stating that "it was a great day in the photographer's trip when the contact prints came in . . . he settled in wherever he could—a room in a business travelers' hotel, most likely . . . and proceeded to do his killing. . . . This was every photographer's privilege: to go over his contact prints and

cross out the pictures he did not want used." Edwin Rosskam, "Not Intended for Framing: The FSA Archive," *Afterimage* 8 (March 1981): 10. Rosskam's comments suggest that while Stryker may have punched holes in the negatives, the selection of images to kill was not a solo endeavor.

23. RA, *First Annual Report* (Washington: 1936).

24. Sidney Baldwin, *Poverty and Politics: The Rise and Decline of the Farm Security Administration* (Chapel Hill: Univ. of North Carolina Press, 1968), 119.

25. RA, *First Annual Report* (Washington: 1936), 32.

26. Ibid., 38–39.

27. Since there are no other images of this family group, it is difficult to determine with certainty the text of the sign.

28. Photographer Dorothea Lange, like other photographers of the period, was conscious of using found lettering, signs, or billboards to enhance the message of the images they took. For example: Margaret Bourke-White's "There's no way like the American Way," flood relief line photograph; or Dorothea Lange's "Next Time Try the Train." James Guimond points out that "the FSA photographers had an aversion to the conservative, big business clichés about American economic life . . . [and] expressed this attitude most clearly in the deliberately ironic photographs they made of certain billboards." James Guimond, *American Photography and the American Dream* (Chapel Hill: Univ. of North Carolina Press, 1991), 112.

29. The woman's appearance, when associated with the word "cleaning," also brings to mind the trademark for Old Dutch Cleanser, a well-known and recognizable symbol of the 1930s. Roland Marchand points out that "agency studies indicated that a majority of Americans were literate in the ideogrammatic language of advertising trademarks" by the late 1920s. Roland Marchand, *Advertising the American Dream: Making Way for Modernity, 1920–1940* (Berkeley: Univ. of California Press, 1985), 335.

30. Call no. LC-USF344-001608-ZB, "Drought Refugees from Oklahoma looking for work in the pea fields," San Jose Mission, Calif. (vicinity), March 1935, P&P.

31. Traits such as laziness, immorality, promiscuity, and physical and emotional degeneracy were characteristics of a southern "po' white" stereotype. John Dollard wrote: "The existence of the lower-class whites or poor white group has been one of the continuous features of southern social organization. One might say of them that they have neither capital, talent, nor ancestry to give them preferential claims on income or prestige. . . . They seem to face the greatest difficulties in gaining status because they do not have the capital to begin making any kind of advance, nor do they have the resolve and tormented determination of some immigrant groups. Since their chances of social advancement are relatively low, they have little to loose in status or economic reward by lax behavior and in general they do not maintain the personal standards of the middle-class whites." John Dollard, *Caste and Class in a Southern Town* (New York: Doubleday, 1957 [1937]), 75. James T. Patterson points out that "the tendency of some people to endow even the Okies with the traits of sloth and shiftlessness revealed the function of stereotypes in chasing away the guilt of more fortunate Americans." James T. Patterson, *America's Struggle against Poverty, 1900–1980* (Cambridge: Harvard Univ. Press, 1981), 46.

The existence of an established stereotype, and its ready application to the potential recipients of government relief, highlights the necessity to project RA clients as "deserving"
of federal assistance.

32. RA, *First Annual Report*, 38.

33. "An effort must be made . . . to organize agricultural production [so] that the advantages of mechanization and mass production . . . can be secured without losing the
social values which have always been associated with rural living." Ibid., 35.

34. Call no. LC-USF34-002948-E, "Resettled farmer and his wife, Ropesville Community, Hockley County, Tex.," April 1936, P&P.

35. RA, *First Annual Report*, 40.

36. There is no photographic series of this couple, so there are no other images to
confirm the woman's condition.

37. RA, *First Annual Report*, 63.

38. The sequence this image is taken from contains a number of images of women engaged in various forms of labor: hanging out washing, canning, and child care. There are
also photographs of men working in the fields or outside, and men and women working
together in the garden (call nos. LC-USF341-011243-B to LC-USF341-011252-B). The content
of the sequence suggests it was taken to illustrate gender roles.

39. Tugwell, "Why Resettlement?" 2.

Poverty Management

Murder, "Convict Flogging Affairs," and Debt Peonage

The Roaring Twenties in the American South

VIVIEN M. L. MILLER

Organized racial violence against African Americans and the perpetuation of debt peonage in Georgia and northern Florida provide a depressing picture of African American and poor white life and labor in the first third of the twentieth century, and of the extent of coercive labor practices. The 1922 death of Martin Tabert in a Florida convict camp drew national attention to the practices of peonage, forced labor, and penal servitude, which nevertheless continued into the 1950s, when the state was simultaneously reinventing itself as a subtropical paradise for northern tourists, snowbirds, and investors.

In April 1923 Florida writer, environmental activist, and champion of the Everglades, Marjory Stoneman Douglas, penned this moving ballad lamenting the fate of Tabert:

Martin Tabert of North Dakota
(A Ballad, to be sung in a minor key, but at the end with shouts)

Martin Tabert of North Dakota is walking Florida now.
O children, hark to his footsteps coming, for he's walking soft and slow.
Through the piney woods and the cypress hollows
A wind creeps up and it's him it follows—
Martin Tabert of North Dakota, walking Florida now.

They took him out to the convict camp, and he's walking Florida now.
O children, the tall pines stood and heard him when he was moaning low.
The other convicts they stood around him

When the length of the black strap cracked and found him,—
Martin Tabert of North Dakota,—and he's walking Florida now.

They nailed his coffin boards together and he's walking Florida now.
O children, the dark night saw where they buried him, buried him, buried him low.
The tall pines heard when they went to hide him
And the wind crept up to moan beside him,
Martin Tabert of North Dakota. And he's walking Florida now.

The whip is still in the convict camp. For Florida's rising now.
Children, from Key West to Pensacola you can hear the great wind go.
The wind he roused when he lay dying,
The angry voice of Florida crying,

> "Martin Tabert of North Dakota,
>   Martin Tabert of North Dakota,
>   Martin Tabert of North Dakota,
>   You can rest from your walking now." [1]

On February 1, 1922, twenty-two-year-old Tabert, a white farm worker from North Dakota, died in a convict camp run by the Putnam Lumber Company and located near Clara, Dixie County, in northern Florida, from a severe flogging inflicted by thirty-five-year-old camp prison guard and "whipping boss" Thomas Walter Higginbotham. [2] Higginbotham was later charged with murder. During his trial in June 1923, J. W. Tyson, formerly a guard at the Clara camp, but then serving a prison sentence for larceny, testified that he had witnessed Higginbotham striking Tabert with a leather strap and counted ninety-seven blows. Former prisoner Eddie Waters, who stated that after the punishment Tabert was laid out on a bunk in the guardhouse and "was smeared with blood from many cuts and bruises," corroborated Tyson's testimony. [3] Other witnesses testifying before a legislative investigating committee in April 1923 described Tabert's back as "a bloody pulp." [4] The lumber company's letter to Martin's brother, E. D. Tabert, gave the official cause of death as a "complication of diseases" and stated that Martin had been "given a Christian burial in a cemetery at the camp." [5] It was not clear what Tabert had done to so enrage Higginbotham, but one report suggested that he had complained about his prison-issue shoes. Further, Higginbotham had a reputation for excessive violence toward prisoners; Tyson claimed that he quit working at the Clara camp after "Higginbotham came out of the wood and whipped almost every negro I had in my squad." [6]

At the time, many Floridians believed convict leasing had been abolished in 1919, when state prisoners convicted of felonies were relocated to the state prison farm at Raiford and the State Road Department camps. Tabert's death, however, exposed the continued practice of leasing for white and black county misdemeanant prisoners, the horrific camp conditions, and the longevity of peonage. In early 1923, the political and economic fallout from the Tabert case and sensational exposés of the enduring peonage in Florida's lumber, turpentine, and citrus industries led to fundamental reorganization of convict labor practices in the state. State legislators were presented with an opportunity to discard traditional forms of public punishment. Yet the economically depressed and materially poor state was ultimately unable to contemplate the financial burden of a modern penitentiary system. Economic growth boomed in 1924 and 1925, but financial collapse and a September hurricane known as the Big Blow both arrived in 1926. Even in prosperous times, Floridians opposed spending money on a predominately black inmate population when there were profits to be made from continuing public labor programs. Their reluctance to embrace penal modernity rested also on particular historical attitudes toward African Americans and poor white males.

Following the return of his elder brother from service in World War I, Martin Tabert had decided to leave the family farm near Munich in northeastern North Dakota to follow numerous young laborers southward in search of adventure and casual wage labor.[7] He left Munich in the late summer of 1921, and finding manual labor hard to come by, hopped on and off freight trains without paying his fare. On December 15, 1921, he was arrested by a Leon County deputy sheriff for "stealing a ride."[8] He was taken before Judge B. F. Willis of Leon County, found guilty of vagrancy, and ordered to pay a fine of $25 plus court costs. Tabert telegraphed his parents for $50 to be wired care of Sheriff James Robert Jones of Leon County, but they sent a letter and a bank draft for $75, which arrived after the 48-hour deadline. The letter was returned unopened and the envelope marked "party gone."[9] All "able-bodied prisoners" who failed to pay their fines within the allotted two days were leased to the Putnam Lumber Company (PLC), a Wisconsin-based company and one of several northern corporations that worked southern convict laborers in Florida. Company agents paid Tabert's fine, so he was indebted to Putnam and required to pay off his debt through physical labor for a period of ninety days at a turpentine camp in a neighboring county. Leasing prisoners from a county sheriff was one strategy employed by north Florida businessmen to surmount the serious labor problems that then plagued their industries.[10]

North Dakota Assistant Attorney General Gudmunder Grimson later accused the Leon County Sheriff of running "a squalid racket aimed directly at carefree amateur hobos." Sheriff Jones had agreements with PLC to furnish convict laborers for twenty dollars per head, and with the brakemen on freight trains to wire ahead information as to the number of fare dodgers aboard. The sheriff and his officers would meet the train, make the arrests, and take the defendants before Judge Willis, who always found them guilty. The extensive political connections and economic clout of PLC in central Florida were also highlighted by Grimson, who charged that the company "needed all the men it could get to work a new lumber camp in the swamp near Clara, Florida. Putnam liked to have a man for at least 90 days, a condition Jones met through his tame judge. And the company did not ask questions, not even when Jones managed to corral a staggering total of 100 strong men in the last three months of 1921 alone." In his study of the north Florida lumber industry, Jeffrey Drobney observes that collaboration between local law enforcement and local employers to secure cheap labor through the arrest of African Americans and, less frequently, whites on vagrancy or a similar charge was commonplace in northern and central Florida. Vagrancy laws also "fueled the county lease system" by enabling local sheriffs to make money for themselves and their counties. Handwritten notes in Grimson's papers showed that the assistant attorney general tallied numbers of persons arrested for vagrancy by Jones and his deputies in the months before and after the Leon County Board of County Commissioners had entered into contract with PLC in August 1921. Significant increases in arrests had occurred in the last three months of 1921 and the early part of 1922. According to the *Tampa Tribune*, Jones had arrested only 20 "vagrants" in the months prior to the August 1921 agreement, but 154 in the following seven months. Jones later admitted to legislative committee members investigating the Tabert case that he had delivered 163 men to PLC at a personal profit, after expenses, of fifteen dollars per prisoner.[11]

At the same time, Florida sheriffs, like their counterparts in many states and counties across the United States, were not paid a regular salary but were dependent on the state fee system for their livelihoods. While county officials set the level of fine for various offenses: "The sheriff, often a county's single most powerful governmental official, undoubtedly had input into framing the ordinances. The sheriff and his deputies were the men who made the arrests, and the sheriff often kept his own fine book that listed the offense, the offenders, and the amount they were fined."[12] Despite attempts to reform the practice in 1919 and 1925, the fee system survived in Florida into the 1930s.

Tabert was taken to a convict camp in Dixie County to serve out his sentence. Brooklyn fireman Max Grimm revealed details about conditions at Clara to the *New York World* newspaper. A former short-term prisoner who had labored alongside Tabert in January 1922, Grimm had been arrested near Greenville, Madison County, in November 1921 also for "stealing a ride" on a train bound for Jacksonville.[13] He recalled being "thrown into a dirty coop, and after a while was taken out and brought in an automobile about seven miles out in the woods before the county judge," who sentenced him . . . to sixty days in the county jail, "the biggest birthday present I ever got." On December 12, he and another prisoner were leased to a turpentine camp, owned by Florida State Senator T. J. Knabb, near Glen St. Mary.

On January 6, 1922, Grimm wrote of his transfer to the PLC camp at Clara, but "camp is little better than Glen St. Mary." He worked with a section gang hauling heavy logs through swamps under threat of the strap. Ten days after his transfer, he was punished by Higginbotham for breaking a hoe handle, "Captain Higginbotham . . . got off his horse, took the leather, and called me out of the ditch. He told me to lie down and I didn't want to lie down . . . and he called me a vile name and gave me one lick across my back." He continued: "I thought it best to lie down, as I knew I could not get away, so I lay down and he gave me first about seven lashes and I said nothing the first seven, but then he got mad and plied the lash harder and I received altogether about twenty-five licks on my back. Then he told me to get up and go back to work. It was the custom to run back to work always, but I was half crazy with pain and started in the opposite direction and he ran after me and gave me about a dozen lashes on my back, neck and head." Grimm was discharged in January 1922 nine days before Tabert died, but was aware of Tabert's declining health: "Tabert at one time worked in a ditch with me and we stood in water up to our thighs. He was weak and trembling so he could hardly lift his shovel. His eyes glittered like those of a half crazy man and he could hardly speak." Tabert, it turned out, was suffering from malaria.[14]

In 1924, sociologist Frank Tannenbaum drew on official reports, inmate testimony, and his own field studies to paint a vivid picture of southern bunkhouses, cages and tents, the torn, unwashed, and vermin-infested bedding, the meager rations of substandard and unwholesome food—molasses, cornbread, pork fat, and coffee—swarming with flies from nearby soil pits and middens, and the lack of sanitation that ensured prisoners' vulnerability to skin, eye, and venereal infections, tuberculosis, and pneumonia. In this world of negligence, brutality, and callous disregard, ill health did not excuse poor work or provide relief from punishments for minor infractions of the rules. Sick inmates were compelled to work, and for this corporal punishment was central: leather straps lacerated the flesh and left "abraded surfaces" and raw wounds discharging blood and pus. Former U.S. government inspector of prisons Joseph F. Fishman was equally scathing in his assessments of county jails: "I declare that a jail is a debauch of dirt, disease and degeneracy." The county jails that furnished misdemeanants like Tabert with their formative experiences of southern penal conditions were for Fishman, places of "neglect, indifference and brutality," rife with corruption and disease, both moral and physical.[15] Grimm's diary showed that conditions in county convict camps were no better.

In July 1922, Glen Thompson, another short-term prisoner recently discharged from the Clara camp, wrote to the postmaster at Munich, asking if he would "please find out whether the parents or kinsfolk of Martin Tabert know or care to know the particulars of Martin's death in February. I was an eye witness in the boy's death and I am doubting whether any particulars were sent to the folks."[16] Thompson and several other witnesses to the beating, including former guards A. B. Shiver and W. O. McCullers, former prisoners John Gardner and Stanley Martin, and former Clara whipping boss J. B. Baruch, corresponded with the Taberts throughout the summer and fall of 1922. Their letters and affidavits provided Grimson and sympathetic Florida lawyers with enough evidence to force legislative and grand-jury investigations the following spring that revealed that "those in control of the prisoners had been guilty of wanton cruelty and callous disregard for the health, and even lives, of their charges."[17] They also provided the Taberts with a full and shocking picture of Martin's last days. Higginbotham punished Tabert with at least fifty blows of the leather strap on the night of Friday, January 27, 1922 (there was no agreement among witnesses on the actual number of blows delivered). On Saturday morning, Tabert was delirious but had to drag himself from his bunk to report for work duty or suffer another punishment beating. On Sunday he was consumed with fever and died on Tuesday morning.[18] Former Alabama convict Ned Cobb would later advise inmates to "be good, obey orders and get out of prison," but this was not always possible for even the most hapless prisoner.[19]

Fourteen months after Tabert's death, the North Dakota legislature passed a resolution demanding the Florida legislature investigate fully, including allegations that the Leon County sheriff and lumber camp operators were involved in a conspiracy to convict men for minor offenses.[20] The issue was made even more sensitive by the fact that the county seat of Leon County was Tallahassee, the state capital: these events had occurred under the legislators' noses. Governor Cary Hardee denounced the resolution and complained to Grimson that North Dakota senators had taken one isolated incident "as a basis for general indictment of the State. With 1500 convicts it is entirely possible that there will occasionally occur some mistreatment, but no State in the Union is more humane to their prisoners than Florida."[21] Yet he ordered the suspensions of Sheriff Jones and Judge Willis. Further, after much legislative hand-wringing, a special legislative session was convened in Tallahassee in early April 1923.[22] The legislature then created a joint senate-house committee with three senators and two legislators who pledged to thoroughly investigate the circumstances of Tabert's death.[23] Exhumation, repatriation, and reburial expenses were also to be paid by the State of Florida, fearful of losing vital northern economic investment and deeply sensitive to any slights to the "honor" of the state. A hundred witnesses testified before the Florida Joint Legislative Committee between April 13 and May 10, 1923. Their statements and testimony were printed widely, giving national publicity to the committee's work and ensuring that parties outside the state would monitor Florida's response.

Tabert's plight in the Florida turpentine camps was brought to the attention of the national press by North Dakota's assistant attorney general, Gudmunder Grimson, and was detailed by *New York World* journalist Samuel D. McCoy. The paper was later awarded a Pulitzer Prize for the articles on the Tabert case and Florida's convict system.[24] Under the banner headline " 'Worse Than Penal Servitude,' Is Characterization of Evil State Protects," McCoy declared that aside from a few long ignored protesters, "Until now the people of Florida themselves have not heard that awful screaming" of "a human being under the lash of a convict captain." But: "It comes from prisoners, white men as well as Negroes, leased out to labor under convict guards in lumber camps and phosphate mines. They are too far away to be heard," and were especially out of the earshot of the half million tourists who visited Florida each winter. McCoy continued, "A few have protested, a few have been sick with shame, but a million people have been either ignorant of the system or have closed their eyes to what was going on about them, have shrugged their shoulders and turned away carelessly."[25]

As the committee heard testimony and the legislators discussed convict matters, the scope of the investigation was enlarged to examine other incidences of inhumane treatment at county and state convict camps. It was clear that the corporal punishment of prisoners was commonplace in Florida. McCoy later recalled, "Among other things, the *World* published the state's own records, showing irrefutably that the treatment of Tabert, far from being an isolated case, was merely one of 94 similar lashings that had been administered to prisoners in the preceding three months alone."[26]

In the early 1920s there had been a torrent of additional evidence of guards killing prisoners and of official complicity in penal servitude and peonage. For example, the 1923 legislative investigating committee considered evidence of brutal labor conditions and peonage in turpentine camps run by the Knabb Turpentine Company (owned by Senator T. J. Knabb and his brother).[27] On May 11, the commissioners of Alachua County canceled their leasing contract with Knabb and demanded the return of all county inmates following revelations over the treatment of nineteen-year-old Paul Revere White from Washington, D.C. Arrested while walking along a highway, White had been convicted of vagrancy. The local justice of the peace sentenced him to six months' imprisonment, and he was leased to the Knabb camp at Glen St. Mary.[28] White's affidavit read: "I was whipped the third day after I arrived. I was kicked, beaten and whipped practically every day during the time I was there."[29] He had been rescued from certain death by convict inspector John B. Thomas, who described the Knabb camp as a "human slaughter pen" (but later retracted this statement). White was beaten for not working hard enough and subjected to other deprivations and cruelties, which were brought to the attention of the commissioner of agriculture by Thomas. Camp "captain" John Roddenbury was indicted for cruel and inhumane treatment by the Baker County grand jury, but Knabb was not charged.

As subsequent testimony of the legislative committee members revealed, those who lived near convict camps were acutely aware of conditions and abuses, but the web of patronage that surrounded county politics and penal issues limited exposure or protest. Thelma Franklin, wife of the postmaster at Glen St. Mary, however, spoke out against White's treatment and claimed that the deaths of another nine inmates at the camp had yet to be investigated.[30] Florida's four state prison inspectors would periodically visit state and county camps and interview prisoners, then report their findings to the commissioner of agriculture, but only some of those observations were recorded in official reports. After 1923, they were required to inspect convict camps and county jails every twenty-one days.[31] Inspector Thomas' suspicions had been raised by several cases of suspicious deaths at the Knabb camp, including one where, in a fourteen-day period, a black male prisoner had been convicted, sentenced, leased, and found dead. The coroner recorded a verdict of "death by natural causes," but Thomas's report stated that the prisoner was in good physical condition at the time he was leased. When Knabb was permitted to continue to lease prisoners on the promise that conditions would be greatly improved, local businessmen paid the fines of Baker County convicts in protest, thereby emptying the county jail.[32] In the mid-1930s the U.S. solicitor general declared that the Department of Justice was again interested in the Knabb Company employment practices, "partly because conditions in the Florida turpentine camps . . . have been a fertile source of complaints of involuntary servitude and peonage."[33] Knabb was eventually forced to sell the camp.

The Tabert investigation had forced legislators to acknowledge the serious structural problems at the heart of Florida's penal system. A letter to the editor of the St. Louis Star decried: "The marvel as well as moral of the Tabert murder and peonage case in Florida consists in the fact that such an incident did not materialize long ago. Just how many unfortunate victims of legalized slavery like young Tabert are rotting in uncoffined and unknown graves in the Southland, is hard to conjecture."[34] Yet, Tabert's treatment as a convict laborer was not unusual; corporal and physical punishments formed an intrinsic part of the disciplinary apparatus of the convict lease and prison regimes across the southern United States. Writing of the regime at Parchman in Mississippi, William Banks Taylor remarks, "Felons were punished by the denial of freedom and by an exacting regimen of discipline; and the hall marks of convict life were unpleasant enough to discourage recidivism in rational beings."[35] And, of course, they encouraged escape in the most desperate.

New Yorker Robert E. Burns, a shell-shocked war veteran wandering the southern United States in 1922, was sentenced to ten years' hard labor on a Georgia chain gang (Georgia didn't build a penitentiary until 1938) after being tricked into participating in an armed robbery in Atlanta. In his memoir, *I Am a Fugitive from a Georgia Chain Gang!* he described being beaten by "illiterate, coarse and brutal" guards who used a six-foot-long leather strap, three inches wide and a quarter inch thick across prisoners' bare buttocks. Prisoners were usually given ten "licks" for petty offenses such as answering back, being disorderly, or refusing to work. After the punishment, half-conscious prisoners with blood running down their legs were carried to the sleeping quarters. The wounds were left untreated and "the dirty filthy stripes [two-piece convict suit] would stick to the wounds on the buttocks and cause inflammation and torture," but as Burns declared: "that is what the chain gang is for, torture! Torture every day."[36]

All prisons and labor camps operated regimes of labor subordination and discipline in which physical punishments to the body were commonplace and floggings were routine. Guards in early twentieth-century Alabama prison mines recalled brutalizing prisoners regularly: "I know we whooped niggers jes to have fun. . . . I've seen niggers with their rumps looking like a piece of raw beef. Some of 'em would pass out like a light but they'd all put up a awful howl, beggin' us to stop. It wasn't right fer us to do that. The company had lots of ways to make a bad convict work but us guards didn't follow 'em much. Didn't nobody want to put a convict in the sweat box, or feed him on bread and water, fer they wasn't no fun in watchin that."[37] However, corporal punishment was not unique to prisons in the Deep South.

Corroborating the guard's memories and revealing that women prisoners were not spared such brutality is the story of forty-year-old Kate Richards O'Hare, a socialist opposed to American participation in World War I, who served fourteen months (1919 to 1921) of a five-year sentence as a political prisoner of the United States. As there was no federal women's prison in the United States until 1927, she was housed at the Missouri State Penitentiary at Jefferson City. O'Hare listed the range of punishments inflicted on female prisoners: from verbal abuse to bread and water rations to denial of privileges such as communication with other inmates, loss of recreation time, and the withholding of letters and food parcels. More serious infractions of the rules could result in physical punishments such as handcuffing women to cell doors, whippings, beatings with fists and clubs, kickings, and the use of a bridle or metal gag placed over the mouth. Incorrigibles could face confinement in "the hole," an ice-cold cement cell, for two to fifteen days, where they were fed two slices of bread and half a cup of water per day.[38] Following her release after receiving a presidential pardon in 1921, O'Hare committed herself to exposing the horrors of U.S. prisons and to working to ending the prison contract labor system.

Early twentieth-century exposés of prison life underlined that floggings, water torture, or confinements in "cribs" were found in every jail and prison. Edgardo Rotman observed that in Joliet, Illinois, male prisoners were held in solitary cells for up to a week on a daily diet of four ounces of bread and a quart of water. In Ohio, prisoners stood for eight or more hours a day confined in a close-fitting, semicircular steel cage. In Colorado, in early 1925, the Civil Service Commission declared flogging a legal form of punishment. Prisoners could also be punished by wearing a heavy ball and chain, riveted to the ankle, for ninety days or longer. Thus the progressive goal of eradicating corporal punishments was not fully achieved until well into the twentieth century. The last whipping recorded in Delaware was in 1954, but the law sanctioning it remained on the books for another eighteen years.[39]

Southern prisons and jails were particularly violent and brutal, partly because of the continuance of traditions of hard labor performed in semipublic settings—when Burns was sent to prison in Georgia in 1922 he expected to see a large stone building "surrounded by a huge wall," but found a collection of filthy and dilapidated wooden buildings and a chain gang—the associations with pre–Civil War slavery, the retention of "stripes," the ubiquitous chains encasing the inmate's body, and use of physical punishments. In Mississippi, Parchman prison farm, "a typical Delta plantation," also had no walls or guard towers, cellblocks or stockades, as did Raiford in Florida.[40] To some extent, northerners' "civilized sensibilities" were not as offended by the condition of northern inmates because they were hidden from public gaze behind the large stone walls of penitentiaries and reformatories. As David Garland observes: "The wince of pain or the scream of agony announce the fact of violence and render it visible, whereas the mental anguish and gradual deterioration of an incarcerated inmate is much more difficult to observe and much easier to overlook. The crucial difference between corporal punishments which are banned, and other punishments . . . is a matter of the form which that violence takes, and the extent to which it impinges upon public sensibilities. Modern sensibilities display a definite selectivity."[41]

Early twentieth-century southern sensibilities also displayed selectivity when it came to matters of race and punishment. Most southern prisoners were African Americans. Convict labor in phosphate or coal mines, lumber camps, or turpentine camps required enormous physical strength and stamina in order for a prisoner to meet a daily quota or task, and leasees in Florida preferred black inmate laborers because they constituted a more dependable and capable workforce.[42] Public outrage at chain gangs and prisoner treatment usually occurred only after exposés featuring respectable white prisoners. Black defendants were generally regarded as misplaced members of a race that was believed to be ignorant, superstitious, immoral, degenerate, totally lacking in self-control, and with a congenital tendency toward crime. In the decades after emancipation, the deep association between race and criminality was still firmly established in the minds of many white southerners. Debates over prisoners, race, and criminality in the early twentieth century were dominated by eugenics, the genetic theory of crime, feeblemindedness, and the pseudoscience of criminal anthropology.[43] For Oshinsky, in this context, the leather strap "seemed the perfect instrument of discipline in a prison populated by the wayward children of former slaves." In Mississippi, corporal punishment garnered strong public support from prison officials, sheriffs, politicians, judges, church groups, and newspaper editors.[44]

Guards, administrators, and white inmates all lived in a society that preached and practiced white supremacy, but when a white guard killed a member of his own race, racialized penal rationales were threatened. Further, those who wrote personal accounts of their imprisonment during the late nineteenth and the first third of the twentieth centuries tended to be white male former prisoners, like Burns, thus giving greater publicity and attention to and garnering public sympathy for this group.[45] Less literate and well-connected black and white prisoners protested their treatment and made allegations of cruelty, physical abuse, and other deprivations to prison inspectors, the National Association for the Advancement of Colored People (NAACP), and other interested parties. In an effort to protest against the conditions of their confinement, others resorted to self-mutilation, such as chopping off fingers, toes, and hands, or slicing tendons, actions that continued into the 1940s in Florida, Louisiana, and Texas, for example.[46]

Although the race of White and Tabert was essentially the catalyst for legislative action—at one level the deaths of black prisoners were considered natural or unsurprising—the issue of proportionality also contributed. It was ultimately indefensible that county prisoners—men and women convicted of misdemeanors and petty crimes, and therefore sentenced to terms of eighteen months or less—should suffer what were in effect death sentences, whereas "hardened" state felons convicted of murder and armed robbery, and serving lengthier terms, survived under better state regulation at state prison farms or in state-run road camps. Further questions—as to how punitive a penitentiary or prison system should be, establishing the line between acceptable chastisement to achieve an efficient and disciplined convict labor force and unwarranted brutality, and the extent to which a prison constituted a zone of power and immunity from the law in which wardens and guards could do as they pleased—were also open to debate.

Many southern penal systems came under severe criticism in the 1920s from penal reformers, former prisoners, and even state officials, including Governor Miriam Ferguson of Texas, for the perpetuation of brutal treatments, inhumane conditions, and political corruption. In Alabama in 1923 the death of another white prisoner provoked further national indignation and public outcry over Deep South penal practices and conditions. James Knox was serving a short sentence for forging a thirty-dollar check when he died at Flat Top prison mine. A prison mining camp doctor identified suicide as the cause of death, but the state attorney general's report revealed that Knox had died during a form of punishment known as *watering*. According to the report: "James Knox died in a laundering vat, located in the yard of the prison near the hospital, where he was placed by two negroes. . . . It seems most likely that [he] died as a result of heart failure, which probably was caused by a combination of unusual exertion and fear. . . . After death it seems that a poison was injected artificially into his stomach in order to simulate accidental death or suicide." The prison warden and four sergeants were indicted for murder but none were convicted. Mary Ellen Curtin argues that "this single incident sparked off an explosion in public outrage that finally dealt a death blow to the system."[47] The similarities between the Knox and Tabert cases, both involving short-term white male prisoners from other states, were lost neither on Alabama and Florida politicians nor on the interested public. The deaths of Tabert and Knox were instrumental in convincing legislators and voters that it was now time to end convict leasing in Florida and Alabama in 1924 and 1928 respectively, and in pushing those states some way toward penal modernity.

Class was as important as race in shaping attitudes toward prisoners, especially as states like Florida, Mississippi, Georgia, and Louisiana were seeing increasing numbers of poor whites in their prison populations, although the majority of prisoners continued to be African American. Thus, for most middle-class or working-class white and black southerners, those who formed the "criminal class"—"po' white trash" and "worthless niggers"—constituted an underclass beyond the pale of civilization and consisted of persons for whom they could feel either no compassion, or only a little compassion at a distance.[48] O'Hare argued that "the whole system of criminal law has become a voracious cormorant that devours the bodies, brains, and souls of the poor."[49] While railing against the class inequities of the U.S. justice system, O'Hare nevertheless considered herself socially, racially, and intellectually superior to the ordinary prisoners and was particularly hostile to the "ignorant, brutal and degenerate black stool pigeons."[50] Tabert's death offended northern and southern sensibilities because he died in a convict labor system designed to control the African American labor force, and in which "routine violence and suffering" could "be tolerated on condition it [was] discreet, disguised or somehow removed from view" (or perhaps practiced on a predominately black male prison population).[51] The legacy of slavery endured: even the most sympathetic white southerners did not automatically recoil from the crack of the strap on the black male body.

Although the state's major cities all had large African American populations, many black Floridians (34 percent of Florida's population of 1.5 million by 1930) also lived in the backcountry, far from the gaze of snowbirds, tourists, and developers. They were exposed to white supremacy, Jim Crow laws, vagrancy legislation, inferior schools, were barred from the Democratic primaries, and endured a seemingly endless cycle of economic exploitation and poverty (exacerbated by the boll weevil), physical violence, and racial harassment (between 1918 and 1927, forty-seven black citizens were lynched in Florida).[52] Approximately forty thousand African Americans had left northern Florida counties between 1916 and 1920; some moved to Miami and southern counties, but most boarded trains in Tampa and Jacksonville bound for the Northeast and Midwest.[53] At the same time that the Tabert case, the peonage investigations, and the debates over prisons and punishment were taking place, black Floridians were being targeted in organized racial attacks. For example, in December 1922 a white female school teacher in Perry was allegedly murdered by an escaped black prisoner, Charlie Wright, who was in effect burned at the stake by a mob of local men and accomplices from Georgia and South Carolina, and the nearby black community was burned out.[54] During the first week of January 1923, following claims by a white woman in Sumner that she had been assaulted by a black male, a white mob attacked black residents of nearby Rosewood. Rosewood, a black township near Cedar Key, was home to eighteen to twenty-five black families, most of whom owned their own homes and property. Some residents were farmers, some labored at the Cummer Lumber Mill, and others, mainly women, worked as domestic servants. At least six African Americans and two whites were killed when Rosewood was destroyed.[55] A similar incident had occurred in Ocoee in November 1920 when racial violence erupted after African

Americans tried to vote.[56] White businessmen feared that the racial violence at Perry and Rosewood would discourage tourism in the Sunshine State. Few wanted to jeopardize the first real chance of prosperity in the economic boom of the 1920s. Business leaders pressured the state's political representatives to stop the violence and restore law and order, which was not achieved but rather better hidden from public view.[57]

The paternalistic character of black–white relations was most enduring in rural and backwoods counties. The perpetuation of debt peonage in Florida underlined the extent to which few of the material and social developments of the 1920s touched the lives of Florida's African American population. During the 1920s and 1930s, approximately 15,000 to 20,000 African American (and some white) workers, both men and women, lived in company towns operated by phosphate companies, and lumber, turpentine, and other naval stores operators. Located deep in the vast pine forests of northern and central Florida, the turpentine and lumber industries subjected many of these workers to forced labor or peonage. The State of Florida was considered one of the worst peonage offenders and indeed one special agent of the U.S. Department of Justice as early as 1906 likened the state to one giant peonage camp.[58]

The Tabert case had highlighted the links between law enforcement and peonage, a practice outlawed under federal statutes passed after the Civil War. But the practice of peonage was perpetuated through state laws, frequent collusion of local government officials, including sheriffs, with turpentine and lumber operators, and the enduring custom of white employers using force to coerce black workers. Also, nonconvict and convict labor camps were often run by the same companies, such as, the Putnam Lumber Company or Florida Pine Company. In 1919, the same year it ended the leasing of state prisoners to private contractors, the state legislature passed a law empowering employers to hold workers for debt.[59] This meant that lumber and turpentine operators requiring laborers could recruit individuals, furnish them with transportation to the work site, assess an advance charge for the service, and subsequently hold the worker and compel him to labor in the piney woods until he paid his debt. Anyone who failed to perform labor or reneged on the debt was guilty of a misdemeanor and liable for a fine of $500. Although demobilization in 1919 had brought a surplus of skilled workmen to Florida, the continued exodus of unskilled black laborers led timber, turpentine, and agricultural employers to complain of labor shortages, and in part accounted for deteriorating race relations in Florida. The *Chicago Defender* charged that there was official connivance in industry plans to keep African Americans in the South and to encourage migrants to leave northern cities, "to get the people back, get them declared vagrants by the courts and then immediately pay their fines and put them to work under the peonage system."[60]

Individuals found it impossible to keep track of their debt or to pay up. Most camps operated their own commissaries, so workers drew their supplies at inflated prices and on credit. The worker's annual bill for food, clothes, and tools inevitably added up to more than his or her wages. Debts were manipulated by the company's bookkeeping methods, and because the system ensured that the black and lower-class white workers would never be out of debt, it was impossible for them to quit. Despite high-profile peonage prosecutions in Florida in 1901, 1906, 1908, and the early 1920s, turpentine operators in Florida were not persuaded to change their labor practices.[61]

A strict caste system prevailed in western and northern Florida camps, and later company towns, from the 1890s to 1930s; hands were black while woodsriders and guards were predominately white.[62] Many black turpentine workers of the 1920s were descendants of slaves, and generations of the same family had often labored in camps since Reconstruction. They lived in company shanties in stockades surrounded by miles of pine forests, in close proximity to camp managers and guards. They usually received company scrip or metal tokens as wages (graded according to skill, age, and gender). The duties of women living in the stockades included child rearing, boiling and cleaning gum-stiff clothing, cooking, and nursing the sick.[63] Children received only rudimentary education (some camps had combination school and church houses) and labored in violation of state child labor laws. Over the years, turpentine workers created a distinct culture with its own rhythms of labor and language, and including religion, gambling, dancing, and fighting. One woodsrider recalled: "Turpentine niggers are a class by themselves. They are different from town niggers, farm laborers, or any other kind. Mostly they are born and raised in the camps, and don't know much about anything else. They seldom go to town, and few of them ever saw the inside of a schoolhouse."[64] Whereas the socially constructed "mill family" did not include black men, women, and children, the "turpentine family" of northern Florida was primarily black.[65]

Drobney's study of the lives of men and women in the lumber company towns of northern Florida between 1900 and 1940 illustrates that "separate and unequal facilities" were the norm for black workers, and labor practices varied widely. Company-built houses were usually equipped with electricity, indoor plumbing, space, and access to certain recreational facilities including theaters, churches, and organized sports teams, although "jook joints" with illegal gambling, dancing, and prostitution remained firmly in the black sections. The emergence of corporate paternalism in the 1910s and 1920s could provide an alternative to peonage for more progressive employers seeking a stable and loyal workforce. PLC company towns at Cross City and Shamrock offered a work experience far different from that at the nearby Clara convict camp.[66]

In his now dated but still valuable study of peonage in the twentieth-century American South, Pete Daniel identified the two main sources of peonage complaints in the late nineteenth and early twentieth centuries as the cotton belt from the Carolinas to Texas, including the Mississippi Delta, and the turpentine areas of northern Florida, southern Georgia, Alabama, and Mississippi. By 1920, "each southern state was enmeshed in a tangle of virtually countless cases and complaints."[67] In Florida these included the former governor, Sidney J. Catts, who was acquitted of peonage charges in 1922, the year after his gubernatorial term ended. Coercive labor practices in lumber and turpentine camps infused the prolonged crusade against peonage by Gainesville District Attorney and later U.S. Attorney General Fred C. Cubberly.[68] At the end of April 1923 the federal government became involved in what the *New York Times* called "Florida's convict flogging affairs." Cubberly set up a federal grand jury peonage investigation in Pensacola, centering on the leasing of a sixty-five-year-old African American prisoner, Ned Thompson, and the complicity of Sheriff Jones and Judge Willis of Leon County.[69]

In many respects it is easy to imagine few differences between conditions during Reconstruction and those in the first half of the twentieth century, although there was at least one major innovation in naval stores production in the early twentieth century: the use of the "Herty cup" for tapping and extracting pine resin to effect more rapid exploration of southern pine forests. Further, camps were not completely isolated from the forces of modernism; 1920s and 1930s photographs show evidence of automobiles as well as a range of canned goods for sale at commissaries.[70] Drobney describes the company stores in Foley and Shamrock as "showcases of modern facilities" that were "large and well lighted" and "carried a diversified stock of merchandise and the quality compared favorably with goods found in an independent store." Customers found groceries, drugstores, a meat market, and a barbershop. The long front porches were meeting places to swap gossip and news, thus the store "was a crossroads where people of different classes, races, and gender came into close contact with one another."[71] In the 1930s WPA interviewers in Florida noted the presence of the "mechanical, nickel phonograph" in remote turpentine, logging, and phosphate camps. They noted also the availability of phonograph records at company stores in Hernando County, and lamented the gradual loss of older and localized workaday songs as recorded numbers and vocal recordings grew in popularity.[72] But only a small percentage of company business involved cash even in the 1930s and workers remained in a chronic state of indebtedness.

The inventories of company stores changed with the times, but attitudes toward lower-class laborers were slower to adjust. Many southern landowners thought that acquiring bonded black laborers from the local jail, working them, and holding them for debt was neither illegal nor wrong, as revealed in one peonage trial in Georgia in the early 1920s that was detailed by Daniel. Following complaints by former prisoners Gus Chapman and James Strickland, two federal agents from the Department of Justice visited the 2,000-acre plantation in Jasper County, Georgia, belonging to John S. Williams. Strickland had escaped from the Williams's plantation on Labor Day 1920, and Gus Chapman had fled under threat of death on Thanksgiving Day 1920. During Williams's subsequent trial, it was revealed that to secure laborers, he or one of his four sons who lived on neighboring plantations would travel to a local jail, pay the fine of a black misdemeanant, and take him to Jasper County. Thus indebted for their bond, laborers worked as long as Williams could hold them, regardless of whether the debt had been repaid. They were warned that if they tried to escape they would be killed—those who did escape were tracked with bloodhounds, brought back, and beaten; some were murdered.

Most such men were uneducated, illiterate, and unfamiliar with the law, and had virtually no recourse, so they did not know how to extract themselves from peonage. There are numerous cases in the 1920s and 1930s of black workers trying to escape their indebtedness, being caught and forcibly returned to camps or plantations, sometimes with the approval of the courts. Up to thirteen prisoners were kept at a time by Williams, and two African American foremen, Clyde Manning and Claude Freemen, were responsible for guarding the "stockade Negroes." The peons were subject to frequent beatings from both their white and black captors. Following the agents' visit of February 1921, Williams coerced Manning into destroying the "evidence" of peonage on the plantation by murdering the peons. Usually this was done with an ax, but some were bound, weighted, and tossed alive into the Alcovy River.[73] On March 24, 1921, Clyde Manning, then under Department of Justice protection, confessed that he and John S. Williams had murdered eleven peons. Manning's disclosures provoked horror and denunciations from neighbors in Jasper and Newton counties, labor unions, journalists (including one from the *New York World*), demands for a legislative investigation, and a publicity campaign by the NAACP. Williams was found guilty of first-degree murder and sentenced to life imprisonment.[74]

Clyde Manning also stood trial for first-degree murder in May 1921, was convicted and sentenced to life imprisonment, but the conviction was overturned on appeal. At the second trial in July 1922, his defense was that "he had been compelled to murder for fear of his own life." To support this claim, the court heard testimony from the other African American residents of Williams's plantation that "revealed the hopeless desperation, the terror, and the ignorance that characterized the vertiginous world of peonage." Most of these men and women had spent their adult lives on Williams's property but did not know of the location (or in some cases the existence) of a local store only five miles from the farm. They could not leave because they were unfamiliar with the surrounding countryside and would have faced beatings or even death if caught. They reasoned that if the "stockade Negroes" who had knowledge of the outside world could not successfully flee, what chance did they have? Manning was again convicted and sentenced to life imprisonment; he died on a Georgia chain gang in the mid-1920s.[75]

Increasing numbers of peonage cases were being prosecuted in the state courts and by federal prosecutors, including Cubberly. Yet, as late as 1949 the Workers Defense League found fourteen turpentine camps in Alachua County, Florida, where "the practice of peonage is open and notorious."[76] In the 1940s a lawsuit charged that a similar debt peonage system, affecting migrant black canecutters, existed in the sugar fields around Lake Okeechobee in southern Florida.[77] Whereas most laborers in the southern states enjoyed freedom of movement in some form and were able to escape poverty and debt, many black sharecroppers and turpentine workers remained trapped in a cycle of debt peonage and poverty. Not until 1942 and 1944 did the U.S. Supreme Court strike down contract labor laws in Georgia and Florida.[78] The continued existence of peonage therefore provided a sobering parallel to the "migration narrative" with its implicit promise of black agency of the post–World War I African American world.

Although the Tabert case did not fundamentally alter the plight of turpentine or lumber laborers, it did herald significant changes to the state's penal regime. At the end of April 1923, Florida legislators debated the abolition of corporal punishment in convict camps as well as measures to improve the pay of guards and physicians, more rigorous inspections, and punishments of up to ten years' imprisonment for prison personnel who mistreated inmates. Florida senators were also forced to consider the circumstances in which use of the strap was appropriate or acceptable. Several argued for the retention of the whipping boss and of corporal punishment as essential to discipline. McCoy declared that Florida "crackers" and men of wealth alike had been "ingrained from birth with the stubborn belief that prisoners, and especially Negro prisoners, cannot be controlled without the frequent use of the lash."[79] This view was shared by Senator N. J. Wicker, who declared: "There are a lot of things I don't know anything about[,] but there are two thins I do know a lot about. They are mules and niggers. You want to abolish the flogging of convicts, and I tell you corporal punishment is the only way a convict nigger can be controlled."[80] The alternative method of punishment was the sweatbox, used across the South in the 1920s and 1930s. Prisoners could spend hours or days on reduced rations in a cramped wooden box, rather like an upright coffin, with no room to move or sit down, where the heat of the sun penetrated the ventilation holes in the roof. Ultimately, legislators voted for the immediate and permanent cessation of the whipping of county and state prisoners in early May 1923. The *New York Times* viewed these developments as an important victory for reformers and humanitarians.[81] On May 15, the antiflogging bill was sent to Governor Hardee for signature.[82]

Yet the abolition of corporal punishment and the use of the sweatbox to discipline uncooperative and incorrigible prisoners had a dramatic impact on prisoners and guards alike. Officials struggled to control the gun men, whose renewed sense of their disruptive potential resulted in several road camp strikes and protests, prisoners' work slowdowns, and increased insubordination. Fallout from the Tabert case temporarily gave state and county prisoners greater leverage within the penal system as continued public and press scrutiny meant that their complaints of brutal or excessive treatment were more likely to be believed. It took nearly two years from June 1923 for prison authorities to fully reassert control over prisoners and four years for productivity to return to pre-abolition levels. Guards and camp captains believed solitary confinement was largely ineffectual and open to prisoner abuse.[83]

Under mounting public and press pressure, the Florida legislature also formally abolished the convict lease in May 1923, to take effect on January 1, 1924.[84] The Tabert case had garnered support for abolition from the major newspapers in the state, civic organizations, women's groups (women had been enfranchised only three years previously), black civil rights organizations, and boosters, and the general public at mass meetings across the state in April and May 1923. McCoy accused Florida newspapers of lukewarm response to the exposé and penal reforms. However, most major state newspapers, their editors, and readership supported the reforms and "housecleaning." They also supported the bill to abolish convict leasing, a practice they had opposed for several years. The *Miami Metropolis* editor optimistically announced, "As a result of publicity it is altogether probable there will be no recurrence of the terrible acts such as were practised in the camp at Clara, where the North Dakota youth lost his life."[85] The vote for abolition was significant given that members from western and northern counties dominated the state legislature.

Not only did the legislature abolish the convict lease, it transformed the practice of capital punishment and attempted to push the state further toward penal modernity. The Florida Board of Commissioners of State Institutions (consisting of the governor and cabinet members) oversaw the construction of the three-legged electric chair, named "old Sparky," by inmates in the carpentry shop at the state prison farm. It became operational in August 1924.[86] Prior to 1924, legal executions in Florida were carried out in the counties where the crimes occurred and under the direction of local sheriffs. Prisoners were hanged on makeshift wooden gallows within the walls of county jail yards or inside jail buildings. Technological changes in the method of execution—the shift from hanging to the electric chair or gas chamber—accelerated the trend toward centralization of state executions into one location in each state; both the electric chair and the gas chamber were difficult to maintain locally.[87] County sheriffs lost jurisdiction over executions to state prison wardens; thus these changes served to limit the arbitrary power of sheriffs and enhance that of the state. Nonetheless, the electric chair bill was part of a reform package supported by the Florida Federation of Women's Clubs and endorsed by Florida sheriffs at their annual conventions in 1915 and 1923.[88]

The *Tampa Tribune* declared that the governor's signature on bills to abolish the lash and leasing delivered Florida from her "detractors and defamers." It announced: "The lease and lash leaders gave a few expiring gasps and they pass out of Florida history forever. They are as dead as the iniquitous, barbarous system they defended and fought to preserve. Florida has again righted herself. She has always come clean. Out of this, her most humiliating situation, she emerges unafraid, smiling with the consciousness of duty done."[89] The problem was that the state-run road labor camps of the 1920s, 1930s, and 1940s bore an uncanny resemblance to their leasing predecessors. In 1919 Florida's state prison population of 1,100 was divided into grade 1 prisoners for road labor and grade 2 for work on the 18,000-acre prison farm. In January 1921, 628 prisoners were located in twenty-four road camps, and 422 prisoners labored at the farm. By 1934, there were 1,500 inmates in thirty-one road prisons around the state.[90]

In the 1920s and 1930s, native-born Floridians and tourists motoring along county roads and state highways would pass lines of dirty, sweaty, and exhausted, bare-chested men, wearing the trousers of their black and white striped "zebra suits" and twenty pounds of chains. Both Spivak and Burns described "keeping the lick," the synchronized labor of the chain men in Georgia and the "rhythmical cadence" of their pickaxes, as bodies, muscles, and work tools moved in time to the tempo and speed of a work song.[91] In Florida as in Georgia, African Americans arrested on feeble charges of vagrancy and disorderly conduct constituted a ready supply of labor to build the roads for white planters and politicians. Inmate road labor remained the most visible and dramatic continuation of daily public punishment and public spectacle in twentieth-century Florida, and penal conditions in road labor camps were as difficult as those encountered in the phosphate mines or turpentine farms before 1923. Further, after the Tabert case, most Florida counties used prison labor to build and maintain roads, and some leased their prisoners to other county sheriffs. Road camps offered no opportunities for education, training, or self-improvement, and systems of classification, rehabilitation, or individualized treatment were nonexistent. Yet, as Alex Lichtenstein observes, "The brutal regime endured by African-Americans working the southern roads in the 1920s and 1930s, so forcefully described by Tannenbaum as one of the 'darker phases' of the South, was actually conceived as a model of regional reform and progress, the direct result of the abolition of convict leasing."[92]

In Florida, women campaigners voiced their concerns over road camp conditions to successive governors. For example, Mrs. W. H. Baker of Jacksonville informed Governor Doyle E. Carlton by telegram in May 1930: "Group of women here intensely interested state road camps period long been familiar with inhumane conditions existing in these camps your efforts for rectification will be heartily endorsed hope to discuss with you sometime."[93] The governor replied that investigations by the Board of Commissioners of State Institutions into camp 27 at Freeport had resulted in the suspension of the camp captain.[94] Such responses, however, did not alter the basic conditions of life and labor in the road camps in general. Further, African American male inmates in particular continued to receive the worst treatment, laboring in malaria-infested swamps to build a highway system that would open the state for land development and tourism.

In contrast, Raiford, established in 1913 on 18,000 acres of land in Bradford and Union Counties, forty miles southwest of Jacksonville, was the third largest state prison in the United States, next to Parchman, Mississippi, and Angola in Louisiana.[95] It was the triumph of progressive penal policy in Florida, extolled as an example of humane treatment, effecting restraint and rehabilitation through agricultural labor, complete with rewards for "good and faithful service," and segregation of inmates from "the so-called worldly pleasures."[96] For Oshinsky, the prison farm was a re-created slave plantation symbolic of the contempt that white Mississippians had for African Americans. Compared to Parchman and Angola, which were immense cotton and sugar plantations worked by gangs of stooped black labor under the watchful eye of overseers, Raiford conformed more to the neoplantation model based on mixed grain-dairy-livestock production as described by Jack Temple Kirby as the key to modernization and scientific agriculture in the pre- and post-Depression South.[97] As the boll weevil devastated cotton production across north Florida, the prison farm offered a model for commercial and experimental farming. It was able to do this because of the absence of troublesome landlord-tenant credit arrangements, and there was a plentiful supply of labor for farming, and machinery, electricity, and other tools necessary for capital-intensive agriculture.

However, prisoners in 1920s Florida worked in overcrowded, inadequately staffed, and educationally starved institutions. Raiford had cell house capacity for 1,200 prisoners in wooden dormitory buildings that were gradually replaced in the later 1920s and 1930s by more secure structures with eighteen-inch-thick walls filled with concrete, rock, and scrap metal. There were over 1,500 prisoners by the mid-1930s, when inmates were housed in small cells for six men that often held eighteen in triple bunks, with a single toilet and no ventilation. Prisoners developed elaborate systems of barter, commodity exchange, and sale of personal services, including sex, thus they were not isolated from "the so-called worldly pleasures." Raiford is perhaps best described as a hybrid of the old convict lease system and elements of the "Big House."[98] Certain characteristics of convict camp surveillance and inmate culture made the transition from the older system to the state prison farm, and indeed the road camps of the twentieth century, but were also supplemented by other forms of correction and punishment, particularly solitary confinement, as popularly illustrated in the 1967 movie *Cool Hand Luke*; after all, inmates had few rights or protections in courts of law.

In June 1923, the editorial of the *Tallahassee Daily Democrat* noted that Tabert's death had not been in vain: "Tabert's death resulted in the removal of the sheriff who arrested him and the judge who sentenced him, the abolishment of the system which made a slave of him, and the prohibition of the whip with which he was whipt. The whipper, T. W. Higginbotham, is now being tried for first-degree murder, and if guilty he will no doubt be punished accordingly."[99] Higginbotham's trial took place at Cross City, a PLC town in Dixie County, and lasted for thirteen days in June 1923, during which time some of the prosecution witnesses met untimely deaths. While he admitted punishing Tabert, Higginbotham denied that he had flogged him so excessively as to cause his death. On July 7, after deliberating for eighty minutes, the jury declared Higginbotham guilty of second-degree murder, and the judge sentenced him to twenty years in the state prison. He was immediately released on $10,000 bond pending appeal, which was successful. As historian Jerrell H. Shofner reveals, Higginbotham was never imprisoned and continued to work for PLC at their Shamrock Camp in Dixie County. In March 1925, he was one of six men (including the Dixie County deputy sheriff) indicted for the first-degree murder of Lewis "Peanut" Barker, an African American turpentine worker.[100] Higginbotham was put on trial a second time for Tabert's murder at Cross City, but press and lawyers alike anticipated the verdict of not guilty. Higginbotham continued to work in

PLC camps until 1937. Sheriff Jones of Leon County was voted out of office in 1923 but returned in 1927, and legislative investigators found evidence that he continued to arrest persons on vagrancy charges to fulfill an agreement with PLC to furnish workers.[101]

The revelations of mistreatment of prisoners, the continued practice of peonage, and the death of Martin Tabert did not impede Florida's economic development in the early 1920s. As early as December 1920, roads in the Sunshine State roared with the sound of hundreds of "tin-can tourists" in campers and tent-equipped Model T's arriving after a two-week journey down the new Dixie Highway from Chicago to Florida. These northern snowbirds were the advance guard of the Florida land rush and building boom of 1924–26.[102] Central and southern Florida had become more accessible by the 1920s because of increased internal and external railroad connections and the accelerated construction of a statewide system of public roads, often built with county and state convict labor. In a continuing effort to attract people with capital to settle in Florida, the 1924 legislature passed, and the voters approved, a constitutional prohibition on state income and inheritance taxes.[103] This helped fuel an economic boom centered in what is now Miami–Dade County, especially Miami, Miami Beach, and Coral Gables. Reports of phenomenal profits to be made in Florida real estate and property filtered northward. Real estate had become an important industry partly because of Florida's ambitious program of Everglades reclamation.[104] Historian Raymond Vickers declares: "California's gold rush of 1849 and the Klondike gold rush of 1898 pale when compared to the Florida land rush of 1925. Florida's boom was the greatest speculative frenzy in history. The madness in the Sunshine State reflected the mood of the country during the Roaring Twenties."[105] Intense speculation occurred because of the availability of easy credit—anyone could put down 10 percent on a parcel of land, then sell it at a profit—and the belief that real-estate values would continue to skyrocket. Land holdings sold to northern investors were actually filled-in mangrove swamps, rough-scraped dirt roads, and cleared pinelands. Some plots had yet to be dredged, and much of what was being sold was paper, not land. Building projects could not be completed fast enough to keep up with the mass population influx, and an acute housing shortage in the Miami area saw many investors sleeping in tent cities and parks.[106]

Even though Florida had abandoned local option and gone dry in November 1918, a year before national prohibition came into effect, the liquor business was also booming due to the spread of illegal gambling and the lucrative profits to be made from smuggling alcohol from the Bahamas and Cuba.[107] Boosterism was rampant. The mayors of Miami, Miami Beach, Hialeah, and Coral Gables issued a joint proclamation boasting that Dade County was "the most Richly Blessed

Community of the most Bountifully Endowed State of the most Highly Enterprising People of the Universe."[108] But businessmen in northern communities
had already begun to voice concerns over the migration of money and people to
Florida, and some started an active anti-Florida campaign.[109] The boom began
to wane in late 1925 as federal tax laws began to eat into speculators' profits; the
overburdened Florida East Coast Railway declared an embargo on incoming
freight, including building supplies; the port of Miami was temporarily closed
by a sunken cabaret boat and labor shortages continued. Contributing to the
plunge were a decline in stock market prices in early 1926 and increasing numbers of people defaulting on real estate payments.[110] By spring 1926 a mass exodus of bankrupt investors blocked the roads northward. The real estate collapse
of 1926 had pitched Florida's economy into deep depression and resulted in at
least forty bank failures; thus the state was already suffering financial ruin three
years before the Wall Street Crash in 1929.

Nearly 400 Floridians were killed, hundreds more were missing and presumed dead, over 6,000 were injured, and 43,000 were made homeless, including residents of the remaining tent cities and tourist camps, when a cate-
gory 4 hurricane struck Miami and Miami Beach on September 18, 1926. Many
victims were unidentified black migrant farm workers and their families who
worked on the edge of the Everglades, picking fruit and beans. The influx of
these black workers doubled the usual African American populations of Miami,
Orlando, and southern counties from November to April.[111] Two years later, on
September 16, 1928, a second hurricane devastated Palm Beach and communities further inland. At least 75 percent of the estimated 3,000 people killed were
again black migrant farm laborers, thus reminding Floridians of the contrasting economic characteristics of the state in the 1920s.[112] Survivors talked of rural
roadbeds and dikes being littered with bodies. So-called "idle" black men were
then rounded up into work gangs by armed white "man hunters" to clear roads
and canals, and for body recovery and burial work. In West Palm Beach, black
recovery crews were supervised by white National Guardsmen.[113] The storms,
the thousands of dead, the collapse of land deals, and near bankruptcy ensured
the end of the period of prosperity and reform in Florida.

The treatment of Tabert, Knox, and Burns, and the less-famous African
American inmates named in grand-jury investigations and federal peonage in-
quiries did offend the sensibilities of important segments of the southern populations increasingly unhappy with the open displays of violence and aggression in their midst. Before 1923 Florida authorities had limited powers over the
punishment and treatment of county prisoners, and the Tabert case gave them
the necessary leverage to curtail the arbitrary powers of sheriffs and county
commissioners and to enhance that of a centralizing and bureaucratizing state

desperate to embrace modernity in some of its forms. Yet, at the same time, official and popular views were highly selective and differentiated according to issues of race, class, and gender, and general disregard for prisoner populations.

As historian Matthew Mancini observes, "humanitarianism, like any motive, requires certain enabling conditions to render it efficacious."[114] Thus in 1920s Florida, even after the flogging and peonage scandals, convict road labor, forced labor, and lynching were still tolerated. They were also part of a political compromise whereby legislators could initiate a partial shift to penal modernity if they turned a blind eye to continuing forms of public spectacle and punishment supported and practiced by certain sectors of the populace. Modernity had its limits. Modernization in the South was also clearly to be a process "for whites only" but that paradoxically required forced black labor.[115] When in April 1923 journalist Samuel D. McCoy argued that in the past few weeks Floridians had been "awakened" or shaken out of their ignorance by the Tabert case—"To the credit of the whole State be it said a wave of anger and indignation [following the death of one white prisoner] is rolling up to-day which may blot out in an instant which should have been ended years ago"[116]—even he sounded too optimistic and did not envisage that it would take another three decades for the "instant" to occur. Further, Tabert would not be the last prisoner, white or black, to meet an untimely death in a Florida prison camp. National outrage over the revelations of mistreatment of southern prisoners ultimately did not reduce the unwarranted brutality and degradation of these prison populations. Without the strap, prison guards and captains found other ways to punish their charges physically.

NOTES

1. *New York World*, 24 April 1923, p. 9.

2. Historians N. Gordon Carper and Jerrell H. Shofner addressed the story of Martin Tabert's death in the *Florida Historical Quarterly*. See N. Gordon Carper, "Martin Tabert, Martyr of an Era," *Florida Historical Quarterly* 52 (Oct. 1973): 115–31; Jerrell H. Shofner, "Postscript to the Martin Tabert Case: Peonage as Usual in the Florida Turpentine Camps," *Florida Historical Quarterly* 60 (Oct. 1981): 161–73. My article, "The Icelandic Man Cometh: North Dakota State Attorney Gudmunder Grimson and a Reassessment of the Martin Tabert Case," *Florida Historical Quarterly* 81 (winter 2003): 279–315, drew heavily on the North Dakota records to argue that an assessment of Grimson's role in the Tabert case was long overdue, that he was a key figure in bringing Tabert's treatment to national attention and in forcing the State of Florida to investigate Tabert's death, and that Grimson deserved more credit from historians for his efforts than previously acknowledged.

3. *New York Times*, 30 June 1923, p. 13.

4. *Pensacola News*, 2 June 1923, clipping in *Governor Cary A. Hardee Scrapbooks*, Manuscript Collection MS 86–39, carton 2, Florida State Archives, Tallahassee, hereafter referred to as MS 86–39(2).

5. Putnam Lumber Co. to Mr. E. D. Talbert, 2 Feb. 1922, Gudmunder Grimson Papers (1923–49), record series 10120, box 1, folder 5, North Dakota Historical Society, Bismarck; hereafter referred to as RS 10120. Microfilm copies of these papers are also located in the Florida State Library, Tallahassee. *Florida Times Union*, 10 April 1923, p. 4.

6. *New York Times*, 30 June 1923, p. 13.

7. Gudmunder Grimson and Irving Wallace, "Whipping Boss," *North Dakota History* 31 (April 1964): 127.

8. In the context of Florida's expanding railroad network, "stealing a ride" or "beating a train" had become a misdemeanor punishable by a fine in 1897 at the request of the recently formed Florida Sheriff's Association in response to the growing problem of thrill-seekers riding trains for a short distance, then jumping off while the train was still in motion, and the resulting increase in accidents. See William Warren Rogers and James M. Denham, *Florida Sheriffs: A History 1821–1945*, (Tallahassee: Sentry, 2001), 180.

9. *Florida Times Union*, 10 April 1923, p. 4.

10. Jeffrey A. Drobney, *Lumbermen and Log Sawyers: Life, Labor, and Culture in the North Florida Timber Industry, 1830–1930* (Macon GA: Mercer Univ. Press, 1997), 149.

11. Grimson and Wallace, "Whipping Boss," 129; Drobney, *Lumbermen and Log Sawyers*, 175; on arrest increases, see RS 10120, box 1, folder 3; Carper 117n9. *Tampa Tribune*, 25 April 1923, as noted by Carper, 123; E. Lassande to Samuel McCoy, no date, in Samuel Duff McCoy (1882–1964) Papers, Manuscript Collection 54 (1922–23, 1955), Florida State Library, Tallahassee, hereafter referred to as MS54.

12. Rogers and Denham, *Florida Sheriffs*, 197.

13. See *New York World*, 2 April 1923, p. 1 in MS 86–9(2).

14. Ibid.

15. Frank Tannenbaum, *Darker Phases of the South* (New York: Negro Universities Press, 1969), 84–102, 107–8; Joseph F. Fishman, *Crucibles of Crime: The Shocking Story of the American Jail* (New York: Cosmopolis Press, 1923), 20, 49.

16. Glen Thompson to Munich postmaster, Plerna, Kan., no date, RS 10120, box 1, folder 4; "Can Americans Stand for This?" in MS54; *Florida Times Union*, 10 April 1923, p. 4.

17. *Literary Digest*, 16 June 1923, newspaper clipping in MS 86–39(2).

18. Glen Thompson to Mr. Talberta [sic], 25 Aug. 1922, RS 10120, box 1, folder 4.

19. Theodore Rosengarten, *All God's Dangers: The Life of Nate Shaw* (London: Cape, 1975), 352.

20. "North Dakota Senate Asks Florida Officials Investigate Death of Martin Tabert," *Tallahassee Daily Democrat*, 28 Feb. 1923, p. 1.

21. Cary A. Hardee, Governor, to Mr. G. Grimson, 1 March 1923, RS 10120, box 1, folder 5.

22. "First Display of Fireworks and Legislature Over Tabert Affair," *Tallahassee Daily Democrat*, 4 April 1923, p. 4. In April 1923 a grand jury in Dixie County met to investi-

gate the circumstances of Tabert's death and to indict Thomas Walter Higginbotham for murder. State attorney J. R. Kelly was assisted by Judge W. K. Kneeshaw of North Dakota. See *Florida Times Union*, 10 April 1923, p. 4.

23. *Journal of the State Senate of Florida of the Session of 1923*, 61–62; *Florida Times Union*, 10 April 1923, p. 8. The Joint Senate-Legislative Committee consisted of St. Augustine attorney W. A. MacWilliams, Pensacola attorney John P. Stokes, Palatka attorney Senator C. H. Kennerly, Citrus County crate manufacturer Senator Frederic Van Roy, and Pensacola attorney Senator John Clay Smith. It was also reported that legislators were considering repealing the law which made riding on a railroad train without paying the fare a misdemeanor and repeal of the laws which permitted the leasing of county convicts. See *Florida Times Union*, 10 April 1923, p. 8.

24. Pulitzer Prizes, 1924 Journalism Public Service award, www.pulitzer.org, accessed 7 July 2005.

25. "Tragedy of Convict Camp Stirs Florida; Saw Tabert Lashed," *New York World*, 2 April 1923, p. 1, in MS 86–39(2).

26. *Journal of the House of Representatives of the State of Florida of the Session of 1923*, 435–36, House Concurrent Resolution no. 5; Samuel D. McCoy, unpublished manuscript, prepared for *Reader's Digest*, 1955, MS 54.

27. "Senator Knabb Called to Tallahassee to Account for Conditions at Prison Camp," *Tallahassee Daily Democrat*, 13 March 1923, p. 1; "Tabert Case Threatens to Involve Higher Ups," *Tallahassee Daily Democrat*, 14 April 1923, p. 1; Shofner, "Postscript," 171.

28. "Alachua Cancels Knabb's Contract for Prisoners," *Florida Times Union*, 12 May 1923, p. 4.

29. *New York Times*, 29 April 1923, p. 15. Alongside this piece in the *New York Times* is a report that "whipping boss" S. M. Rogers had been arrested for cruelty to convicts and the information in the indictment was being investigated by the Lee County grand jury. "Prisoners were forced to work twelve to fourteen hours a day and were whipped for no apparent reasons [according to investigators in Lee County]. They told of instances of convicts being lashed until they fell, as many as 150 blows being administered." The Mars Turpentine Co. was permitted to retain their leased convicts despite recommendations from Commissioner of Agriculture William McRae that they be removed from the camp in Lee County.

30. "Sensational Testimony of Mrs. Franklin Regarding the Knabb Convict Camp; Prison Inspector [J. B. Thomas] Is Declared Unfit," *Florida Times Union*, 9 May 1923, p. 8.

31. "Drastic Change in Law for the Inspection of Convicts," *Tallahassee Daily Democrat*, 29 May 1923, p. 1.

32. *Florida Times Union*, 1 May 1923, p. 8.

33. Quoted in Shofner, "Postscript," 171.

34. See clipping, no date, in RS 10120, box 1, folder 5. Grimson's papers include numerous newspaper clippings from a range of state publications covering the Tabert case, gathered from news clipping services. However, the dates of publication are not always recorded, and page numbers are usually absent.

35. William Banks Taylor, *Down on Parchman Farm: The Great Prison in the Mississippi Delta* (Columbus: Ohio State Univ. Press, 1999), 64.

36. Robert E. Burns, *I Am a Fugitive from a Georgia Chain Gang!* (Athens: Univ. of Georgia Press, 1997 [1932]), 54–56.

37. Quoted in Mary Ellen Curtin, *Black Prisoners and Their World, Alabama, 1865–1900* (Charlottesville: Univ. Press of Virginia, 2000), 166–67.

38. The issue that disturbed O'Hare most was the absence of segregation, particularly of sick inmates, as revealed in her infamous "bathhouse letter," which also detailed the horrors of shared bathing facilities, and the prevalence of venereal disease. Kate Richards O'Hare, *In Prison* (Seattle: Univ. of Washington Press, 1976 [1923]), 65–67, 109–10.

39. Edgardo Rotman, "The Failure of Reform: United States, 1865–1965," in Norval Morris and David J. Rothman, eds., *The Oxford History of the Prison: The Practice of Punishment in Western Society* (Oxford: Oxford Univ. Press, 1998), 165.

40. David M. Oshinsky, *"Worse Than Slavery": Parchman Farm and the Ordeal of Jim Crow Justice* (New York: Free Press, 1996), 137.

41. David Garland, *Punishment and Modern Society: A Study in Social Theory* (Oxford: Clarendon Press, 1997), 243.

42. Vivien M. L. Miller, *Crime, Sexual Violence, and Clemency: Florida's Pardon Board and Penal System in the Progressive Era* (Gainesville: Univ. Press of Florida, 2000), 32–33.

43. For a discussion of the rise and decline of eugenic criminology, see Nicole Hahn Rafter, *Creating Born Criminals* (Urbana: Univ. of Illinois Press, 1997).

44. Oshinsky, *"Worse Than Slavery,"* 151.

45. See also the series of prison narratives discussed in Gary Brown, *Texas Gulag: The Chain Gang Years, 1875–1925* (Plano: Republic of Texas Press, 2002).

46. Brown, 8, 94; Mark T. Carlton, *Politics and Punishment: The History of the Louisiana State Penal System* (Baton Rouge: Louisiana State Univ., 1971), 150; "Convict Camp Investigation Made Public," *Florida Times Union*, 30 July 1942; "Probe Reveals Brutality at Convict Camp," *Fort Pierce News Tribune*, 30 July 1942.

47. See Matthew J. Mancini, *One Dies, Get Another: Convict Leasing in the American South, 1866–1928* (Columbia: Univ. of South Carolina Press, 1996), 115 n. 53; Curtin, *Black Prisoners*, 167.

48. Taylor, *Down on Parchman Farm*, 30.

49. O'Hare, *In Prison*, 48.

50. Ibid., 70.

51. Garland, *Punishment and Modern Society*, 243.

52. Michael Gannon, *Florida: A Short History* (Gainesville: Univ. Press of Florida, 1993), 86.

53. Jerrell H. Shofner, "Florida and the Black Migration," *Florida Historical Quarterly* 57 (Jan. 1979): 267–68.

54. David R. Colburn and Richard K. Scher, *Florida's Gubernatorial Politics in the 20th Century* (Gainesville: Univ. Press of Florida, 1980), 190–91.

55. See Maxine D. Jones, "The Rosewood Massacre and the Women Who Survived It," *Florida Historical Quarterly* 76 (fall 1997): 193–208.

56. Shofner, "Black Migration," 285–86; Gary W. Donogh, ed., *The Florida Negro: A Federal Writers' Project Legacy* (Jackson: Univ. Press of Mississippi, 1993), xx.

57. Colburn and Scher, *Florida's Gubernatorial Politics*, 192.

58. Ibid., 38.

59. Laws of Florida, 1919, 286; Shofner, "Black Migration," 284.

60. *Chicago Defender*, 17 May 1919, quoted in Shofner, "Black Migration," 283.

61. The first test case of the 1867 federal peonage statute occurred in November 1901 when Samuel M. Clyatt was indicted in Leon County, Florida. Clyatt was convicted and sentenced to four years in a federal penitentiary but did not go to prison. The case was appealed to the U.S. Supreme Court in 1904, and the court ordered a new trial in March 1905, but the Justice Department in 1909 eventually dropped the case. See Pete Daniel, *The Shadow of Slavery: Peonage in the South, 1901–1969* (Urbana: Univ. of Illinois Press, 1972), 4–18. The Justice Department did secure an important victory with the conviction for peonage of William S. Harlan, manager of the Jackson Lumber Company, together with four other employees, in 1906. But a further case in 1908, originating with labor practices on the construction of Henry M. Flagler's Florida East Coast Railroad to Key West (1904–13) failed. See Daniel, 83–90, 103–7. In contrast, complaints of peonage in Alabama declined dramatically after the U.S. Supreme Court ruled the state's contract labor law unconstitutional in 1914.

62. Shofner, "Postscript," 163; Gannon, *Florida*, 87–88.

63. See Robert N. Lauriault, " 'From Can't to Can't': The North Florida Turpentine Camp, 1900–1950." *Florida Historical Quarterly* 57 (Jan. 1989): 310–28.

64. Stetson Kennedy, *Palmetto Country* (Tallahassee: Florida A&M Univ. Press, 1989), 265.

65. Jacqueline Jones, *American Work: Four Centuries of Black and White Labor* (New York: W. W. Norton, 1998), 315.

66. Drobney, *Lumbermen and Log Sawyers*, 179–89.

67. Daniel, *Shadow of Slavery*, 21–23.

68. See Lauriault, " 'From Can't to Can't,' " 321. The extent of peonage in Florida turpentine camps was brought to public attention by various commentators including New York attorney Mary Grace Quackenbos who came to Florida to gather evidence against corrupt New York labor agents who recruited several thousand newly arrived immigrants and delivered them to southern employers, such as the Florida East Coast Railroad, for a fee. A series of prosecutions were brought against the Jackson Lumber Company of Pensacola. See Shofner, "Postscript," 17; Daniel, *Shadow of Slavery*, 95–109; Mary Church Terrell, "Peonage in the United States: The Convict Lease System and the Chain Gangs," *Nineteenth Century* 68 (Aug. 1907): 306–22.

69. *New York Times*, 29 April 1923, p. 15; *New York Times*, 30 April 1923, p. 7.

70. Grace Elizabeth Hale noted that Farm Security Administration photographs provide evidence that by the late 1930s a national consumer culture had penetrated even the smallest dirt crossroads in southern communities. See Grace Elizabeth Hale, *Making Whiteness: The Culture of Segregation in the South* (New York: Pantheon, 1998), 137.

71. Drobney, *Lumbermen and Log Sawyers*, 194–95.

72. Gary W. McDonogh, ed., *The Florida Negro: A Federal Writers' Project Legacy* (Jackson: Univ. Press of Mississippi, 1993) 53.

73. Daniel, *Shadow of Slavery*, 110–16.

74. Ibid., 121–26.

75. Ibid., 128–30.

76. Shofner, "Postscript," 172.

77. Gannon, *Florida*, 73.

78. Daniel, *Shadow of Slavery*, 80.

79. *New York World*, 28 April 1923, p. 1.

80. *Florida Times Union*, 21 April 1923, p. 8.

81. *New York Times*, 13 May 1923, p. 23.

82. *New York Times*, 16 May 1923, p. 3.

83. See *Reports of the Commissioner of Agriculture, 1923–1928*, Florida State Library, Tallahassee.

84. Colburn and Scher, *Florida's Gubernatorial Politics*, 263.

85. Newspaper clipping, n.d., MS 86–39(2).

86. Ken Driggs, "A Current of Electricity Sufficient in Intensity to Cause Immediate Death: A Pre-*Furman* History of Florida's Electric Chair," *Stetson Law Review* 22 (summer 1993): 1,183. Although one state, Alabama, did use a portable electric chair for several years, and one Florida governor, Sidney J. Catts (1917–21), a native of Alabama, had advocated that Florida follow suit.

87. William J. Bowers, *Legal Homicide* (Boston: Northeastern Univ. Press, 1974), 12, 14, 52.

88. Driggs, "A Current of Electricity," 1,179–80; Rogers and Denham, *Florida Sheriffs*, 202, 234.

89. *Tampa Tribune*, June 1923, newspaper clipping in MS 86–39(2).

90. *16th Biennial Report of the Prison Division of the Department of Agriculture of the State of Florida, 1919–1920*, 7–8; Baynard Kendrick, *Florida Trails to Turnpikes, 1914–1964* (Gainesville: Univ. of Florida Press, 1964), 19.

91. Burns, *I Am a Fugitive*, 143–144; John L. Spivak, *On the Chain Gang*, 2nd ed. (New York: International Pamphlets, 1934), 6.

92. Alex Lichtenstein, *Twice the Work of Free Labor: The Political Economy of Convict Labor in the New South* (New York: Verso, 1996), 159–60.

93. Mrs. W. H. Baker to Gov. Doyle Carlton, 15 May 1930, series 204: *Governor Doyle E. Carlton, 1929–1932: Administrative Correspondence*, box 76, file 10: Road Department Investigation, Florida State Archives, Tallahassee.

94. Gov. Doyle Carlton to Mrs. W. H. Baker, 17 May 1930, as above.

95. The most recent studies of state prison farm labor focus on Parchman. See Oshinsky, "*Worse Than Slavery*," and Taylor, *Down on Parchman Farm*.

96. *Proceedings of the American Prison Association*, Jacksonville, Fla., 1921, p. 40, Florida State Library, Tallahassee; Herman B. Walker, "The State Prison Farm at Raiford," 1928 newspaper clipping, P. K. Yonge Library, University of Florida, Gainesville.

97. Jack Temple Kirby, *Rural Worlds Lost: The American South, 1920–1960* (Baton Rouge: Louisiana State Univ. Press, 1987).

98. In the 1920s and 1930s a new type of prison emerged, the Big House (as at Sing Sing in New York), managed by professionals rather than short-term political appointees and designed to eliminate the abusive forms of corporal punishment and prison labor. See Rotman, "The Failure of Reform," 165.

99. Newspaper clipping, June 1923, in MS 86–39(2).

100. *New York World*, 8 July 1923, RS 10120, box 1, folder 2; *Tallahassee Daily Democrat*, 9 July 1923, p. 1; Shofner, "Postscript," 162.

101. Shofner, "Postscript," 161–62.

102. Gannon, *Florida*, 76.

103. Paul S. George, "Brokers, Binders, and Builders: Greater Miami's Boom of the Mid-1920s," *Florida Historical Quarterly* 65 (July 1986), 31, 35; Charlton W. Tebeau, *A History of Florida*, 3rd ed. (Miami: Univ. of Miami Press, 1991), 382.

104. George, "Brokers, Binders, and Builders," 27.

105. Raymond B. Vickers, *Panic in Paradise: Florida's Banking Crash of 1926*, (Tuscaloosa: Univ. of Alabama Press, 1994), 17.

106. George, "Brokers, Binders, and Builders," 43; Gannon, *Florida*, 80–81.

107. George, "Brokers, Binders, and Builders," 45.

108. Quoted in Gannon, *Florida*, 79.

109. Tebeau, *History of Florida*, 386.

110. George, "Brokers, Binders, and Builders," 46–49.

111. McDonogh, *Florida Negro*, 40.

112. Gannon, *Florida*, 83–84.

113. Robert Mykle, *Killer 'Cane: The Deadly Hurricane of 1928* (New York: Cooper Square Press, 2002), 188–213.

114. Mancini, *One Dies, Get Another*, 221.

115. Jones, *American Work*, 329: "In the United States, Modernization Wore a White Face."

116. *New York World*, 2 April 1923, p. 1 in MS 86–39(2).

"Ain't Worth a Damn for Nothin'"

The New Deal and Child Labor
in Southern Textiles

CLIVE WEBB

On July 24, 1933, millions of Americans tuned their radios to listen to Franklin D. Roosevelt deliver the third of his "fireside chats." In his intimate yet authoritative tone, the president outlined the initiatives taken by his administration to promote social improvement and economic recovery. Roosevelt was particularly proud of the abolition of child labor in the textile industry: "That makes me personally happier," he pronounced, "than any other one thing with which I have been connected since I came to Washington." It was neither the first nor the last time Roosevelt would proclaim his accomplishment. When the reform was initially announced two weeks earlier, the president boasted to reporters that after "years of fruitless effort and discussion" his administration had finally eliminated "this ancient atrocity." The following month, Roosevelt spoke in almost spiritual terms of how he had "saved" thousands of American children by delivering them from an "old evil."[1]

The abolition of child labor was accomplished under the auspices of the newly established National Recovery Administration (NRA). The NRA sought to stabilize American industry by encouraging business leaders to adopt new codes of practice that restricted production and established maximum hours and minimum wages. When the textile industry submitted its draft code in July 1933, there was no explicit mention of child labor. The employment of children was nonetheless rendered redundant by the establishment of a $12 minimum weekly wage. Under sustained pressure, industry representatives then inserted an explicit clause prohibiting the employment of anyone under the age of sixteen. As a result, twenty thousand children left the mills. Although the Supreme Court invalidated the NRA two years later, mill owners continued to abide by the provision. The employment of children under sixteen was again outlawed under the 1938 Fair Labor Standards Act.[2]

When industry representatives at the public hearing on the new code announced their intention to abolish child labor, a "thunderous burst of applause" filled the room. The most enthusiastic cheers came from social activists who had lobbied long and hard for a change in the law. During the early decades of the twentieth century, the campaign to outlaw child labor gathered a relentless momentum. Reformers invested much of their efforts in fighting what Supreme Court Justice Felix Frankfurter described as "the stubborn black spots of the South."[3]

The blackest spot of all was the southern textile industry. Reform campaigns at a national and state level ingrained on the public consciousness a stark image of young mill workers: the long hours and low wages, the limited educational opportunities, and the physically ruinous exposure to lint and dust.[4] Child labor reformers showed little linguistic restraint in describing the conditions of the mill. One typically inflammatory piece of reportage, titled "Slaughter of the Innocents," proclaimed that child labor was worse than slavery.[5] With a similar melodramatic flair, the authors of another study wrote of "The Crimson in Our Cotton."[6] More immediate than the written word, the photography of muckraker Lewis Hine imparted to the American public the degradations endured by mill children. The young workers in Hine's photographs captured the popular imagination, their plaintive expressions contrasting with the industrial machinery towering around them.[7]

To many observers, the abolition of child labor thus appeared a moral imperative. During the early twentieth century, the state assumed a new custodial responsibility for the nation's youth. Acting as a "superparent," that is, assuming an interventionist role, it sought to protect children from present hardship in order that they might grow into a talented new generation of American citizens. The removal of children from the mills therefore seemed an act of moral guardianship on the part of the Roosevelt administration.[8]

Although the president's rhetoric implied that the repeal of child labor was entirely a matter of high principle, the situation was more complex. As David Kennedy observes, the actions of the Roosevelt administration were motivated by not only a basic humanitarianism but also "a cold economic logic." The removal of children from the mills secured a living wage for many adult laborers who would otherwise be jobless.[9] Despite the moral certainties of the president, the abolition of child labor also had an ambiguous impact on mill families. Insensitive to the appeals of textile workers, the Roosevelt administration failed to anticipate the longer-term consequences of reform. New Deal policy was determined by a misguided paternalism that precluded a more empathetic understanding of poverty.

Children contributed significantly to the southern textile boom of the late nineteenth century. Employers saw in the recruitment of children a solution to the problem of chronic labor shortages. They also appreciated that the exploitation of cheap labor would enable them to undercut their northern competitors, who generally employed far fewer children (table 1). Mill owners therefore actively recruited whole families. Recruitment agents portrayed the employment of children as a philanthropic measure that enabled otherwise destitute farming families to raise their standard of living. Mill owners provided rented accommodation to families and schooling to children. The success of these recruitment drives is clear from the employment statistics. By 1900, an estimated 25 percent of all employees in southern cotton mills were children aged between ten and sixteen. These juvenile laborers worked principally as doffers, spinners, and sweepers. Many had long been initiated into mill work by the time they actually became wage laborers; under the "helper system," small children tended or cleaned machinery while their parents rested during the much-needed dinner break.[10]

The abolition of child labor under the cotton textile code represented the culmination of a legal battle that dated to the late nineteenth century. The introduction of legislative reforms owed much to the relentless campaigning of the National Child Labor Committee (NCLC). By 1910, only six years after the establishment of the NCLC, every southern state had established a minimum employment age. The adoption of compulsory school laws also reduced child labor.[11] Political pressure by mill owners nonetheless succeeded in blunting the teeth of the reforms. While every state established a minimum working age, only four went as high as fourteen. Young workers continued to toil up to sixty hours a week for little pay. Although supposedly prohibited by law, many also continued to work night shifts. Enforcement of child labor legislation was undermined by the failure to provide for proper inspection of the work place. A study by the Bureau of Labor in 1907–8 found that 75 percent of mills in North Carolina and 92 percent in South Carolina failed to observe the law.[12] Progressive reformers successfully lobbied for child labor legislation in 1916 and 1919. Yet the U.S. Supreme Court stole their triumph when it struck down both laws. Southern opposition also ensured the defeat of a federal constitutional amendment on child labor approved by Congress in 1924.

The decision to abolish child labor in 1933 nonetheless met with little opposition from mill owners. Since the turn of the century, management had bitterly resisted state encroachment on employment practices. Mill owners feared that a federal initiative on child labor would open the way to other protective laws, which would undermine their commercial advantage over northern competitors. In response, industry representatives condemned the public campaign to eliminate child labor as part of a conspiracy by New England mill interests,

Table 1. Children Under Sixteen in U.S. Cotton Mills as
Percentage of Total Workforce

Year	New England	South
1899	6.7	25.0
1904	6.0	22.9
1909	5.3	17.9
1914	3.7	15.0
1919	5.0	4.9
1930	1.6	3.8

Adapted from Herbert J. Lahne, *The Cotton Mill Worker* (New York: Farrar &
Rinehart, 1944), 290.

claiming that federal legislation represented a "strained interpretation" of the
Constitution and a "communist" threat to states' rights.[13]

Yet by the time the cotton textile code was introduced, southern mill owners
had themselves assumed the initiative in discarding child labor. Several factors
account for this shift in employment practice. First, the textile industry suffered
an economic depression as a result of overproduction after World War I, which
led mill owners to prioritize cheap adult labor over children. Second, the enactment of a Child Labor Tax in 1922 acted as an additional financial disincentive.
Third, the introduction of new and improved machinery, operating at higher
speeds, increased the need for skilled adults, a need more than met by the sudden labor surplus created during the Great Depression.[14] In 1914, children accounted for 15 percent of the southern textile workforce. By 1930, the figure had
fallen to 3.8 percent. The age at which children first entered the workplace also
increased. At the turn of the century, 21 percent of children employed in southern textile mills were aged fifteen or older; by the onset of the Great Depression
it had risen to almost 70 percent. In terms of sheer numbers, more children were
still employed in textiles than in any other manufacturing industry. Nonetheless, the abolition of child labor no longer constituted such a serious concession on the part of employers. As one textile industry spokesman observed, "No
cotton-millman wants to employ under sixteen. Every cotton-millman knows
that employment of people under sixteen is a losing proposition."[15]

Ironically, the only people who did not add their voices to the chorus of approval for the abolition of child labor were the mill operatives. As Paul Blanshard observed in the 1920s, "In many cases the conscience of the employer in
relation to child labor is superior to the conscience of the parents."[16]

Many social commentators assumed that the equivocal response of southern mill hands to child labor legislation stemmed from their social conservatism and moral degeneracy. It is true that the first generation of workers who abandoned the depressed farming communities for the mills accepted child labor with little or no moral reservation. Rural families relied on the children's income to attain a subsistence income. Through long-standing tradition, child labor came to be seen as both a natural and necessary element of rural life. When families migrated from the farms to the mills, their children also transitioned from one form of labor to another, substituting the spinning machine for the plow.[17] The opposition of mill parents to child labor reform was also determined by their resentment at what they perceived as interference of the state in their private affairs. In regulating the lives of mill children, the federal government assumed a supervisory role at odds with traditional parental authority. As one mill hand asserted, "You can't have the law tellin' a man what to do with his children."[18] In truth, mill workers nursed legitimate grievances about the social and economic consequences of reform.

However, mill parents who opposed child labor reform were not, as some critics accused, idle layabouts who lived off the hard work of their offspring, nor were they simply being stubborn in resisting the interference of the state. The first generation of textile workers may have tolerated or even welcomed the opportunity for their children to work in the mills. However, by the time those children had themselves become parents, they were acutely conscious of the hardships the factory system inflicted on young laborers and no doubt hoped for something better for their sons and daughters.

The standpoint of this second generation is revealed in the songs that emerged from the factory floor. Next only to miners, no American workers composed more songs about their experiences than did cotton mill operatives. Through lyrics that commented—sometimes with wry humor and, at others, with unconcealed bitterness—on their condition, mill hands constructed a collective folk memory.[19] The titles of the songs reveal a stark awareness of their degraded social and economic status: "Hard Times Cotton Mill Girls," "Mill Mother's Lament," "Winnsboro Cotton Mill Blues."

Several songs comment specifically upon the use of child labor in the mills. The most conspicuous is "Babies in the Mill" by Dorsey Dixon. Dixon entered the workforce at the Darlington, South Carolina, mill when he was nine years old. These experiences inform the lyrical themes of the song. First, Dixon sings of the physical stress imposed by the relentless call of the factory whistle and the long hours of the working day.

> I used to be a factory hand when things were moving slow
> When children worked in cotton mills, each morning had to go

Every morning just at five the whistle blew on time
And called them babies out of bed at the age of eight and nine.

Come out of bed, little sleepy head,
And get your bite to eat.
The factory whistle's calling you,
There's no more time to sleep.

The singer then expresses resentment at the restricted opportunities mill children had to receive an education. The last two lines capture the essential spirit of the song. Dixon remains haunted by the hardships that stole away his childhood.

Those babies all grew up unlearned, they never went to school.
They never learned to read or write, but learned to spin and spool.
Every time I close my eyes, I see that picture still
When textile work was carried on with babies in the mill.

Finally, the song turns to the physical mistreatment of children.

To their jobs those little ones was strictly forced to go.
Those babies had to be on time through rain and sleet and snow.
Many times when things went wrong their bosses often frowned
Many times those little ones was kicked and shoved around.[20]

The sentiments expressed by Dixon about limited educational opportunities and physical cruelty are sharply echoed in another mill worker song, "Let Them Wear Their Watches Fine":

Our children they grow up unlearned
No time to go to school;
Almost before they've learned to walk
They learn to spin or spool.

The boss man jerks them round and round
And whistles very keen;
I'll tell you what, the factory kids
Are really treated mean.[21]

As powerful as the social commentary in these songs may be, they do not capture the complexity of parental attitudes toward child labor. The sentimentalization of childhood attained an increasingly powerful cultural influence during the second half of the nineteenth century, particularly among the urban middle classes. Popular rhetoric promoted the concept of the "economically worthless

but emotionally priceless" child, protected from hardship and therefore preserved in the innocence of youth.[22] The criticisms of child labor contained in
songs such as "Babies in the Mill" suggest that textile workers shared the progressive values of middle-class social reformers. In principle, many parents recognized the need to safeguard their children from manual labor. But in practice
they literally could not afford such idealism. Social reformers who sought to
impose their class-bound assumptions upon mill parents failed to appreciate
the relentless economic pressures that compelled child labor.[23] The lyrics to another song, "The Mill Has Shut Down," underscore the financial realities that
mill families faced:

> Last year with patience a lessened wage
> They helplessly took—better than none;
> More children worked, at tenderer age—
> Even their mite helped the lessened wage.[24]

Criticisms of progressive reformers that the responsibility for child labor
rested with lazy and avaricious parents[25] were exaggerated but not entirely without substance. In response to the introduction of minimum age legislation,
parents sometimes lied about the age of their children or failed to register a
new birth. "I lied so much about my age," asserted North Carolina mill worker
Gladys Griffin, "I like to never have got my age sorted out."[26] Some families
eluded the census by constantly moving from one mill village to the next. Others resorted to hiding their children in water closets or waste boxes when the
factory inspector called.[27]

Such tales do not, however, prove that parents lived parasitically off their children's incomes. The increasingly desperate tactics deployed by parents under-
lines a more fundamental truth about child labor: that for most mill families
it was a matter not of choice but necessity. The financial contributions of children sustained low-income families. As North Carolina mill worker Ida Allen
observed, "They never made much but put together it was enough to feed us."
The role of children was even more important in the absence of welfare provisions such as disability insurance and retirement benefits. When Mary Smith
and her husband both suffered serious illness, their family came close to destitution. "We was in such bad shape," she recalled, "that the two younguns was
forced to go in the mill though I'd hoped to keep 'em out until they'd had a
little more chance for schoolin'." A textile worker near Greenville, South Carolina, similarly asserted that she first entered the mill at the age of eight when
her father suffered a stroke.[28]

Parents therefore despaired at the 1935 repeal of child labor under the cotton
textile code. The code was perceived as stripping an important source of income

from families straining under the burden of the Great Depression. In order to reduce overproduction, mills drastically cut machine hours or regularly shut down. As James Hodges has observed, the introduction of the $12 minimum weekly wage was barely sufficient to sustain the families of full-time workers. The plight of mill laborers forced to work restricted hours was therefore appalling.[29] The NRA received numerous letters of complaint from mill families, including children who asserted their need to support old or disabled parents.[30] More than twenty years later, John Kenneth Morland encountered the same response. While North Carolina mill workers accepted that restrictions on child labor were "good things," they regretted that their offspring "cannot help with the family income as they had been able to help when they were children."[31]

Child labor legislation had another unforeseen impact upon mill families. Traditionally, when mill women took maternity leave they assumed responsibility not only for their own infant but for their neighbors'. This network of mutual support enabled mill communities to ease their collective social and economic burden. The abolition of child labor necessitated the employment of all family members above the minimum working age, including mothers. As a result, children too young to work in the mills assumed responsibility for domestic chores. According to author Sinclair Lewis, "Where there are younger children, the oldest—often it is a girl of eight or nine—has to wash the dishes, make the beds, try to clean the house and sweep the porch, and amuse the still younger slaves all day long." Although mill children no longer supplemented the incomes of their parents, they continued to perform an important role in family life. The realities of mill life still imposed responsibilities that forced children into premature adulthood, a predicament that points to the failure of the New Deal to address the systemic roots of poverty. Paid or unpaid, the labor performed by mill children limited their opportunities to escape the grip of the textile industry. Jeanette Nichols observed of the mill hand's daughter: "She may do remarkably well under the circumstances; but, herself supposed to be at school part of the time, and quite untaught in the essentials of child care and feeding, she can't do a good job. The result is that it is a poorly-cared-for, undernourished child that falls into the hands of the school teacher."[32]

More positively, the abolition of child labor promised new educational opportunities for the sons and daughters of mill operatives. The schools set up by mill owners in the late nineteenth century were in most instances a substantial improvement on the rural establishments children would otherwise have attended. Nonetheless, these schools suffered from intrinsic shortcomings. Mill owners were motivated less by an innate interest in child welfare than a conviction that improved education created a more productive class of employee. School curricula reflected this crudely functionalist attitude. Most mill schools were also seriously underresourced and teachers poorly trained. Moreover, management remained erratic in its enforcement of attendance.[33]

Several decades later the situation had only marginally improved. Despite increased resources and the introduction of compulsory school attendance laws, mill children remained seriously undereducated, even by the relatively low standards of the southern states. The new laws did not mandate attendance for more than a few months a year; they did not apply at all to children over the age of fourteen. A study conducted in North Carolina during the 1920s disclosed that less than half of fourteen-year-old mill children were enrolled in school.[34]

As a result of these educational deficiencies, illiteracy rates among mill children were two to three times higher than for the southern population as a whole.[35] "Education?" mused North Carolina mill worker Jones Freeze. "Don't ask me about that 'cause I never did have none to amount to anything." By the 1920s only 3 percent of southern mill workers were high school graduates. Over half the North Carolina mill children studied by sociologist Jennings Rhyne were at least a year behind in school.[36] Born into poverty, with little or no prospect of social and economic advancement, the sons and daughters of southern textile workers were forced to follow their parents into the mill. The cycle of poverty and limited opportunity repeated itself endlessly with each new generation. "They will tell you that once a mill-worker, always a mill-worker," mused Frank Tannenbaum. "Not only you, but your children and children's children forever and ever."[37]

Progressive reformers often criticized mill worker parents for their reluctance to send their children to school. According to John Harrison Cook, mill parents "consider the children as immediate economic contributors rather than those to whom they should provide further opportunities for growth and development." A number of studies noted the irony that the primary obstacle to school attendance was not the avarice of employers but the prejudice of parents.[38]

Indeed it was not uncommon for parents to have a fatalistic attitude about their children's ability to break out of the cycle of poverty. As one father remarked, what use was an education to his illiterate children when "about all they can do is work in the cotton mill anyway."[39] Such words represented the opinion of an older generation of textile workers who saw the mill as a distinct improvement upon rural drudgery. The generation who attained adulthood during the Depression, and who knew only the low pay and poor working conditions of the mill, nursed greater ambitions for their children. Less sanguine about the social and moral acceptability of child labor, they strove to educate their sons and daughters in order to ensure them better futures.

A recurrent theme in the interviews with mill operatives conducted by the Works Progress Administration (WPA) is the desire to see children stay off the factory floor long enough to graduate from high school. Sarah Wall, a mill worker from Wake Forest, North Carolina, had been out of work for three months. Standing in her small, fly-infested house surrounded by six children, Sarah wondered how she would ever afford so many school clothes. Nonetheless, she was determined to see all her children through school. "I hope never to see a youngun I've got in the mill for even one day's work." These sentiments were shared by many mill parents. Josephine Wallace, for instance, asserted that her sole ambition was "to keep her five children, more particularly her two daughters, out of the mill."[40]

The same parents who spoke enthusiastically about securing an education for their children nevertheless worried that their wages would not cover the costs. Since mill schools seldom provided an education beyond the seventh grade, older children had to attend municipal schools, incurring additional costs in transportation and tuition fees.[41] Whereas children had once provided an important additional source of family income, now, at a time of low wages and increasing lay-offs, they imposed a new financial burden. Nina Boone agonized over the issue with her husband. "Jim wants all the children to go through high school," she asserted, "but I don't know whether we can keep 'em in school that long or not." Elsie and Jim Wall were even more pessimistic about their own situation, according to the WPA interviewer: "if he can manage to send them through school[,] perhaps they will find something else besides cotton mill work to do. Well, it's Jim's problem. She can't figure it on six dollars a week."[42] Among many mill hands there remained a profound disparity between their abstract hopes and their actual expectations. According to Myra Page, 60 percent of parents at the Hutchins Hill mill in South Carolina expressed a "definite opposition" to child labor. Few, however, believed that their children would remain in school long enough to avoid the inevitability of mill work. These unrealized desires were articulated in the common refrain, "What else kin they be?"[43]

Many mill children certainly aspired to more rewarding careers than their parents had. Some, like the daughter of textile workers in Cromerton, North Carolina, sought employment outside the mill that would allow them to find personal fulfillment while still supplementing their family income. However, this was all but impossible in a depressed labor market, particularly without greater government investment in job training programs. "Mrs Roosevelt," the girl wrote the first lady, " I don't want to spend my life working in a cotton mill. My parents before me have had to do that, and I've seen what they have gone threw [sic]. I want to get a job to make enough, so my dear mother wont have to stand on her tired legs and work until she dies." To this end, the girl requested a loan to pay the cost of her training as a beautician. Inevitably, the money was not forthcoming.[44]

The financial strain that school costs imposed upon parents often forced them to push their children into mill work as soon as they graduated, and oftentimes even sooner. A survey of 385 mill families in the 1920s disclosed that the children had a 90 percent chance of entering the same profession as their parents. The situation did not improve significantly after the enactment of New Deal legislation. In a survey conducted after World War II, over 65 percent of mill children still entered the textile industry upon completing high school. As the author of the survey observed, textile workers remained an "inbred occupational group."[45] The cycle of poverty and limited occupational choice may not have turned so swiftly, but it had by no means been broken.

Parents worried how to keep their children not only in the schools but off the streets. The abolition of child labor increased concerns about juvenile delinquency. The introduction of restrictive legislation in the early decades of the twentieth century led more women into the mills in order to compensate for the loss of family income.[46] With neither parent home, children strayed into trouble. According to the 1920 census, 11.3 percent of white workers in North Carolina were cotton mill operatives. The children of these workers nonetheless accounted for 22.9 percent of boys and 20.4 percent of girls at state reform schools.[47]

The prohibition of child labor under the cotton textile code compounded this social problem. Although many mothers assumed that the restrictions imposed on working hours would enable them to spend more time tending their children, economic exigencies soon dictated otherwise. As long as children were in school, parents could be more or less confident that they would not lapse into delinquency. However, children were without supervision for weeks at a time during school vacations. Still, parents disapproved of the very places where children most commonly fraternized. Movie houses and swimming pools, they asserted, provided "practically unlimited possibilities for evil." This observation suggests some parental overreaction. Their concern about such establishments to some extent reflected the social conservatism of their Protestant faith. As Bryant Simon observes, a culture clash emerged between traditionalist parents and children socialized into the world of mass consumerism.[48] The problems were nevertheless sufficiently acute that these parents claimed their children would be saved from corruption were they allowed to work during the long summer vacation. "Father figured hard work never hurt anybody," recalled the child of one such parent. "He thought we were better off in the mill than gallivanting around getting into mischief." Large numbers of children dropped out of school as soon as they reached the compulsory age limit of fourteen; still too young to work in the mills, they sought other means to occupy themselves. According to one retired textile worker, "these children wander up and down the streets or thinks of nothing but dressing up, and wasting their time in the moving picture houses. If the children was taught to work when they are young, and was made to work hard, there wouldn't be so many people here to depend on the Government, now." Although protective of young children, mill parents opined that those between the ages of fourteen and sixteen should be eligible for paid employment. The fact that financial difficulties forced many of these teenagers to drop out of school therefore underscores the failure of the New Deal to address the social and economic consequences of child labor reform.[49] The delinquent social behavior of mill children continued to concern parents in the postwar era. As one mill hand caustically observed, now that children no longer worked in the mills, they "ain't worth a damn for nothin.' "[50]

The abolition of child labor was a watershed in the history of southern textiles. In broad societal terms, it contributed to the dissolution of the mill village. Employers traditionally leased company houses on the condition that families provide one worker for each room. The decline in child laborers rendered this system unsustainable. By the 1920s, the average family furnished only half a worker for each room; by 1940, the figure had fallen to a third. The subsequent cut in profit margins compelled mill owners to sell off company houses.[51] As Jeanette Nichols asserted, the system ironically discriminated against those children who secured employment outside the mill, since their families were expelled from the company home. According to Nichols, "the mill village simply purges itself of its undesirables, those who vary from the established norm, who have an initiative and an imagination which seek different work."[52]

For mill families the prohibition of child labor had a profoundly ambiguous impact. The New Deal failed to provide the proper infrastructure that would enable children to exploit the new educational opportunities open to them. State intervention simultaneously cut incomes and increased expenditure. For many mill families, the New Deal administration seemed less like a benevolent superparent than an interfering relative who claims to know what is best for a child but only disturbs the domestic order of a household. Throughout the reforms of the interwar era, mill operatives retained a somber attitude toward their impoverished status, placing their faith not in secular reform but spiritual redemption. "I memba what th' Good Book says about th' rich 'n' th' poor," asserted one employee. " 'They'll get theirs when they die.' " Other mill workers took more practical measures to ease their economic problems. In the face of financial pressure, many men and women concluded that their only hope in the long term was to have fewer children. Bill and Helen Branch were among the couples who abandoned the traditional resistance of mill families to birth control. When interviewed by the WPA, both Bill and Helen had been out of work for months. Helen contemplated the uncertainty of their children's futures: "These two are all I want. It seems to me the world's too full of people already or there wouldn't be so many out of jobs. Big families don't belong in this changing world."[53]

The limitations of New Deal legislation ultimately bear relevance not only to the lives of mill workers during the Great Depression but also to the contemporary discourse on child labor in the developing world. The abolition of child labor under textile industry codes betrayed a naive humanitarianism among reformers, who failed to foresee the turbulent social and economic impact of their actions upon mill families. Similar criticisms can be made of the modern campaign by Western reformers to boycott child labor in developing countries. In 1993, the U.S. Congress passed the Child Labor Deterrence Act, which resulted in the removal of thousands of children from the garment factories of Bangladesh. Although applauded by reformers, the act demonstrated a misunderstanding about the realities of child labor akin to that of the Roosevelt Administration six decades earlier. The employment of children is, under current economic conditions, essential to the subsistence of many Bangladeshi families. Their removal from the factory floor therefore threatened serious economic consequences. As a result, the United Nations Children's Fund and the International Labor Organization established a Memorandum of Understanding that encourages children to attend schools by compensating them for lost income.[54] Social reformers of the interwar era acted on the mistaken assumption that child labor was caused by the shortcomings of mill parents rather than structural deficiencies in the southern economy. As a recent conference of child workers in Kundapur, India, made clear, the plight of the poor can only be resolved by addressing "the root causes of our situation, primarily poverty."[55] The lesson of the New Deal needs to be learned in order to prevent reformers perpetuating the mistakes of the past.

NOTES

1. "The Simple Purposes and the Solid Foundations of Our Recovery Program," 24 July 1933; "The President Hails the First N.R.A. Code," 9 July 1933; "A Wider Opportunity for the Average Man," 4 Aug. 1934, in Samuel I. Rosenman, comp., *The Public Papers and Addresses of Franklin D. Roosevelt*, vol. 2, *The Year of Crisis, 1933* (New York: Random House, 1938), 299, 275, 373–74. See also Irving Bernstein, *A Caring Society: The New Deal, the Worker, and the Great Depression* (Boston: Houghton Mifflin, 1985), 117.

2. In contrast to textiles, the number of child laborers in other industries, such as lumber, increased after the abolition of the NRA codes. *New Republic*, 2 Dec. 1936, 131.

3. Hugh S. Johnson, *The Blue Eagle from Egg to Earth* (Garden City: Doubleday, Doran, 1935), 233; Felix Frankfurter, "Child Labor and the Court," *New Republic*, 26 July 1922, 249.

4. See, for example, the physical description of a twelve-year-old girl, "more fit for a hospital than for a spinning-room," in Mary Applewhite Bacon, "The Problem of the Southern Cotton Mill," *Atlantic Monthly* 99 (Feb. 1907): 227.

5. Walter I. Trattner, *Crusade for the Children: A History of the National Child Labor Committee and Child Labor Reform in America* (Chicago: Quadrangle, 1970), 99. The condition of mill children was also compared with that of slaves by reformer Lenora Beck Ellis. See Edna D. Bullock, comp., *Selected Articles on Child Labor* (White Plains NY: n.p., 1915), 9.

6. Edwin Markham, Benjamin B. Lindsey, and George Creel, *Children in Bondage: A Complete and Careful Presentation of the Anxious Problem of Child Labor—Its Causes, Its Crimes, and Its Cure* (New York: Hearst's International Library, 1914), 40–57. For a further example of sensationalist reporting, see Thomas Robinson Dawley Jr., *The Child That Toileth Not: The Story of a Government Investigation* (New York: Gracia Publishing, 1912).

7. Among the many studies of Lewis Hine are Russell Freedman, *Kids at Work: Lewis Hine and the Crusade against Child Labor* (New York: Clarion Books, 1994); Judith Mara Gutman, *Lewis W. Hine and the American Social Conscience* (New York: Walker, 1967); and John R. Kemp, ed., *Lewis Hine: Photographs of Child Labor in the New South* (Jackson: Univ. of Mississippi Press, 1986).

8. Mary Ann Mason, "The State as Superparent," in Paula S. Fass and Mary Ann Mason, eds., *Childhood in America* (New York: New York Univ. Press, 2000), 549–54.

9. David M. Kennedy, *Freedom from Fear: The American People in Depression and War, 1929–1945* (New York: Oxford Univ. Press, 1999), 257, 371. Roosevelt made this point explicitly when he urged passage of the National Industrial Recovery Act. See Rosenman, *Public Papers* 2:205.

10. Cathy L. McHugh, *Mill Family: The Labor System in the Southern Cotton Textile Industry, 1880–1915* (New York: Oxford Univ. Press, 1988), 14, 37–39; Shelley Sallee, *The Whiteness of Child Labor Reform in the New South* (Athens: Univ. of Georgia Press, 2004), 10–11; Hugh D. Hickman, *Child Labor: An American History* (Armonk NY: M. E. Sharpe, 2002), 54, 154–56; Allan DuMar Jones, "The Child Labor Reform Movement in Georgia," *Georgia Historical Quarterly* 49 (Dec. 1965): 398; Trattner, *Crusade for the Children,* 38–39; Broadus Mitchell, *The Rise of Cotton Mills in the South* (Gloucester MA: Peter Smith, 1966 [1921]), 95.

11. Further information about the NCLC can be found in Trattner, *Crusade for the Children*; Hugh C. Bailey, *Edgar Gardner Murphy: Gentle Progressive* (Coral Gables: Univ. Press of Florida, 1968); and Herbert J. Doherty, "Alexander J. McKelway: Preacher to Progressive," *Journal of Southern History* 24 (May 1958): 177–90.

12. W. J. Cash, *The Mind of the South* (New York: Vintage Books, 1991 [1941]), 225–26; Paul Blanshard, *Labor in Southern Cotton Mills* (New York: New Republic, 1927), 14; Jacquelyn Dowd Hall et al., *Like a Family: The Making of a Southern Cotton Mill World* (Chapel Hill: Univ. of North Carolina Press, 1987), 58.

13. Arden J. Lea, "Cotton Textiles and the Federal Child Labor Act of 1916," *Labor History* 16 (fall 1975): 485–94; Anne Firor Scott, "After Suffrage: Southern Women in the Twenties," *Journal of Southern History* 30 (Aug. 1964): 305; Dewey W. Grantham, *Southern Progressivism: The Reconciliation of Progress and Tradition* (Knoxville: Univ. of Tennessee Press, 1983), 189–90; Katharine Du Pre Lumpkin and Dorothy Wolff Douglas, *Child Workers in America* (New York: R. M. McBride, 1937), 219–20, 228, 231; Jones, "Child

Labor Reform," 397, 400; Dewey Grantham Jr., *Hoke Smith and the Politics of the New South* (Baton Rouge: Louisiana State Univ. Press, 1958), 300; William E. Gonzales, "An Unnecessary Amendment," *Forum* (Jan. 1925), 21; Hindman, *Child Labor*, 170–71. For further details of organized resistance to federal reform, see Grace Abbott, *The Child and the State*, vol. 1, *Legal Status in the Family Apprenticeship and Child Labor* (Chicago: Univ. of Chicago Press, 1938), 537–42; and Richard B. Sherman, "The Rejection of the Child Labor Amendment," *Mid-America* 45 (Jan. 1963): 10–11.

14. Glen Gilman, *Human Relations in the Industrial Southeast* (Chapel Hill: Univ. of North Carolina Press, 1956), 162–63; Hall et al., *Like a Family*, 59.

15. James A. Hodges, *New Deal Labor Policy and the Southern Cotton Textile Industry 1933–1941* (Knoxville: Univ. of Tennessee Press, 1986), 31; Herbert Jay Lahne, *The Cotton Mill Worker in the Twentieth Century* (New York: Farrar & Rinehart, 1944), 107; Liston Pope, *Millhands and Preachers: A Study of Gastonia* (New Haven: Yale Univ. Press, 1942), 195.

16. Blanshard, *Labor in Southern Cotton Mills*, 11.

17. Gilman, *Human Relations*, 159; Lahne, *Cotton Mill Worker*, 122–23, Gavin Wright, *Old South, New South: Revolutions in the Southern Economy Since the Civil War* (Baton Rouge: Louisiana State Univ. Press, 1996 [1986]), 145–46.

18. Bryant Simon, *A Fabric of Defeat: The Politics of South Carolina Millhands, 1910–1948* (Chapel Hill: Univ. of North Carolina Press, 1998), 19–20; Lois MacDonald, "Social and Economic Forces in Southern Mill Villages" (Ph.D. diss., New York University, 1929), 113.

19. John Greenway, *American Folk Songs of Protest* (New York: Octagon, 1960 [1953]), 121; Bill C. Malone, *Country Music U.S.A.* (Austin: Univ. of Texas Press, 1968), 142.

20. Dorsey Dixon, "Babies in the Mill" (HighTone Records, HMG 2502). Further details about the life and music of Dorsey Dixon can be found in Patrick Huber and Kathleen Drowne, "'I Don't Want Nothin' 'Bout My Life Wrote Out, Because I Had It Too Rough in Life': Dorsey Dixon's Autobiographical Writings," *Southern Cultures* 6 (summer 2000): 94–100.

21. Greenway, *American Folksongs*, 140–41. A recording of this song is available on Pete Seeger's album *American Industrial Ballads* (Smithsonian Folkways 40058).

22. Viviana A. Zelizer, *Pricing the Priceless Child: The Changing Social Value of Children* (Princeton: Princeton Univ. Press, 1994 [1985]), 5, 57.

23. I. A. Newby, *Plain Folk in the New South: Social Change and Cultural Persistence, 1880–1915* (Baton Rouge: Louisiana State Univ. Press, 1989), 494.

24. Greenway, *American Folksongs*, 139–40.

25. Melvin Thomas Copeland, *The Cotton Manufacturing Industry of the United States* (New York: A. M. Kelley, 1966 [1917]), 43–44; David L. Carlton, *Mill and Town in South Carolina 1880–1920* (Baton Rouge: Louisiana State Univ. Press, 1982), 196; Newby, *Plain Folk*, 498–502.

26. Marjorie A. Potwin, *Cotton Mill People of the Piedmont: A Study in Social Change* (New York: Columbia Univ. Press, 1968 [1927]), 137; undated interview with Mr. Trout, *American Life Histories: Manuscripts from the Federal Writers' Project, 1936–1940*, http://

memory.loc.gov/ammem/wpaintro/wpahome.html, accessed 1 Aug. 2000; Victoria Byerly, *Hard Times Cotton Mill Girls: Personal Histories of Womanhood and Poverty in the South* (Ithaca: ILR Press, 1986), 168–69.

27. Jennings J. Rhyne, *Some Southern Cotton Mill Workers and Their Villages* (Chapel Hill: Univ. of North Carolina Press, 1930), 201; U.S. Department of Commerce and Labor, *Report on Condition of Women and Child Wage-Earners in the United States*, 61st Cong., 2nd sess. (1910), 188–96.

28. Interview with Ida Allen (9 Sept. 1938), *American Life Histories*; interview with Mary Smith (15 July 1938), *American Life Histories*; Myra Page, *Southern Cotton Mills and Labor* (New York: Workers Library, 1929), 25–26. For further details on the severe financial constraints that compelled the employment of children, see Byerly, *Hard Times Cotton Mill Girls*, 17–18; Sallee, *Whiteness of Child Labor Reform*, 38–40; Jeremy P. Felt, "The Child Labor Provisions of the Fair Labor Standards Act," *Labor History* 11 (fall 1970): 471; Dolores E. Janiewski, *Sisterhood Denied: Race, Gender, and Class in a New South Community* (Philadelphia: Temple Univ. Press, 1985), 147; Lumpkin and Douglas, *Child Workers in America*, 164–67; Terrill and Hirsch, *Such As Us: Southern Voices of the Thirties* (Chapel Hill: Univ. of North Carolina Press, 1978), 149.

29. Hodges, *New Deal Labor Policy*, 32.

30. Hall et al., *Like a Family*, 316.

31. John Kenneth Morland, *Millways of Kent* (Chapel Hill: Univ. of North Carolina Press, 1958), 69–70, 96.

32. Page, *Southern Cotton Mills and Labor*, 25; Sinclair Lewis, *Cheap and Contented Labor: The Picture of a Southern Mill Town in 1929* (New York: United Textile Workers of America, 1929), 18, 30; Jeanette Paddock Nichols, "Does the Mill Village Foster Any Social Types?" *Social Forces* 2 (March 1924): 354.

33. Harriet L. Herring, "Tracing the Development of Welfare Work in the North Carolina Textile Industry," *Social Forces* 6 (June 1928): 593–94; William Hays Simpson, *Life in Mill Communities* (Clinton SC: n.p., 1943), 35; Frank Tannenbaum, *Darker Phases of the South* (New York: Negro Universities Press, 1969 [1924]), 45; Carlton, *Mill and Town*, 94–99, Page, *Southern Cotton Mills*, 51–53.

34. Blanshard, *Labor in Southern Cotton Mills*, 13, 15; John Harrison Cook, *A Study of the Mill Schools of North Carolina* (New York: Columbia Univ. Press, 1925), 39–41.

35. Page, *Southern Cotton Mills*, 52. These reforms rendered some improvement in the education of mill children. See Harriet L. Herring, "Industrial Relations in the South and the NIRA," *Social Forces* 12 (Oct. 1933): 127.

36. Hodges, *New Deal Labor Policy*, 28; Rhyne, *Some Southern Cotton Mill Workers*, 144–45, 149–50, 156.

37. Tannenbaum, *Darker Phases*, 43–44. See also Rhyne, *Some Southern Cotton Mill Workers*, 18.

38. Cook, *Study of the Mill Schools*, 51; Simpson, Life in Mill Communities, 36–37; Harriet L. Herring, *Welfare Work in Mill Villages: The Story of Extra-Mill Activities in North Carolina* (Chapel Hill: Univ. of North Carolina Press, 1929), 32, 58–59.

39. Rhyne, *Some Southern Cotton Mill Workers*, 155, 203.

40. Interviews with Sarah Wall (25 July 1938) and Josephine Wallace (5 July 1938), *American Life Histories*. Similar sentiments were expressed in the WPA interviews with Mrs. Teddy Lucille Keller (14 June 1939) and Margie Rushing (27 Oct. 1939). See also Byerly, *Hard Times Cotton Mill Girls*, 65.

41. Lumpkin and Douglas, *Child Workers in America*, 147–48; Cook, *Study of the Mill Schools*, 38.

42. Interviews with Nina Boone (26 Sept. 1938) and Elsie Wall (27 July 1938), *American Life Histories*. The financial pressure on parents is also discussed in the WPA interviews with Mary Smith (15 July 1938) and Edgar Wynce (1 Oct. 1939).

43. Page, *Southern Cotton Mills*, 27, 30, 67–68. Lois MacDonald encountered a similarly resigned response from mill workers. Although supportive of compulsory education, they considered that "There is no chance for the children of such as us." MacDonald, "Social and Economic Forces," 82–83, 116–17, 144–45.

44. Robert Cohen, ed., *Dear Mrs. Roosevelt: Letters from Children of the Great Depression* (Chapel Hill: Univ. of North Carolina Press, 2002), 140–41.

45. Page, *Southern Cotton Mills*, 58; Morland, *Millways of Kent*, 100, 37, 51.

46. Blanshard, *Labor in Southern Cotton Mills*, 22–23; Hall et al., *Like a Family*, 154.

47. Lahne, *Cotton Mill Worker*, 105; Rhyne, *Some Southern Cotton Mill Workers*, 180–83, 198–99. Manufacturers warned that the prohibition of child labor would result in the moral corruption of mill youth. Broadus Mitchell and George Sinclair Mitchell, *The Industrial Revolution in the South* (Baltimore: Johns Hopkins Univ. Press, 1930), 218–21.

48. Simon, *Fabric of Defeat*, 24. According to Myra Page, mill communities imposed a "religious taboo" on modern entertainments. Page, *Southern Cotton Mills*, 51.

49. Rhyne, *Some Southern Cotton Mill Workers*, 199, 184, 204; Gilman, *Human Relations*, 160; interviews with the Farlows (16 Dec. 1938) and Blansh Gibson (26 Sept. 1939), *American Life Histories*; Blanshard, *Labor in Southern Cotton Mills*, 14–15.

50. Morland, *Millways of Kent*, 95.

51. Blanshard, *Labor in Southern Cotton Mills*, 22; Carlton, *Mill and Town*, 102, 191; Janiewski, *Sisterhood Denied*, 74–75; Douglas L. Flamming, *Creating the Modern South: Millhands and Manager in Dalton, Georgia, 1884–1984* (Chapel Hill: Univ. of North Carolina Press, 1992); Harriet L. Herring, *Passing of the Mill Village: Revolution in a Southern Institution* (Chapel Hill: Univ. of North Carolina Press, 1949), 20–21.

52. McDonald, "Social and Economic Forces," 25–26; Nichols, "Does the Mill Village Foster Any Social Types?" 355.

53. Page, *Southern Cotton Mills*, 24; interview with Bill and Helen Branch (1 Aug. 1938), *American Life Histories*. On the long-term impact of reform on the size of mill families, see Morland, *Millways of Kent*, 82–83.

54. "Thank You, Mr Harkin, Sir!" *New Internationalist*, July 1997, 12, www.oneworld .org/ni/issue292/than.htm, accessed 1 Aug. 2000.

55. "We, the Working Children of the Third World, Propose . . ." *New Internationalist*, July 1997, 24, www.oneworld.org/ni/issue292/simply.html, accessed 1 Aug. 2000.

From Memphis to Bandung

The Political Uses of Hunger in

Richard Wright's Black Boy

ANDREW WARNES

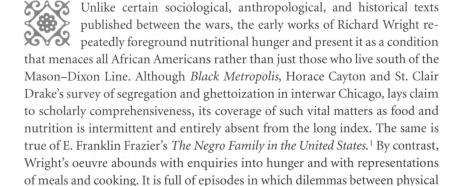 Unlike certain sociological, anthropological, and historical texts published between the wars, the early works of Richard Wright repeatedly foreground nutritional hunger and present it as a condition that menaces all African Americans rather than just those who live south of the Mason–Dixon Line. Although *Black Metropolis*, Horace Cayton and St. Clair Drake's survey of segregation and ghettoization in interwar Chicago, lays claim to scholarly comprehensiveness, its coverage of such vital matters as food and nutrition is intermittent and entirely absent from the long index. The same is true of E. Franklin Frazier's *The Negro Family in the United States*.[1] By contrast, Wright's oeuvre abounds with enquiries into hunger and with representations of meals and cooking. It is full of episodes in which dilemmas between physical safety and nutritional satiety become fraught. And it continually insists that the condition plagues African Americans at both the departure and arrival points of the Great Migration.

As we will see, Wright's insistence that a hunger many U.S. readers associated only with the South actually held national proportions is visible throughout his autobiography, *Black Boy*, and not least in its first, fully restored publication in 1991 as *Black Boy (American Hunger)*. But this insistence is also clear in *Native Son*, a novel Wright characterized as an attempt to distill "the emotional and cultural hunger" of American slum experience into the single, nihilistic personality of Bigger Thomas, the protagonist. It is conceivable that *Black Metropolis*, although published scarcely a year before *Native Son*, influenced this rigorous profiling of nutritional and psychological want. In his 1945 introduction to a reissue of the work, Wright certainly acknowledged the connections between the study and the novel, paying tribute to Cayton and Drake for picturing "the environment out of which the Bigger Thomases of our nation come."[2] Yet the methodological representation this environment received at the hands of these social scientists includes far fewer references to food and hunger than the austere fictionalization it received in *Native Son*. Even *Black Metropolis*'s description of African Americans' special susceptibility to "lean times," although constituting one of Cayton and Drake's few references to the diet of an urban population they otherwise exhaustively survey, points specifically to unemployment but not to any impact such redundancy had upon nutritional intake. *Native Son*, by contrast, pictures a scene in which Bigger Thomas, having half-accidentally murdered his white employers' daughter, finds his equally amateurish attempts to extract a ransom obstructed by food's visual promise of imminent physical satisfaction. By so viscerally intensifying Bigger's conflicting impulses for satiety and for flight, the sensory presence of this tantalizing meal establishes concerns about the disciplinary usefulness of food to which Wright, unlike many contemporary social scientists, consistently returns:

> [Bigger Thomas] had strained himself from a too long lack of sleep and food; and the excitement was sapping his energy. He should go to the kitchen and ask for his dinner. Surely, he should not starve like this. . . . On a table were spread several white napkins under which was something that looked like plates of food. . . . There were sliced bread and steak and fried potatoes and gravy and string beans and spinach and a huge piece of chocolate cake. . . . He rested his black fingers on the white table and a silent laugh burst from his parted lips as he saw himself for a split second in a lurid objective light: he had killed a rich white girl and had burned her body after cutting her head off . . . and yet he stood here afraid to touch food on the table, food which undoubtedly was his own. (175)

Alive to the agony that food arouses in the hungry, *Native Son* offers a corrective to the contemporary scholarly tendency to invoke hunger rhetorically without exploring its impact upon behavior or personality. This tendency is evident when Cayton and Drake's *Black Metropolis* characterizes the Great Depression as "the Lean Years":

> [Before 1929, Chicago's] white papers talked of unending prosperity and were advertising a second World's Fair to celebrate a Century of Progress. But Negroes were a barometer sensitive to the approaching storm. They had reason to fear, while most of the Midwest Metropolis seemed to suspect nothing, that the Fat Years were about to end.
>
> Chicago's banking structure broke at its weakest link—in the Black Belt. In July of 1930, Binga's bank closed its doors, while mobs cried in the streets for their savings. Within a month every bank in Black Metropolis was closed. As white housewives balanced the budget, their Negro servants were often the first casualties.

When factories cut production, unskilled Negro labor was usually the first to go. . . . The Depression had come to Midwest Metropolis and Black Metropolis reflected the general disaster. The Lean Years were at hand. (84)

THIS CHAPTER INVESTIGATES the ways in which the representations of hunger supplied by Wright's narratives intersect with and disrupt those of more methodological analyses of poverty produced in the Depression era. It is important to begin by stating that this involves more than simply contrasting the formidable presence hunger achieves in Wright's oeuvre with its absence in much contemporary scholarship. It involves more than simply pointing out that Wright's work explodes the former invisibility of northern hunger, calling attention to its similarities with its more recognized incidence in the South. This argument also requires us to engage with those statements on nutrition that *were* issued by contemporary scholars and to clarify the structural aspects, beyond those of region, that distinguish them from Wright's imagery.

Of these structural differences, among the most noteworthy is the challenge Wright's literary narratives lodge against the tendency among many contemporary social scientists to characterize hunger as a byproduct of poverty. Evidence of this causational perspective arises from *Black Metropolis* itself. As the previous quotation attests, Cayton and Drake's survey parlayed contemporary assumptions that hunger was symptomatic, a branch sprouted from the malignant root of economic inequality. Characterizing the fractious transition from Boom to Bust as one from "fat" to "lean times," Cayton and Drake vividly establish an economic cause—unemployment—that then has a direct effect upon the waistbands of those turned away from Chicago's warehouses and factories. Nor does the sequential link that this passage constructs proceed from a single economic cause to a single nutritional effect, since, manifestly, the phrase *lean times* synecdochically refers to an economic climate in which African Americans found not just food but *everything* scarce. Thus, while Cayton and Drake's metaphor prioritizes nutritional concerns, it also encompasses many other shortfalls, many other "branches," all of which, as elements within a generalized dispossession, face back to the one malignant root of economic deprivation. Consequently, like so many rashes, spells of dizziness, and bouts of nausea, shortfalls in shelter, insurance, health care, housing, and, explicitly, food all function symptomatically as diagnosable signs of a single malaise: poverty.

In its length, its combination of interviews and statistical evidence, and its insistence that racism is antidemocratic, Gunnar Myrdal's *American Dilemma* shares much with *Black Metropolis*. And yet, as though to compound the impression that hunger was a strictly southern phenomenon, *American Dilemma*'s treatment of the issue is neither fleeting nor rhetorical; Myrdal offers extensive discussions of diet, malnutrition, and poverty. However, even Myrdal's inquiry into southern disfranchisement—though conceding that noneconomic factors can differentiate nutritional intake even when "income is kept constant"— nonetheless broadly reiterates Cayton and Drake's symptomatic conceptualization of hunger. *American Dilemma* characterizes hunger as one among many symptoms of poverty, not just by claiming that "deficiencies in diet [. . . are] highly dependent on income," but by bracketing its discussion of such diet alongside subheadings like "The Family Budget" and "Housing Conditions" within an overarching chapter on money.[3]

THERE IS NO EVIDENCE to suggest that Wright considered the causational approach to hunger typified by *Black Metropolis* and *American Dilemma* to be anything other than useful, not to mention necessary. Accordingly, my intention is not to attack those postwar social scientists who endorse the causational view embodied, for instance, in the subtitle of Isobel Cole-Hamilton and Tim Lang's *Tightening Belts: A Report on the Impact of Poverty on Food.*[4] It is, after all, obvious that, in those economies of the urban North and rural South that experienced rapid industrialization between the wars, hunger all but invariably results from a prior economic setback. Manifestly, those who sought the alleviation of relief stations and were thus forced into what *Black Boy* terms "a public confession of . . . hunger" (352–53) had only been brought to such a low following a collapse in income.[5]

Justifiable and necessary though these symptomatic conceptualizations are, however, they are rarely reiterated in Wright's oeuvre. What one often encounters instead is a figurative approach in which Wright isolates hunger from other symptoms of poverty and, having established it as a "disease" in its own right, engages with it as a political condition. This approach can be detected even in Wright's introduction to *Black Metropolis*, which begins with his memory of how, after fleeing the South for Chicago, he "lived half hungry and afraid."[6] This prefatory focus on a word so seldomly or metaphorically mentioned on subsequent pages is made explicit as Wright observes:

> Current American thought . . . has quite forgot the reality of the passion and hunger of millions of exploited workers and dissatisfied minorities. . . . Let us disentangle in our minds Hitler's deeds from what Hitler exploited. His deeds were crimes; but the hunger he exploited in the hearts of Europe's millions was a valid hunger and is still there. Indeed, the war has but deepened that hunger, made it more acute.[7]

If these words are placed into a temporal rather than a textual relationship with *Black Metropolis*, they become interpretable less as an introduction to the sociological investigation and more as a critical postscript in which Wright voices his responses to it. This accomplished, one might speculate that, given Cayton and Drake's failure to include an extended discussion of nutrition in their text, Wright is actually implicating *Black Metropolis* in his criticism of the significant silences "current American thought" displays on the "passion and hunger" of the "exploited." Whether this is true or not, Wright significantly follows this criticism with a renewed concentration on hunger, which not only isolates it from other social "symptoms" but almost treats it as *Black Metropolis* treats poverty: as an organizational umbrella under which material shortfalls can be grouped. Equally, although Wright's phrase "valid hunger" recalls Cayton and Drake's metaphoric use of "lean times," his countervailing refusal to anchor this signifying hunger to a specific economic referent actually releases it from any rigidly causational conceptualization in which it would synecdochically invoke distinct symptomatic shortfalls in housing, insurance, or healthcare. Nor does Wright here conceive hunger as a merely metaphorical referent for political desire: rather, by affirming its reality, validity, venality, and inexorability, he presents a broader, more fluid condition able to accommodate nutritional desires together with those political passions with which they now become blurred. In the process, this new fluidity and breadth remind us that, psychologically, the desire for economic reform and the desire for food might actually resist the clear compartmentalization premised by the causational, symptomatic approach of certain social scientists. They remind us that neither the hungry nor the revolutionary might as efficiently distinguish the perception of political oppression from the experience of malnutrition— that, within such "exploited" personalities, reformism and hunger may overlap and, as mutable desires, coalesce to become as inseparable as yeast and flour in dough.

IN A 1969 ESSAY TITLED "Black Studies and the Contemporary Student," C. L. R. James has recounted a dinner in France that Richard Wright, who "fancied himself as a bit of a cook," prepared "in some Southern way." Before this expatriated soul food meal's commencement, James received a guided tour of his host's temporary European home. Pausing before some bookshelves, Wright declared to his fellow writer: " 'Look here, Nello, you see those books there? They are by Kierkegaard. . . . I want to tell you something. Everything that he writes about in these books, I knew before I had them.' " James insists that Wright's remark was intended, not egotistically, but to attribute intellectual foresight to African Americans in general. Understanding Wright in social terms, James concludes: "What he was telling me was that he was a black man in the United States and that gave him an insight into what today is the universal opinion and attitude of the modern personality." A quarter century later, Paul Gilroy confirms James's view, noting that "Wright's apparently intuitive fore-knowledge of the issues raised by Kierkegaard was not intuitive at all. It was an elementary product of his historical experiences as a black growing up in the United States between the wars."[8] In other words, this sharpened intellectual foresight derived from a position imposed on Wright by America as a whole: the lesson of its white supremacy and acute nutritional inequality, though first taught to the young writer by Jim Crow, was monotonously repeated in Chicago's daily grind.

In some ways, Wright's introduction to *Black Metropolis* demonstrates the insight into modernity that his commentary on Kierkegaard assigns to much African American cultural production. Rather as James and Gilroy suggest that American racial hierarchies foreshadowed elements explored by Kierkegaard, so his introduction's representation of a hunger bound by these hierarchies foreshadows directions pursued by Western intellectualism after the war. For example, by subtly resisting Cayton and Drake's causational approach, Wright's introduction forms a rich and sustainable bridge to research undertaken by Raymond Williams in the 1970s. Particularly, the introduction's tacit subversion of foregoing efforts to categorically separate the desire for food from the desire for political change exemplify Williams's insistence in *Marxism and Literature* that "practical consciousness is almost always different from official consciousness." Wright rejects the "handling of fixed forms and units" that *Marxism and Literature* assigns to "official" thinking, and his embrace of political and nutritional desires as mutable facets within an overarching "hunger" anticipates Williams's reemphasis on "what is actually being lived, and not only [on] what it is thought is being lived."

Episodes from *Black Boy* further substantiate these interconnections. Describing the days immediately following his flight to Chicago, for instance, Wright recalls that he "hungered for a grasp of the framework of contemporary living, for a knowledge of the forms of life about me, for eyes to see the bony structures of personality" (334). Such terms virtually paraphrase those by which *Marxism and Literature* sets out what Edward Said terms the "seminal phrase 'structures of feeling.'" Almost uncannily, they call to mind Williams's advocacy of a new intellectual engagement with "meanings and values as they are actually lived and felt."[9] Nor are *Marxism and Literature*'s "structures of feeling" and *Black Boy*'s "structures of personality" comparable only semantically, but because both recommend lived experience as the ideal guide for future intellectual engagements.

The first manuscript of Wright's autobiography was titled *American Hunger*, began by recounting his Mississippi boyhood, and ended by exposing his disaffection with Communism and encounters with racism in Chicago. However, the prospect of a deal with the Book of the Month Club persuaded Wright to change this original title to *Black Boy*, limit it to the South, and publish the Chicago section elsewhere. The BOMC wished to repeat the success of its earlier edition of *Native Son* but not the controversy. Interested in "only the first section of the work" titled "Southern Night," this liberal northern organization clearly felt far more comfortable about Wright's jeremiad against Jim Crow than they were with his narrative's subsequent insistence that the North was racist, too.[10] And yet, even as it mutilated and limited Wright's manuscript to a southern geography, this crude abridgment could not prevent his trope of hunger from assuming national proportions. Even before its 1991 restoration, Wright's original title palimpsestically burnished *Black Boy*'s "official" version, resurfacing in renegade phrases that signaled a concern with "the plight of the Negro in America" as a whole rather than in a particular part of it (321). Not only hunger but a once-eponymous "American hunger" in this way survived the mutilation of Wright's autobiography, remaining as testimony to his principal concern. Throughout, Wright imbues the condition of hunger with a certain determinism: his very "consciousness" is "riveted upon obtaining a loaf of bread"(274); he asserts that "I lived on what I did not eat" (161); he describes hunger as "my daily companion" (307). Constantly positioning hunger as an omnipresent experience, *Black Boy* thus uses it to shape a lens through which the living, moving world is filtered—a lens, indeed, that exerts such influence on Wright's perception as to qualify under Williams's "structure of feeling" designation.

In turn, the differences between the representations of hunger by certain social scientists and by Wright crystallize. On one hand, many scholarly texts published by liberals or socialists in the Depression and New Deal eras present malnutrition as a kind of human boll weevil: a southern disease. Those who do acknowledge the presence of hunger in northern cities, meanwhile, tend to concur with the causational and symptomatic understanding of the condition employed by analysts of southern life. Most accordingly arrive at a familiar conclusion: that the need to reform American capitalism is demonstrated by the many intolerable symptoms that it almost incidentally creates, one of which happens to be hunger. By contrast, even the part of Wright's autobiography that the BOMC published collapses the economic fulcrum at the heart of this construction, concentrating its terms, to establish an equivalency between the desire for bread and the desire for political change. Hunger, in Wright's oeuvre, *is* reformism: it *is* radicalism; and, if exploited with sufficiently Machiavellian intelligence, it can even become the totalitarianism that, in its fascist and Stalinist forms, preoccupies much of *Black Boy*.

ONE RESPONSE TO THIS treatment of hunger is to say that, far from realizing a "structure of feeling," it merely manifests a rhetorical conceit that blurs mean-

ingful distinctions between income and nutrition in order to capture a particular political temperament more succinctly. Such a response could certainly be
bolstered by the fact that, as a novelist, Wright's trade was in the imaginative
use of language, whereas Cayton and Drake's lay in its uses as an analytic tool.
Evidence that Wright's representation of hunger results from more than mere
aesthetic considerations is, however, supplied by *Black Boy*'s dramatization of
the uses underfeeding offers to social authorities wanting to force the potentially troublesome into acquiescence. This dramatization of hunger as a disciplinary tool first emerges in the autobiography's opening pages, which recount
childhood experiences when Wright knew that he was hungry but did not yet
know that he was poor. Among other things, Wright's use of childhood naïveté
facilitates a reversal in the cause-and-effect sequence that informs much of the
period's scholarly writing on hunger. It establishes hunger instead as a foundation upon which a postponed yet inevitable realization of poverty can be subsequently constructed. This, in turn, allows *Black Boy* to position hunger, not
as an "incidental" symptom of poverty, but as a condition that exerts pressures
and sets limits that maintain social acquiescence.

Of these childhood years, Wright admits, "I was not aware of what hunger
really meant"—was not yet cognizant either of its potential for enforcing subordination or of its profundity as a perspective filter for an emergent "structure
of feeling" (16). Yet although it resists explanation, and although it remains a
"cloudy notion," hunger is nevertheless recognized by the young Wright as a
guide to his initial encounters with white-dominated social authorities and institutions (10). The privileges of white Americans, that Wright later denounces
in analytical terms, are first forced into his consciousness because of their un-
explained access to an unimaginable supply of food. Mystification mixes with
an inarticulate sense of injustice as Wright recalls that, if his mother's white
employers "left anything, my brother and I would eat well; but if they did not,
we would have our usual bread and tea. Watching the white people eat would
make my empty stomach churn and I would grow vaguely angry" (22). Even
Wright's attitude to the black church is critically influenced by an anger borne
of this vague and as yet unstructured hunger. Preachers—who, again, *Black Boy*
later denounces in an extensive and sophisticated diatribe—are not at first condemned due to problems of faith or dogma, but because these representatives
on earth are, in a word, gourmands:

> In the center of the table was a huge platter of golden-brown fried chicken. I com-
> pared the bowl of soup that sat before me with the crispy chicken and decided in
> favor of the chicken. . . .
> "Eat your soup," my mother said.

"I don't want any," I said. . . .

The preacher had finished his soup and had asked that the platter of chicken be passed to him. It galled me. He smiled, cocked his head this way and that, picking out choice pieces. I forced a spoonful of soup down my throat and looked to see if my speed matched that of the preacher. It did not. . . . As piece after piece of chicken was taken, I was unable to eat my soup at all. I grew hot with anger. The preacher was laughing and joking and the grownups were hanging on his words. My growing hate of the preacher finally became more important than God or religion and I could no longer contain myself. I . . . screamed, running blindly from the room.

"That preacher's going to eat *all* the chicken!" I bawled. (30–31)

Thus, years before his adoption of Marxism, and decades before his adoption of existentialism, Wright is converted to the atheism that customarily partners these philosophical ideologies by hunger, and hunger alone. The complex and extensive analyses by which Wright elsewhere condemns white southerners and black preachers are prefigured, in *Black Boy*'s narrative sequence, by the accusation that neither group intervened to assuage his "American hunger."

Following this scene, *Black Boy* details those years of late childhood when the mental and physical deterioration of Wright's mother stripped his family life of the small semblance of security it once possessed. Chronicling his relatives' failed attempts to keep him within the family circle, Wright turns to the representation of what he calls a Methodist "orphan home" in Memphis. The fact that, although his parents are alive, Wright must be designated an orphan in order to qualify for state guardianship primes the narrative for a representation that in some ways signifies upon foregoing portrayals of institutional life.

The orphan home was a two-story frame building set amid trees in a wide, green field. . . . The house was crowded with children and there was always a storm of noise. The daily routine was blurred to me and I never quite grasped it. The most abiding feeling I had each day was hunger and fear. The meals were skimpy and there were only two of them. Just before we went to bed each night we were given a slice of bread smeared with molasses. The children were silent, hostile, vindictive, continuously complaining of hunger. There was an over-all atmosphere of nervousness and intrigue, of children telling tales upon others, of children being deprived of food to punish them. . . . Each morning after we had eaten a breakfast that seemed like no breakfast at all, an older child would lead a herd of us to the vast lawn and we would get to our knees and wrench the grass loose from the dirt with our fingers. . . . Many mornings I was too weak from hunger to pull out the grass; I would grow dizzy and my mind would become blank. (33–34)

In its Puritanical atmosphere, which actively intensifies and exploits the guilt orphans are expected to feel about their orphanhood, *Black Boy*'s Memphis institution recalls Lowood House in Charlotte Brontë's *Jane Eyre* as well as the "branch-workhouse" that introduces Charles Dickens' *Oliver Twist*. Implicitly, by signifying upon British representations issued from the early phase of what Michel Foucault termed the Great Confinement, *Black Boy*'s orphanage scene effects a necessary racial complication, which emphasizes the disproportionate presence African Americans assume within this imprisoning movement's later cycles in the United States. That this orphanage scene bridges the class dynamics of the utilitarian workhouse with the class and race dynamics of the penitentiary is confirmed as Wright autobiographically locates it in a pre–World War I period that Rayford Logan identified as marking "the nadir of the Negro's status in American society."[11] In *The Betrayal of the Negro*, Logan defends his assertion by noting that this period witnessed: state disfranchisement of African Americans, both constitutionally and by stealth; an escalation in lynchings; record Ku Klux Klan membership numbers; and the consolidation both of segregation and of racial stereotyping. In short, *The Betrayal of the Negro* characterizes a period of racial brutality—a period when almost every conceivable tool of social control at the disposal of white American culture was dedicated to preserving the essentialist hierarchies that once legitimized slavery.

Of these tools of control, it is the distribution of food that Wright pushes to the foreground of *Black Boy*'s orphanage scene. Wright and his fellow inmates "continuously complain of hunger": the "most abiding feeling I had each day was hunger"; hunger even debilitates Wright to the extent that he cannot wrench grass from the ground. Of course, any attempt to attribute this hunger to a disciplinary tool is undermined by the possibility that it merely arises from a financial shortage—that it is merely a symptom of institutional poverty, after all. However, it is significant that such financial restrictions remain unmentioned by *Black Boy* as, indeed, they are by *Oliver Twist*, which describes the regime by which orphans "got thin" as actually being "rather expensive, [. . . owing to the] necessity of taking in the clothes of all the paupers."[12] Nor do *Black Boy*'s accumulating references simply isolate hunger and engage with it as a condition in its own right. They also show that this isolation results from something other than a merely aesthetic motivation. They reveal that *Black Boy*'s isolation of hunger is a verisimilar representation of an isolation first initiated by an orphanage regime eager to enlist such want in its imposition of acquiescence. They suggest, in other words, that *Black Boy*'s prioritization of hunger over poverty results, not from a rhetorical conceit, but from Wright's realist ambition to capture the principal position that nutrition occupied in his early southern life.

In order to clarify this, we must return to the key phrase *great confinement* and to Foucault's empathetic commitment to those subjected to the "institutions of repression, rejection, exclusion, marginalization . . . that permit the fabrication of the disciplinary individual." Indeed, even as Wright claims to anticipate Kierkegaard on behalf of African American experience, so *Black Boy*'s orphanage scene predates Foucault's concern with this institutional limitation of the individual occupant's free will. That is to say, rather as it paraphrases Williams's *Marxism and Literature*, so *Black Boy*—which elsewhere identifies Wright's "need" to "use words to create religious types, criminal types, the warped, the lost, the baffled" (334)—engages with the archive of "marginalization" that Foucault explores in *Discipline and Punish*. Moreover, this interest in the treatment of the socially marginal by the socially authoritative extends, in *Black Boy* and *Discipline and Punish* alike, to the institutional segregation of inmates both into cells and into fixed timetables. What *Black Boy* signals through repetitive phrasing—wherein hunger abides "each day," bread and molasses are served "each night," and grass is uprooted "each morning"—is a "daily routine" that, in the terms of *Discipline and Punish*, regulates "the relations of time, bodies and forces." *Discipline and Punish* argues that such temporal and spatial segregation increases institutional authorities' ability to withhold and to grant, to mete out punishments and to dole out rewards, to turn "need" into "a political instrument meticulously prepared, calculated, and used." Punishment, Foucault suggests, thus becomes "only one element of a double-system: gratification-punishment" that secures acquiescence by defining "behaviour and performance on the basis of the two opposed values of good and evil." In turn, Foucault's identification of this institutional "circulation" both of "debits" and of "awards" reminds us that inmates' desires can be manipulated as profitably as their fears—that beatings, deprivations, isolations, and humiliations can all produce acquiescence; but so can bribery.[13]

Yet it also reminds us that the distribution of food that *Black Boy*'s orphanage imposes, since it determines who will be fed and who will not, is also a distribution of hunger. It, too, is a "circulation" that, by simultaneously parading food's presence as an "award" and threatening food's absence as a "debit," meets both polarities delineated by Foucault's "double-system" of "gratification-punishment." Furthermore, this particular "circulation" becomes intensified since the "debit" of hunger, which can be defined as a desire that solicits its own cessation, inordinately increases the appeal of food's "award." Children are punished by a distribution of hunger—they are "deprived of food to punish them"—yet they are also bribed into submission by the mutual counterweight of hunger's promised termination, which, perhaps, tempts inmates into "telling tales upon others." Functioning complementarily as threat and as promise, the oppositional yet interdependent distributions of hunger and food thus enable the institution to resolve in its favor everyday flashpoints, disputes, and rebellions, securing a regimented, disciplinary tranquility.

GIVEN THAT FOOD and hunger thus unite in this institutionally useful double system of "punishment-gratification," it is perhaps unsurprising that *Black Boy* should then charge the orphanage authorities with attempting to maximize their inmates' feelings of appetite. Certainly, it seems significant that, like Oliver Twist, Richard Wright is underfed rather than unfed. Wright is given food, after all—he is not simply being starved to death. But it is possible that the orphanage regime actually maximizes Wright's appetite via the very paltriness of the food that it promises, via the very inadequacy of the meals that it awards. At any event, literary and academic evidence suggests that the rationing that Wright's orphanage enforces may intensify appetite more effectively than any other dietary regime. Oliver Twist, after all, grows "voracious and wild with hunger" because he is being subjected to the "tortures of slow starvation" rather than to starvation outright.[14] Meanwhile, the biopsychologist Andrew John Hill suggests:

> It is generally recognized that for those people who totally abstain from eating, the feeling of hunger disappears in a matter of days. . . . On the other hand, hunger is a constant presence when people are only semi-starved. . . . The desire . . . to redress the energy deficit spills over into daily life and for some people becomes the central feature of their interest. It is apparent that satiety is a state never achieved in these circumstances.[15]

Hill's remarks indicate that "a breakfast that felt like no breakfast at all" is likely to optimize Wright's psychological desire for food far more efficiently than would *having* "no breakfast at all." Effectively, Hill explains why Wright's morning meal seems to vaporize before his eyes, postponing indefinitely the satiety that it visually promises, thereby revitalizing that promise and reinvigorating the potent memory of adequate nutrition. Foods, as a material within the "circulation" of nutrition, thus become so "meticulously prepared" and "calculated" as to produce a diet that is exactly sufficient to prevent outright starvation, yet exactly insufficient to assuage malnutrition. The evaporating meal, reneging on the promise of satiety, works to promote the hunger that it allegedly abolishes, prompting Wright to follow Twist and ask for more.

THE MEMPHIS ORPHANAGE episode is thus a classic instance of Wright's ability, when preparing *Black Boy* for publication, to smuggle past his censor's gaze representations that exceeded their southern settings and commented on the nation as a whole. What the orphan home episode outlines, after all, is an assessment of the uses of hunger and the manipulation of need that holds a resonance universal to Western societies. And beyond: the later Wright would revisit this same analysis of need, this same insight into how authorities could create and exploit want, when working to understand the problems facing people in the newly postcolonial world. As *The Color Curtain*, Wright's report on the conference of newly independent nations at Bandung, Indonesia, observes:

> As I had discovered in Africa's Gold Coast, so I found in Indonesia that almost every item in the home in which I was staying had been imported from faraway Europe. There is a nervous kind of dependence bred by imperialism: not only are people taught Western law, ethics, and finance; but they are encouraged to develop a taste, yea, a need, for goods which are only to be had from the European mother country. Then, when the natives rise and make a revolution in the name of the values of the West, they find themselves trapped, for they cannot build even a modern house without Western aid. The psychological agony that Indonesia suffers was created by a situation compounded of a fear of the return of Western technical capacities which they feel they need, which in their hearts they adore; yet, how can they have the co-operation of the West and at the same time fend off what they feel to be the desire of the West to dominate?[16]

Here the distribution and management of need that Wright first encountered as a child bleed from the Memphis orphanage's walls, replicating and extending the orphanage's distinctive patterning of power beyond not only its boundaries but beyond America itself. Wright's autobiographical memory of how that Dickensian home punished errant children by denying them food and guaranteed an "over-all atmosphere of nervousness and intrigue" is now resurrected as the postcolonial world is forced into a corresponding shame—is punished for its Westernization, its hunger for advancement, and its presumption of independence. As such, Wright's prioritization of hunger and his inability to see it as a mere symptom of something else drew him toward a conclusion that eluded many more orthodox sociologists or economists. Looking beyond mere statistics, knowing that hunger cannot simply be dismantled into the dry data of calorie counts or nutritional graphs, Wright here grasps that the creation of need remains a weapon of authority even when that authority is talking peace.

On one level, then, it is clear that Wright's understanding of hunger held national and international ramifications and contributed massively to the empathy and kinship he was to extend and receive in turn from leaders of the postcolonial and Pan-Africanist movements. But on another level, it is equally clear that Wright expresses this global understanding in a vocabulary particular to the south. For *Black Boy*'s Memphis home episode indeed writes a peculiarly southern hunger: that most southern of foods, molasses, is by far the most prominent in the scene, and it is the ingredient most responsible for the fact that the children are underfed rather than unfed. Molasses, in other words, is what guarantees that the hunger of these children will remain an "abiding feeling";

produced locally, molasses constructs this latest installment in the Foucauldian Great Confinement, imprisoning its future hosts in a "cell" of nutritional desire.

Molasses is well equipped for this corporal role for three interrelated reasons. First, like the equally calorie-laden white sugar from which it is separated during sugar cane processing, molasses produces an intense rush of energy that rapidly induces a craving for more. Molasses, as such, concentrates the mind on hunger, and especially so in children for whom, like Wright, it is their only source of the nutrition they need for bodily growth.

Moreover, molasses is bound up with the economic histories of U.S. and Caribbean slavery—being as deeply steeped in these histories as cotton and tobacco. The gathering of cane, an undesirable labor that callused the hands and exhausted the spine, was invariably delegated to the poorest—namely the black—sections of southern and Caribbean populations. Meanwhile, the processes that separate canes into molasses and refined sugar were occasionally overseen by slaves or by their descendants—by men like C. L. R. James's "pan-boiler" grandfather or by fictional men like Jean Toomer's David Georgia, whose days were surrounded by "grinding cane and boiling syrup." Upon the completion of this process, plantation owners received two commodities, white sugar and brown molasses, the first of which was valued far more highly by Western markets than the second. By pricing white sugar above brown molasses, these Western markets in essence constructed a commodity hierarchy based on color that not only mirrored but potentially consolidated the preexisting racial hierarchies that, among other things, determined sugar production's racialized demographic in the first place. Molasses, its cheapness attributed to an innate inferiority rather than to entrenched cultural connotations of color, could duly be fed to slaves like Booker T. Washington as if to persuade them, too, that their social inferiority was neither designated nor imposed but natural. Indeed, having recounted in *Up from Slavery* how he had looked forward to the distribution of molasses "once a week from the 'big house,' " Washington then confirms that this food was involved in a racialized culinary binary by noting that only "the whites had been accustomed to use" sugar. The racialized binary of white sugar and brown molasses, confirmed by *Up from Slavery*, is far from unique. Divisions imposed by sugar refinement resemble, for instance, the divisions that pork butchery rather more forcibly imposes upon pig carcasses, as it produces binaries of pork chops and chitterlings, of bacon and pigfeet, which can then be classified by a price hierarchy comparable to that which relegates molasses beneath sugar. Nor should the fact that sugar refinement and pork butchery are often imagined, respectively, as chemical and biological processes mislead us into thinking there is something innate about these price hierarchies. Although we may share cultural preferences for sugar or bacon, we must view these preferences as socially constructed forms of evaluation. Washington's assertion that molasses was "much more enjoyable to me than is a fourteen-course dinner," like Bessie Smith's call for a "pigfoot and a beer," must be seen not as unnatural but as radical reevaluations that destabilize binaries historically segregating diet by income, race, and class.[17]

Having said this, *Black Boy*'s orphanage scene by no means reassesses molasses in the radical manner of *Up from Slavery*. To put it simply: if Washington's assertion questions why molasses should be deemed inferior, Wright's orphanage scene questions why he should be fed something deemed inferior. This distinction brings us to the third factor that qualifies molasses for its corporal role in *Black Boy*'s orphanage scene, namely, its uses in farming and animal husbandry. These uses are signaled by the memory of "silage ricks fed with molasses" introducing Raymond Williams's *The Country and the City* and are confirmed by the food scientists Neil Pennington and Charles Baker's classification of "blackstrap" molasses as "cattle feed."[18] Not only had molasses frequently been distributed to the poorer populations in the South: it is still frequently distributed to cattle throughout the West. This, in itself, invites us to interpret the molasses that so thinly lines Wright's evening sandwiches as the digestible agent, not only of inferiority, but of what Paul Gilroy terms "infrahumanity."[19] A racialized food binary of molasses and sugar sketched by *Up from Slavery* not only subordinates blackness to whiteness, it actually co-opts this ethnic polarity for a new and exclusive equivalence with humanity that, by implication, animalizes the darker side of its binary opposition. This means that, by nominating molasses as the corporal custodian of hunger, Wright's institutional authorities can unsettle their inmates' self-image as humans and can, in the process, prime them for the bovine activities that conclude *Black Boy*'s orphanage scene. For in this concluding image Wright and his fellow orphans are forced out into "the vast lawn" and there required to "get to our knees and [to] wrench the grass loose from the dirt with our fingers. . . . I would grow dizzy and my mind would become blank." Wright and his fellow orphans are, as such, positioned to embody a compromised and contorted infrahumanity presaged in their consumption of cattle feed. Forced to join a "herd," to sink to their "knees," and to make their minds bestially "blank," these orphans submit to caricature, metaphorically assuming a quadruped shape that, by reanimating the intertwined etymologies of *cattle* and *chattel*, finally equates the orphan institution with the peculiar institution of slavery.

ARGUABLY, SLICES OF "bread smeared with molasses" not only consolidate the authority of the orphanage because of their caloric quality and inadequate quantity; they also mirror racial binaries influencing those social hierarchies prevailing throughout the United States. As a foodstuff involved in a binary with a designated "superior," molasses introduces Wright to the broader, racialized role in which Jim Crow has already cast him. By fetishising the brown of the molasses he consumes, the Memphis orphanage forces Wright, as it were, to face the mirror and fetishize his skin—to see himself in essentialist terms, as a boy whose blackness is to whiteness what molasses is to sugar. Thus, via its orphanage scene, *Black Boy* demonstrates that hunger can be imposed as a way of subordinating African Americans to a racial hierarchy that designates them inferior—inferior, cheap, and animal. Hunger in the Memphis orphanage and in *Black Boy* is, in short, more than a symptom arising, as though incidentally, from poverty. Instead, it is a tool of that economy of propaganda and psychological manipulation that, Wright suggests, has been dedicated to preserving the racial foundations upon which national American culture is built.

The significance of Wright's elevation of hunger into a "structure of feeling" or lived experience is not that it discredits but that it complements the causational approach adopted by the social sciences. Wright interrogates hunger as a vital sensory experience, dissecting the impact it has upon individual free will, the pressures it can exert, and the limits it can impose. By so vividly dramatizing and articulating the psychological and physical debilitations that result from malnutrition, this rigorous analysis of hunger actually assists contemporary social scientists' analyses of the economy since it explains exactly why the hunger the latter assumed to be undesirable *is* undesirable. Ostensible discrepancies between the social science approach and that adopted in Wright's oeuvre actually lead to an ultimate agreement upon the urgent need for hunger's cessation. It is simply that Wright reaches this ideological destination via a radical route, via an iconoclastic view that sees poverty as symptomatic of that "structure of feeling" now designated as "American hunger."

NOTES

1. Horace Cayton and St. Clair Drake, *Black Metropolis* (London: Jonathan Cape, 1946), 84; see E. Franklin Frazier, *The Negro Family in the United States* (Chicago: Univ. of Chicago Press, 1947 [1939]), 673–86.

2. Richard Wright, *Native Son* (London: Jonathan Cape, 1970), 175—page numbers are cited in text; Richard Wright, "How Bigger Was Born," in *Native Son*, xiv; Richard Wright, introduction in *Black Metropolis*, xviii.

3. Gunnar Myrdal, *American Dilemma: the Negro Problem and Modern Democracy* (New York: Harper & Row, 1944), 372–73.

4. Isobel Cole-Hamilton and Tim Lang, *Tightening Belts: A Report on the Impact of Poverty on Food* (London: London Food Commission, 1986).

5. Richard Wright, *Black Boy (American Hunger)* (New York: Harper Perennial, 1993 [1945]). Page citations to this edition appear in text.

6. Wright, introduction, in *Black Metropolis*, xvii.

7. Ibid., xxiii–xxv.

8. C. L. R. James, "Black Studies and the Contemporary Student," in *At the Rendezvous of Victory: Selected Writings* (London: Allison & Busby, 1984), 195–96; Paul Gilroy, *Black Atlantic: Modernity and Double Consciousness* (London: Verso, 1993), 159.

9. Edward Said, *Culture and Imperialism* (London: Vintage, 1994), 61; for citations from Williams, see Raymond Williams, *Marxism and Literature* (Oxford: Oxford Univ. Press, 1977), 130–32.

10. Arnold Rampersad, "Note on the Text," in Wright, *Black Boy (American Hunger)*, 487.

11. Charles Dickens, *Oliver Twist* (London: Penguin, 1985 [1837–39]), 48; Rayford W. Logan, *The Betrayal of the Negro: from Rutherford Hayes to Woodrow Wilson* (New York: Da Capo, 1997 [1954]), 52.

12. Dickens, *Oliver Twist*, 55.

13. Michel Foucault, *Discipline and Punish: the Birth of the Prison* (London: Penguin, 1991 [1975]), transl. Alan Sheridan, 308, 157, 26, 180–81.

14. Dickens, *Oliver Twist*, 56.

15. Andrew John Hill, "Investigation of Some Short-Term Influences on Hunger, Satiety and Food Consumption," unpublished Ph.D. dissertation, Department of Psychology, University of Leeds, 1986.

16. Richard Wright, *The Color Curtain: A Report on the Bandung Conference* (Jackson MS: Banner, 1994 [1956]), 112–13.

17. Jean Toomer, *Cane* (New York: Norton, 1988), 8; C. L. R. James, *Beyond a Boundary* (Durham: Duke Univ. Press, 1993), 7; Booker T. Washington, *Up from Slavery* (London: Penguin, 1987 [1901]), 246, 10, 246. Also, transcripts both of Wesley "Six" Wilson's lyrics to "A Pigfoot and a Beer" (1933) and of other Bessie Smith songs can be found via http://blueslyrics.tripod.com, accessed 4 July 2005.

18. See Raymond Williams, *The Country and the City* (New York: Oxford Univ. Press, 1973), 12; Neil L. Pennington and Charles W. Baker, *Sugar: A User's Guide to Sucrose* (New York: Van Nostrand Reinhold, 1990), 18–20.

19. Paul Gilroy, *Between Camps: Race, Identity and Nationalism at the End of the Colour Line* (London: Penguin, 2000), 22.

Poverty Recollected

"All Manner of Defeated, Shiftless,

Shifty, Pathetic, and Interesting

Good People"

Autobiographical Encounters
with Southern Poverty

JOHN C. INSCOE

In *A Tidewater Morning*, his fictionalized memoir of growing up in eastern Virginia in the 1930s, William Styron wrote of his boyhood fascination with the Dabneys, a poor family who lived nearby and with whom he spent a great deal of time as a ten-year-old. They lived in a "rambling weatherworn house that lacked a lawn. . . . On the grassless, graceless terrain of the front yard was a random litter of eviscerated Frigidaires, electric generators, stoves, and the remains of two or three ancient automobiles, whose scavenged carcasses lay abandoned beneath sycamores like huge rusted insects" (42).[1]

The young Styron had found a ready playmate in the youngest of the Dabney children, a boy named Little Mole, who "had never been known to use Lifebuoy soap, or any other cleansing agent" (42). But Styron's real fascination lay in the patriarch of the Dabney clan. While Vernon Dabney dealt in junk and auto parts, his true calling was producing bootleg whiskey. The Dabneys had not always been poor. Theirs was once a name associated with such "first families of Virginia" as the Randolphs, Tuckers, Peytons, and Lees, but due to the unfortunate marriage of his father to a "half-breed Mattaponi or Pamunkey Indian girl from the York River," the family had "long ago slid down the social ladder" and the Dabney name "had lost almost all of its luster" (42–43).

Styron's portrait of the Dabneys is at once comic and poignant, as is the story in which they figure so prominently. It centers on the predicament they face with the 1935 arrival of an ancient black man named Shadrach, who walked from Alabama back to Virginia because he considered himself a Dabney who wanted to die and be buried on the Dabney ground from which he had been sold away in 1850. Despite the hardships—financial and otherwise—that Shadrach's interment imposed on the Dabneys, their dynastic sense of noblesse oblige somehow rose to the surface and they made it their mission to "oversee his swiftly approaching departure, laying him to rest in the earth of their mutual ancestors." Vernon Dabney was not, Styron insisted, "an ill-spirited or ungenerous man (despite his runaway temper)." But he was a "soul beset by many woes in the dingy threadbare year 1935, being hard pressed not merely for dollars but for dimes and quarters, crushed beneath an elephantine and inebriate wife, along with three generally shiftless sons and two knocked-up daughters, plus two more likely to be so." Yet with Shadrach's appearance in Mr. Dabney's yard, Styron writes, "I saw him gaze down at the leathery old dying black face with an expression that mingled compassion and bewilderment and stopped up rage and desperation, and then whisper to himself: "He wants to die on Dabney ground. Well, kiss my ass, just kiss my ass!" (58).

What makes Styron's depiction of southern poverty so distinctive is how appealing a lifestyle it represented to the young boy. "Oh, how I loved the Dabneys!" he wrote in the voice of youthful innocence:

> I actually wanted to *be* a Dabney—wanted to change my name from Paul White-hurst to Paul Dabney. I visited the Dabney homestead as often as I could, basking in its casual squalor. . . . The mother, named Trixie, was a huge sweaty generous sugarloaf of a woman, often drunk. It was she, I am sure, who propagated the domestic sloppiness. But I loved her passionately, just as I loved and envied the whole Dabney tribe and that total absence in them of the bourgeois aspirations and gentility which were my own inheritance. I envied the sheer teeming multitude of the Dabneys—there were seven of them—which made my status as an only child seem so effete, spoiled, and lonesome. Only illicit whiskey kept the family from complete destitution, and I envied their near poverty. (44; original emphasis)

Much of the appeal of being a Dabney lay in the perfectly normal sensibilities of a ten-year-old boy. "They were Baptists," he wrote. "As a Presbyterian, I envied that. To be totally immersed—how wet and natural! They lived in a house devoid of books or any reading matter except funny papers—more envy. I envied their abandoned slovenliness, their sour unmade beds, their roaches, the cracked linoleum on the floor, the homely cur dogs leprous with mange that foraged at will through house and yard." Styron concluded: "My perverse longings were—to turn around a phrase unknown at the time—downwardly mobile. Afflicted at the age of ten by *nostalgia de la boue*, I felt deprived of a certain depravity" (44–45). In re-creating a ten-year-old perspective, Styron's youthful persona takes the Dabney's slovenly lifestyle in stride—there is no epiphany, no shock, no guilt or shame apparent in his matter-of-fact description of their squalor. As we've seen, it's quite the opposite—he revels in it. In some respects, the Dabneys serve as comic counterpoints to the real emotional and moral heart of the story—the experience of this hundred-year-old former slave and the meaning of his return home to die.

STYRON'S YOUTHFUL EXPOSURE to poverty was not unique. A number of middle-class southern whites who came of age in the first half of the twentieth century also wrote vividly and poignantly about the circumstances in which they discovered the socioeconomic differences in their own comfortable lives and those of less-fortunate neighbors. Some, like Styron, were intrigued by this class of people from whom they had either physically or intellectually been insulated until adolescence. Unlike Styron, few others found either the comic dimensions or the personal appeal in the circumstances that accompanied such material deprivation; and certainly no others yearned for their own "downward mobility" in order to enjoy such desolation firsthand. Yet like Styron, for whom the Dabneys provide a mere framework for the more significant story of Shadrach, other writers tied their awareness of and sympathy for poor whites to similar discoveries relating to race.

Southerners have long had a propensity for self-examination through autobiography and memoir; and more so than other Americans, their perspectives on their homeland have been—and still are—closely linked to the impulses that led them to write about themselves, often for confessional or therapeutic purposes. In telling their own stories, these writers became either apologists for or critics of the South as they knew it. The very title of Fred Hobson's book on the subject—*Tell About the South: The Southern Rage to Explain*—aptly describes the phenomenon.[2]

Among the unique features of autobiographical work as a historical genre is that it is one of the few in which the adolescent experience holds so much sway. For southerners, coming of age involved discoveries, often troubling, sometimes traumatic, about the society in which they lived. Individually and collectively, southern autobiographies offer numerous cases of young people struggling with issues and circumstances of historical import—which in the South meant slavery, Civil War, emancipation, Jim Crow, civil rights, and poverty. That formative stage of life and all it encompasses—the learning processes, discovery, experimentation, confusion, and social development, and the questioning, probing, and challenging of ideas and authorities—these are among the most vital and richly expressed components of autobiography.[3]

Matters of race are among the most obvious themes that pervade the life stories of southerners. In his latest book, *But Now I See*, Fred Hobson narrows his focus to what he calls "racial conversion narratives," those works by southern whites who at some point in their lives—often during their teenage years—changed their minds about what it meant to be white and what it meant to be black in the South.[4] They were compelled to explain such revelations in part to repent of past racist sins—their own or their families'. In so doing, the very telling of their stories became acts of contrition and moral indictments of the society in which those personal and communal sins were grounded.

For a few writers, their racial conversions were preceded or accompanied by the discovery that race was not the only factor dividing their society. Through a variety of circumstances, these young southerners were exposed for the first time to poor whites. The impact that discovery had on them either at the time or later in their lives was considerable, and along with their new perspectives on the plight of African Americans in their midst, discovering the poor of their own race made them see themselves and their region in very different terms.

BECAUSE MOST OTHER writers made such discoveries at an older age than did the ten-year-old Styron, their contacts with fellow southerners of a lower class were imbued with far more social consciousness. Katharine Du Pre Lumpkin's *The Making of a Southerner*, published in 1946, was among the first and most definitive of these racial conversion narratives; it is also perhaps the best example of how the discovery of poor whites served as the beginning of the transformative experience that would lead to racial enlightenment as well.[5] Though not as drastically as the Dabneys, the Lumpkins too had once been among the planter elite who experienced considerable "downward mobility"—in their case, as a result of the Civil War and its ruinous economic aftereffects. Katharine grew up in Macon, Georgia, but was immersed in the rural, plantation heritage of her antebellum lineage—her grandparents' plantation, their slaves, and her father's wartime experience in the Confederate army. Referring to herself as "a child of the Lost Cause," Lumpkin never questioned the natural order of the hierarchical social structure of which her family formed the apex until hard times forced her father to leave Macon and purchase a modest farm in rural South Carolina, soon after which he died.

In a chapter titled "Sojourn in the Sand Hills," Lumpkin explained that their farm did not actually lie in "the real Sand Hills," but was "very close to this desolate area, so much so that one could almost believe that the winds of heaven had drifted some of the sand across the border line into our woods and fields—

and some of the inhabitants too . . . with their pasty faces, scrawny necks, an-
gular ill-nourished frames, straw-like hair" (151). Most of the farmers around
them were, Lumpkin noted, white and landowners, but owners "in name only;
the heavy mortgages they carried were ever a threat to their tenure. Most had
few acres and very poor little dwellings. A few more were renters, and some
were croppers who had nothing, not even a mule or plow" (151–52). She recounted her sobering impressions of the field hands—more black than white—
who were hired to work her family's two hundred acres of cotton, and noted
that these "somber strangers coming and going . . . seemed like people carrying
some kind of burden with which they were preoccupied" (156).

But it was in a classroom that Lumpkin most closely observed this new class of
southern whites, and she came to realize just how different their lives and experiences were from her own. As a fifteen-year-old student at the local school, she
became painfully aware of the variety of ways in which her classmates' lower socioeconomic circumstances contrasted with her own. "There was everything,"
she wrote, "to keep us separate and hardly anything to bridge the gap save our
common childhood" (158). She described in detail their clothing, their lunches,
their manners (characterized by reticence and lethargy), their limited knowledge, and even their language. "I was a city child and talked like one," Lumpkin
explained. She bemoaned the fact that she couldn't adopt their speech patterns
and vocabulary, if only because of how "hard they would stare at me when I
talked, as though I were some kind of foreigner, as indeed they regarded me;
and worse, as though I were 'putting on airs' " (159).

Lumpkin was not alone in the advantages she held over most of her classmates. The daughters of the one other relatively affluent landowner in the area
were also in the class, and it disturbed Lumpkin that they seemed to flaunt their
superior knowledge and smugly answer questions that their classmates couldn't.
Such "airs" by her social peers only added to her self-consciousness. "It was as
though I had a pre-arranged advantage in a race which made me always win,"
she wrote. "I longed to hide what I knew if thereby I might escape from always
having the better of them. I felt unfair and that they would think me so" (160).

These observations of her superior background, material circumstances, and
breeding were to Lumpkin "new sensations." "As a city-bred child little of destitution had passed before my protected eyes, or at least it had not impressed me.
Seeing any poverty, I no doubt accepted our spiritual lesson to explain it: 'The
poor ye always have with you.' This would account for the poor whites among
us. Negro poverty I would have taken even more for granted" (160).

If it was this experience through which Lumpkin discovered and came to
sympathize with the plight of white victims of rural poverty, it would take her
return to Georgia as a college student to introduce her to the effects of Jim Crow

and its victimization of southern blacks. That process proved to be a more gradual and ultimately far more significant one in terms of her future activism and writings. Yet as she acknowledged at the end of her memoir, the white destitution and deprivation of the South Carolina sand hills was a crucial prerequisite to her conversion experience.

NO SOUTHERNER CHRONICLED southern poverty to greater effect than did Erskine Caldwell. The publication of *Tobacco Road* and *God's Little Acre* in the early 1930s, along with their subsequent stage and screen adaptations, conveyed to a vast American public the plight of rural white Georgians as deprived and depraved victims of both an agricultural system that had run its course and the exploitative trap of the cotton mills that provided yet another form of economic victimization for those who saw it as their only viable recourse. Among the most prolific of southern writers, Caldwell's massive body of work includes two autobiographies: one from 1951 (*Call It Experience*), the other from 1987 (*With All My Might*).[6] In both, he revealed his own initial exposure to the poor in whose midst he lived.

The son of a Presbyterian minister, Caldwell moved several times with his family across Georgia and the Southeast. In 1918, when Erskine was fifteen, the family moved from western Tennessee to Wrens, a small town in eastern Georgia a few miles southwest of Augusta (only two counties away from the ancestral homeland in Oglethorpe County that Lumpkin described in her autobiography). There he first observed the rural poor around whom he would later construct his most famous novels. Although Wrens was situated amid fertile cotton-growing farmland, Caldwell noted that it was not far from "the barren sand hills and depleted soil of the tobacco lands between Wrens and Augusta." He saw its unfortunate inhabitants both in Wrens and in traveling through the surrounding countryside and described them in his latter autobiography: "The impoverished people from the sand hills and tobacco roads, hungry and ragged, were frequently in town begging from house to house for handouts of food and clothing and a little money with which to buy cure-all medicine. There always seemed to be one or more feebly crying, sickly looking babes in arms among the begging families" (*WAMM* 40). In his first memoir, he wrote of traveling through the country, first with his father as he made ministerial visitations, and later with both a local doctor and the county tax assessor. There he saw many of the same people—tenants and sharecroppers—in their own homes and on the very land that victimized them. "Most of the landowners lived in comparative comfort in the nearby towns of Waynesboro, Louisville, and Wrens, while in the country itself there was poverty on all sides, the only apparent variation being in the degree of it" (*WAMM* 24–25).

Caldwell's teenage consciousness of the plight of these poor farmers seems primarily based on his parents' contrasting reactions to them. "The most persistent mendicants," he wrote, "had perfected the technique of sitting on the doorsteps of a house and, for hours at a time, alternating knocking loudly and moaning in a distressed voice to gain the sympathy of a householder" (WAMM 40). The Caldwell manse was among those on whose steps these so-called Weepers planted themselves, and their presence there soon became so constant that Erskine's mother quickly lost any sympathy for them. Her son recalled that she "became so provoked that she jabbed the tufted end of a broom at a small group of Weepers who had remained on our porch and continued their pathetic moaning long after my father had given them a large sack of sweet potatoes and several cans of pork and beans." Concerned about their own marginal financial status, Mrs. Caldwell insisted that she felt sorry for the Weepers, but that "there's got to be a limit to how kindhearted we can be at this house" (*WAMM* 40).

His father extended his outreach to the needy well beyond his front porch. In his earlier memoir, Caldwell stated, "I do not remember a single occasion when my father was not asked for food during our trips into the country. He made it a habit, even when my mother said was none too much for the three of us, always to carry a sack of potatoes or flour and a bag of grits or black-eyed peas in the car with him wherever he went." Erskine's portrayal of his mother's beneficence was somewhat softer than it would be later. He ended this memory by noting that she "more often than not added a small bag of candy for the old people and children" (*CIE* 26).

There is little sense of revelation, inspiration, or even compassion in these descriptions; Caldwell wrote nonjudgmentally of his mother and father's differing responses to the poor around them (and in two different books). He made little effort to link these early impressions with the vivid personal portraits and the bleak lifestyle he would create in his fiction. It was only in returning to the region years later that he found the inspiration to portray what he observed in his writing. After stints at writing short stories and screenplays while living in Maine and California, he wrote that "I felt that I would never be able to write successfully about other people in other places until first I had written the story of the landless and poverty-stricken families living on East Georgia sand hills and tobacco roads." He returned to his parents' home in Wrens in 1930 and began retraveling the country roads he had ridden so often as a teen. "It was not a pleasant sight," he stated, "more dispiriting to look upon now than it had been several years before" (*CIE* 102).

At last, Caldwell conveyed some real feeling as to what he saw and how it inspired him. "Day after day I went into the country," he wrote, "becoming more and more depressed by what I saw as I traveled farther and farther from settlements and highways. I could not become accustomed to the sight of children's stomachs bloated from hunger and seeing the ill and aged too weak to walk to the fields to search for something to eat." Back home in the evenings, he made notes on what he had seen, but he remained frustrated. "Nothing I had put down on paper succeeded in conveying the full meaning of poverty and hopelessness and degradation as I had observed it. The more I traveled through [these] counties, the less satisfied I became with what I wrote" (*CIE* 102–3).

Just as it had taken a return to Georgia to conceptualize fully the depths of poverty among those who would become his literary subjects, Caldwell decided that only with distance could he do them justice. So he moved to New York, where he began work on his greatest successes—*Tobacco Road* in 1932 and *God's Little Acre* a year later. The physical distance he put between himself and his Georgia characters seemed to restore the emotional detachment of his adolescent years.[7] The unsympathetic and even grotesquely comedic portraits of Jeeter Lester and Ty Ty Walden and their families fully captured the futile, hand-to-mouth existences Caldwell had observed firsthand, but strikingly absent in either novel is any sense of the compassion or sympathy with which he had claimed to view their real-life counterparts just before he began fictionalizing them.

LILLIAN SMITH EMERGED as the white South's most outspoken racial conscience during the 1940s and 1950s, but despite several autobiographical works—most notably, *Killers of the Dream*—she was far more evasive than was Caldwell about the childhood or adolescent roots of the remarkably strong convictions that drove her diatribes, both fictional and nonfictional, on southern racism and class exploitation. She provided only a few tantalizing anecdotes of early experiences that shaped her sensibilities regarding her region's racism and poverty. More in private correspondence than in her autobiographical writings, Smith recalled her unusual powers of observation and empathy toward those around her. "I could walk into a room (at age 9 or 10)," she later confided in a letter, "and feel almost instantly how each person in that room was feeling." She claimed to have been "almost overcome, sometimes, by my vicarious 'suffering.'"[8]

Like Katharine Lumpkin, a family move prompted Smith's raised consciousness of southern poverty. In 1915, the year in which she graduated from high school, the Smiths hit hard times when her father, Calvin, lost his business. They moved from Jasper, a small mill town in northern Florida, to Clayton, in the Blue Ridge mountains of northeast Georgia, where her father opened a hotel and, soon thereafter, a summer camp for girls. There Lillian discovered the desolation of rural mountain life and was shocked by the hand-to-mouth existence, ignorance, and lack of initiative or spirit among the highlanders she observed. After moving to Baltimore to study music at the Peabody Conservatory two years later, she was exposed to the urban poor as well and learned much about "slums, poverty, factories—much I had known nothing about."[9] Curiously, neither mountain whites nor urban industrial workers ever became central to the indignation Smith mustered in her later condemnations of the South's social and economic inequities.

One incident soon after the Smiths' move to Clayton, having nothing to do with poor mountaineers, serves as the most revealing example of Lillian Smith's awakening to the outcasts in southern society. In one of her few flights of nostalgia, she reminisced in a *Life* magazine essay in December 1961 about early Christmases and described a remarkable act of generosity by her father that made one such holiday memorable.[10] As he and his family struggled to make ends meet in what she called "our year of austerity," Calvin Smith invited a chain gang to have Christmas dinner with the family. Disturbed after having encountered the convicts in the shabby railroad cars in which they lived while assigned to state road work in the area, he came home and declared to his wife that "there's more misery in the world than even I know; and a lot of it unnecessary" (60–62). He then proposed the Christmas visit, and Mrs. Smith reluctantly agreed.

At noon on Christmas Day, the Smiths watched forty-eight men in stripes, both white and black, along with their guards, heading toward their house. According to his admiring daughter, Calvin "moved among them with grace and ease," and broke the early awkward moments with a warm welcome. The "wonderful absurdity" of the situation soon had them "all laughing and muttering Merry Christmas, half deriding, half meaning it." Three of the guests— specifically a killer, a rapist, and a bank robber—pitched in to put the meal on the table, Lillian notes wryly. "My sister and I served the plates. The murderer and his two friends passed them to the men. Afterward, the rapist and two bank robbers and the arsonist said they'd be real pleased to wash up the dishes" (62).

While this story comes across as more of an amusing anecdote than is typical of Smith's writing, it is a tale with a moral. When the chain gang left after a satisfying visit for all concerned, Calvin gathered his family around him, as "the old look of having something to say to his children settled across his face." He began his lecture: "We've been through some pretty hard times, lately, and I've been proud of my family. Some folks can take prosperity and can't take poverty; some can take being poor and lose their heads when money comes. I want my children to accept it all: the good and the bad, for that is what life is." He went on to talk about their recent guests, reminding his children that they were merely men who had made mistakes, as each of them would at some point in their lives. "Never look down on a man," he told them. "Never. If you can't look him straight in the eye, then what's wrong is with you" (63).

Despite this sermon, with which Smith closes her story, it is obvious that she has told it more as a tribute to her father than as a transformative moment in her own views. Calvin Smith was key to Lillian's sensitivity toward poor whites, as was Erskine Caldwell's father key to his. But despite the fact that the chain gang he invited into his home included both black and white men, she indicated elsewhere that there were limits to his humanitarianism. In *Killers of the Dream*, she wrote in far more critical terms of her parents' hypocrisy about race.[11] "The father who rebuked me for an air of superiority toward schoolmates from the mill and rounded out his rebuke by gravely reminding me that 'all men are brothers,' trained me in the steel-rigid decorums I must demand of every colored male." As with so much of Smith's commentary, this was an indictment not only of her parents but of southern society in general. "They who taught me to split my body from my mind and both from my 'soul,'" she concluded, "also taught me to split my conscience from my acts and Christianity from southern tradition" (27).

The plight of poor whites never inspired the sympathy or the rage in Smith's adult social conscience to the extent that racism did. This was true of other writers, as well—though it is curious that Smith never chronicled nearly so definitive a turning point in the creation of her racial consciousness as she did with this minor anecdote in a nostalgic holiday piece on a lesson taught about the poor.[12]

AS EDITOR OF THE *Atlanta Constitution* during the civil rights movement, Ralph McGill emerged as one of the South's most influential white voices of liberalism—or at least moderation—during those critical, tension-filled years. In the midst of that era, 1963, he published his autobiography, *The South and the Southerner*, in order to explain himself and his perspective on the region as he had known it through a lifetime of experience and observation.[13] Like Lumpkin and Smith, McGill's exposure as a teenager to the white underclass of southern society served as a prelude to his later sensitivity to the plight of their African American counterparts.

Growing up in a suburb of Chattanooga, Tennessee, McGill wrote of two summer jobs that exposed him to very different types of poor people in the vicinity. He spent one summer working as a flagman for a surveying team. Though the project on which he worked involved running a line up Signal Mountain (now a suburb of Chattanooga), McGill was entranced by the contrast it presented to the comfortable, suburban world he had known. He considered the job "a frontier adventure" and marveled at the "wild beauty of the wilderness through which he surveyed." As part of that adventure, he discovered Appalachian residents as well.

Moving deep into one of the creek valleys where "we felt like pioneers in the new world," the team came across what he described as "an ancient log cabin in a clearing of small fields" (59–60). An old man on the porch and his daughter-in-law welcomed the crew and served them coffee. McGill was fascinated by these people and quick to apply to them all the stereotypical assumptions he knew about "hillbillies." When told that the woman's husband was "away on a job," he said, "we imagined a still or perhaps a prison term for moonshining." Even more intriguing was the family's ancestry: "The old man told us his name was Hesse." He explained that he'd always "heared" that his great-great-grandfather had been a Hessian soldier captured by the British in the American Revolution. When the war ended, "he had made his way down to Tennessee and taken up land. The old fellow had no papers," McGill concluded. "His name was just a story handed down" (59–60).

For McGill, these mountain people intrigued him less for their poverty than for their primitiveness—the "otherness" of their existence; to him, they represented what others have called "yesterday's people," a reference to the timelessness of their simple, premodern lifestyle. In some respects, this encounter only reaffirmed for this teenager the wilderness adventure—the sense of having suddenly discovered a frontier environment complete with frontier inhabitants—and all within easy access to the comfortable, complacent, and modern suburban world of which he was a product.

Equally fascinating but more disturbing for McGill was his discovery of the urban poor. Not only were these encounters more significant in their impact as the future journalist found himself coming to terms with the South in all its facets; it is nearly unique in terms of southern autobiography. (Only Lillian Smith's Baltimore experience, which she never referred to in her published work, comes to mind as another white writer who encountered poverty within a southern urban environment.) The summer before his mountain surveying adventure, at just fourteen and a half years old, McGill took a job collecting overdue bills for a local drugstore, or as one coworker characterized it: collecting "small, mean bills, some of them damned old and mean." In that job McGill "learned all the mean streets and slum neighborhoods." Though he described the characters he encountered as both "weird and wonderful," he noted that "the poverty and squalor about some of the mills and ironworks were a shock. I had seen coal-miners' poverty in Shoddy, Tennessee, but this was worse" (61).

It was not merely the degradation of their surroundings that bothered McGill: he was equally struck by the degeneracy of their lives. "From one of my old accounts," he wrote, "I learned a new word—incest." In listening to a group of men gathered in the store, McGill heard them "damning some man who lived in the neighborhood who had had a child by his daughter. Someone knew the word incest. He said he had once served on a jury which heard a like case. The story and the word depressed me all that summer." Yet his overall impression of Chattanooga's less fortunate residents was more mixed. He summed up the summer as "hot, sweaty, and lonely," and stated, "I met all manner of defeated, shiftless, shifty, pathetic, and interesting good people" (61–62).

McGill dismissed the impact of his exposure to these people at the time by following that summary of his summer as a bill collector with the observation that the company was pleased with his collection results and that all the walking involved in the job built his legs up enough that he made the all-city football team that fall. Only with the Depression's impact over a decade later did McGill fully grasp the lessons of his adolescent summer jobs. Like Caldwell, it took adult sensibilities to appreciate the implications of what he had earlier observed far more innocently. As part of a fact-finding team of academics and journalists, McGill traveled through Georgia in the 1930s, visiting sharecroppers and tenants. "Their wretched cabins and the pitiful meagerness of their possessions and existence were eloquent evidence of the inequities of an agricultural social and economic system which had ground to a halt," he wrote. "I recall thinking, with a surge of pity, on seeing them on the roads, sometimes whole families of them ragged, now and then barefooted, I had never seen despair" (159). Not only did McGill convey their plight with far more feeling than he did that of the mountaineers and slum residents he encountered as a teenager; he was by then also ready to examine the causes of their poverty, which he did with great insight in a chapter of his memoir titled "What the Depression Taught Us."

IF A HEIGHTENED sensitivity to racial inequities and injustice often developed in conjunction with or soon after early encounters with poor whites, only rarely if ever did writers prior to World War II acknowledge any causal link between Jim Crow and black poverty. It was only in the next generation, as rumblings of change in the South's racial order generated new sorts of qualms among white adolescents, that such connections become more obvious—or that writers confronted them more directly. No one has done so more effectively than Melton McLaurin, whose memoir, *Separate Pasts: Growing Up White in the Segregated South*, is one of the most fully articulated depictions of adolescence and the awakening of racial awareness within the vast and growing genre of southern autobiography.[14] In contrast to the writers already mentioned here, who experienced their adolescent years in the 1920s and 1930s, McLaurin's adolescence in the early 1950s posed different issues and different sensibilities. In Wade, a small crossroads in rural eastern North Carolina, McLaurin worked in his grandfather's general store, and in that capacity came to know local African Americans who did business there in a way few white teenagers did in that era. "My appreciation of Wade's blacks as individuals," he wrote, "presented me at an early age with the complex intellectual and emotional dilemmas of segregation" (26).

Separate Pasts consists of character sketches of these individuals, McLaurin's relationships with each, and how in a variety of ways each of them forced him to make difficult moral judgments about the injustices of racism. Not least of such injustices was the poverty to which racism sentenced many accomplished African Americans, who by any other measure would have enjoyed the comforts of a middle-class lifestyle. His most striking character sketch is of Carrie McLean, "the only black woman I ever heard whites address as Miss, the universal term of respect for all mature white women, married or not" (146). Miss Carrie was a retired school teacher who "looked and acted every inch a school marm." When she came into his grandfather's store, McLaurin recalled, "she ordered me about as if I were a student, her voice filled with humor and kindness but sharp enough to command my full attention." Although he knew Miss Carrie and her husband Jerry better than any other black residents of Wade, McLaurin knew them only on his own terms, seeing them outside their homes, in the store or around the community. Black homes, he wrote, "remained private—they formed a world of which I knew little. When delivering groceries to black families I was never asked to carry packages into their homes" (151).

"Since I didn't enter black homes," McLaurin continued, "I assumed they were somewhat like mine and those of my friends. I knew that some poor blacks probably didn't have the furnishings that we did, that their houses were smaller, but if I thought about it at all, I thought that their homes were simply scaled-down versions of my own. Not until I was seventeen did Miss Carrie invite me into her home. I will never forget that visit or the impact it had on me" (151). Entering their sparsely furnished kitchen, he saw a rustic room, with wood-planked walls covered by old newsprint. A newspaper photograph of FDR hung on one wall, a picture of Jesus on another, and a cardboard, hand-lettered sign "God Bless Our Home" on the other.

"Nothing about my relationship with Jerry or Miss Carrie had prepared me for this moment," McLaurin wrote. "The emotional impact of her kitchen produced the physical responses one feels as a roller coaster begins its downward plunge: the tightening of the stomach; the quick gasp for breath; the queasy sinking feeling inside. Stunned by the appearance of the room, I searched for words while bursts of understanding exploded through my brain. . . . Appalled by what I saw, by the realization that these people whom I admired had so little, I wanted to somehow disappear from the scene, to sink through a crack in the floor and avoid this confrontation with reality. I felt as if I had invaded their privacy and discovered some long-kept secret, which I had." McLaurin concludes this story by saying, "My relationship with [Jerry and Miss Carrie] remained unchanged, but the visit to their home had confirmed my growing suspicions that I could not become a part of what had been, that I could never completely accept the racial etiquette that had been an essential reality in the world of my father and grandfather. It thus made inevitable my final rejection of the segregated South" (151–54).

NO ONE SEEMED TO have reached such dual epiphanies—linking black poverty to racism—before the war; nevertheless, one cannot deny the extent to which the discovery of the inequities and misery of a class-based southern society more often than not also led to epiphanies of racial inequities and injustices. Of the writers considered here, Katharine Lumpkin came closest to recognizing the linkages in her own transformation. She summarized the theme of *The Making of a Southerner* and the impact of her adolescent discoveries on its last page: "I was a Southerner nurtured in the Lost Cause, who looked upon my people's history and conduct of affairs as scarcely short of exemplary" (239). And yet, she noted, the "glaring incongruities" of southern life began to seep into even her limited childhood perspective and "began to arouse in me a chronic state of doubt." She went on to explain the key to her full conversion. True, this awakened skepticism might have come to very little, even to being

> stifled by our protecting walls of privilege, had it not been for one thing—the sudden breaking down of my isolation from the realities of Southern life. The Sand Hills intervened, and did so at the very time of my changing teens. Here in actuality was the moment when chance circumstance showed me our native Tree of Life, and had me eat of its revealing fruit . . . once my eyes had been opened, it would seem, I never again could return to the comfortable ignorance which would never let me assume as an unfortunate inevitability the destitution, the drabness of life, the spiritual and material exploitation, which was the lot of so many. (239)

And so it was for most of the other writers considered here. "Chance circumstance" showed them all "their native Tree of Life," and sooner or later "had them eating of its revealing fruit." Their discovery of poor whites as a coming-of-age experience, or as an early stage on the road to southern liberalism, seems to have been a phenomenon limited primarily to the decades after World War I and prior to the civil rights movement. For each of the writers discussed here, the adolescent experiences they recalled so movingly in later years were crucial steps on the road to defining the ideological perspectives and even career courses they later took. For all but Erskine Caldwell, these revelations led to or were integral in their discoveries of racial injustice as well, which became priorities in the novels, memoirs, and newspapers of William Styron, Katharine Lumpkin, Lillian Smith, and Ralph McGill.

Yet there are in these works revealing distinctions between the portrayals of white poverty and black discrimination. It is striking that these writers rarely portrayed poor whites as individuals. With the exception of Styron's Dabneys, none of the descriptions of white poverty involve personality or individuality (and for Styron, it took a fictionalization of his experience to give such vibrant life and depth to his comic characters). For Lumpkin, Caldwell, Smith, and McGill, the poor whites they discovered remained faceless composites, generic entities that the authors more often than not observed at a distance or en masse rather than through the personal encounters with particular men and women that usually characterize racial conversion narratives.

The result is a curious detachment—more of an intellectual or even sociological observation—toward those about whom they wrote that contrasts markedly with, for example, the intimate and emotional incident involving Miss Carrie and Jerry that Melton McLaurin portrays so movingly. Even within the same work, such as Katharine Lumpkin's *The Making of a Southerner*, such contrasts between the treatment of poor whites and blacks are evident. Lumpkin never identified by name or otherwise individualized the poor white school children or tenants she encountered in the South Carolina sand hills; and yet, her discovery of racial inequities hinged almost entirely on a single woman and a single incident. It was a Miss Arthur, a black YWCA official who spoke before a group of white students at Brenau College while Lumpkin was a student there, that she credited with her epiphanal moment about race. (Miss Arthur was an accomplished woman probably not unlike Miss Carrie, the teacher who was the catalyst for McLaurin's epiphany.) For Lillian Smith, none of the forty-eight convicts with whom her family shared Christmas dinner is singled out or portrayed in any detail. Yet her only other childhood memory as fully realized in print is a very personal one: that of Janie, the light-skinned black girl who was assumed to be white and who lived for several weeks with the Smith family until the error in the girl's racial identity was realized.[15]

Perhaps these different approaches to matters of class and race suggest that the first of these discoveries—that those of their own race could be victims of poverty—was merely a precursor to what they found as a more compelling and more personally meaningful discovery: that of Jim Crow and its centrality in making the South distinctive and historically significant, at least in the hindsight from which these authors recalled the youthful shaping of lifelong agendas. Or perhaps it speaks to the different types of circumstances by which affluent southern whites made contact with blacks and poor whites, and thus defies any real pattern in terms of the reasons for which they documented those experiences as they later did.

The racial conversion narratives by southerners continued through the 1960s and 1970s, but far fewer included revelations of white poverty as part of that experience. In the 1960s, American sensibilities toward the poor in their midst were becoming more nationalized. President Lyndon Johnson's quest for a Great Society in part through a War on Poverty revealed to the American public what had once been highly personal, self-generated revelations. Perhaps as an aftereffect of that new public consciousness of want and deprivation in the midst of national prosperity, a new type of autobiography emerged in the 1980s and 1990s: southern whites writing about the poverty of their own early years. Adapting what had long been a staple of African American autobiography—graphic descriptions of the meager circumstances and destitution of their early years and their eventual triumph over them—white authors are now telling their own such stories.

Beginning with Harry Crews's *A Childhood: The Biography of a Place* in 1982, which documents his first six years on a tenant farm in south Georgia, a growing number of white writers have earned both critical and popular acclaim—and even celebrity status—for their narratives of growing up poor in the mid-twentieth-century South. These range from Rick Bragg's *All Over But the Shoutin'*, his best-selling paean to his mother's struggle to survive and keep her family intact in the cotton fields and trailer parks of rural Alabama to Dorothy Allison's *Two or Three Things I Know for Sure*, a harrowing account of her abuse as a child in the slums of Greenville, South Carolina; from Mary Karr, who finds much humor in her turbulent childhood and adolescence as part of a dysfunctional East Texas Gulf Coast family in two books (*The Liars' Club* and *Cherry*) to Linda Scott DeRosier's *Creeker*, a surprisingly upbeat account of her hand-to-mouth existence in the coal camps of Appalachian Kentucky and Janisse Ray's *Ecology of a Cracker Childhood*, recounting her emergence as an environmentalist and writer from roots in a junkyard in the piney woods of southeast Georgia. There is now no shortage of vivid firsthand accounts of what it means to be poor, southern, and white in our own times. And in all of these cases, the authors' childhoods and/or adolescence form the centerpieces of these books, and the poignancy of such youthful traumas accounts for their vast appeal to modern readers.[16]

Southern victims of poverty, it seems, no longer need to be discovered, or exposed, by their socioeconomic betters. They can tell their own stories and do so adeptly. But, as the work of an earlier generation suggests, in the 1920s and 1930s southerners were well insulated by their wealth or by their whiteness from some of the most troubling facets of race and class in their midst. Even during the Depression years, which elevated American awareness of poverty, a number of young people experienced the shock, discomfort, and revelatory effects of their firsthand exposure to those, white or black, less fortunate than themselves.

Such reactions may have been unusual, but one does not read autobiographies for the typicality of their authors' observations or experience. Nor do we value such work now only for the impact it had on the writers' contemporaries; indeed, the influence of these testimonials on other white southerners was minimal. These authors were indeed exceptional in their sensitivity to the misfortune they observed around them at the time, and in the transformative power of their experiences, rousing in them powerful social consciences about their communities and their region. Those consciences drove many of them, in one way or another, to tell their own stories. The intensity—and often compassion—of those stories not only reveal them as moving reflections of specific times, places, and people; they also reveal the inspiration that drove these writers to use their own stories to "tell about the South," to give in to the peculiarly "southern rage to explain."[17]

NOTES

1. William Styron, *A Tidewater Morning: Three Tales from Youth* (New York: Random House, 1993); page citations appear in text. The Dabneys appear in the "Shadrach" chapter, which was originally published in *Esquire* in 1978.

2. Fred Hobson, *Tell About the South: The Southern Rage to Explain* (Baton Rouge: Louisiana State Univ. Press, 1983).

3. Several essays deal with adolescence and southern autobiography, usually within the context of race. See especially Melton McLaurin, "Rituals of Initiation and Rebellion: Adolescent Responses to Segregation in Southern Autobiography," *Southern Cultures* 3 (summer 1997): 5–24; Francis Smith Foster, "Parents and Children in Autobiography by Southern Afro-American Writers," and Lynn Z. Bloom, "Coming of Age in the Segregated South: Autobiographies of Twentieth Century Childhoods, Black and White," both in J. Bill Berry, *Home Ground: Southern Autobiography* (Columbia: Univ. of Missouri Press, 1991), 98–109, 110–22 ; and John C. Inscoe, "Black, White, and Southern: Autobiography and the Complexities of Race," Georgia Humanities Lecture, 12 May 2005, online on the Georgia Humanities Council, www.georgiahumanities.org/programs/gov/lect .html, accessed 1 Aug. 2005.

4. Fred Hobson, *But Now I See: The White Southern Racial Conversion Narrative* (Baton Rouge: Louisiana State Univ. Press, 1999).

5. Katharine Du Pre Lumpkin, *The Making of a Southerner* (Athens: Univ. of Georgia

Press, 1991 [1946]). For an insightful account of Lumpkin's autobiographical writings, see Jacquelyn Dowd Hall, " 'You Must Remember This': Autobiography as Social Critique," *Journal of American History* 85 (Sept. 1998): 439–65.

6. Erskine Caldwell, *With All My Might: An Autobiography* (Atlanta: Peachtree, 1987), abbreviated as *WAMM* in page citations; Erskine Caldwell, *Call It Experience: The Years of Learning How to Write* (New York: Duell, Sloan & Pearce, 1951), abbreviated as *CIE* in page citations.

7. The empowerment of "exile" for writers from the South was not unusual. Caldwell was one of many southern writers who articulated their observations about their native region in either fictional or nonfictional form only after leaving it. New York City in particular was a base from which many other writers—including Styron and Lumpkin—found perspective and inspiration to write about the South and their lives as southerners.

8. Quoted in Anne Loveland, *Lillian Smith, A Southerner Confronting the South: A Biography* (Baton Rouge: Louisiana State Univ. Press, 1986), 9.

9. Ibid., 10–11.

10. Lillian Smith, "Memory of a Large Christmas," *Life* (15 Dec. 1961), 90–94. Cited here is the version that was expanded and published as *Memory of a Large Christmas* (New York: W. W. Norton, 1962); page citations appear in text.

11. Lillian Smith, *Killers of the Dream*, rev. ed. (New York: W. W. Norton, 1961 [1949]). Page citations appear in text.

12. She came closest to doing so in a childhood memory of a young very light-skinned black girl, Janie, who briefly lived with her family when it was assumed she was white and had been kidnapped by a local black family in the community. Ibid., 34–37.

13. Ralph McGill, *The South and the Southerner* (Athens: Univ. of Georgia Press, 1992 [1963]).

14. Melton A. McLaurin, *Separate Pasts: Growing Up White in the Segregated South* (Athens: Univ. of Georgia Press, 1987); page citations appear in text. Though his story is set two decades or more after the others discussed here, McLaurin notes a certain timelessness about his hometown and its development: "The Wade of 1953," he wrote, "differed little from that of 1933, or for that matter, except for the presence of automobiles and electricity, from the Wade of 1893" (3).

15. Lumpkin, *The Making of a Southerner*, 189–93; Smith, *Killers of the Dream*, 34–37.

16. Harry Crews, *A Childhood: The Biography of a Place* (Athens: Univ. of Georgia Press, 1995 [1982]); Rick Bragg, *All Over But the Shoutin'* (New York: Pantheon, 1997); Dorothy Allison, *Two or Three Things I Know for Sure* (New York: Dutton, 1995); Linda Scott DeRosier, *Creeker: A Woman's Journey* (Lexington: Univ. Press of Kentucky, 1999); Mary Karr, *The Liars' Club: A Memoir* (New York: Viking,1995), and *Cherry: A Memoir* (New York: Viking, 2000); and Janisse Ray, *Ecology of a Cracker Childhood* (Minneapolis: Milkweed Editions, 1999).

17. Quotes are from Fred Hobson's book title and subtitle (see note 2).

Creating "Nate Shaw"

The Making and Remaking of

All God's Dangers

JAMES C. GIESEN

 In Leon Litwack's *Trouble in Mind*, a history of African American life in the early-twentieth-century South, there are nearly as many references to Ned Cobb as to Booker T. Washington or W. E. B. DuBois. In a 1994 *Journal of American History* survey, more historians cited Cobb's *All God's Dangers* as an influential book than cited classics like *The Narrative of the Life of Frederick Douglass*, Ralph Ellison's *Invisible Man*, or Richard Wright's *Black Boy*. *All God's Dangers* has become not only the most celebrated firsthand story of rural black poverty in the twentieth century, it has, since its publication in 1974, come to dominate historians' thinking about sharecropping and sharecroppers. This important historiographical impression is the result of several factors: the timing of the book's publication, the somewhat ambiguous manner in which the book was "written," and scholars' initial reaction to its publication. This chapter explores how the creation of, and reaction to, *All God's Dangers* shaped and reshaped historical perspectives on sharecropping.[1]

All God's Dangers is essentially the life story of Ned Cobb as told to historian Theodore Rosengarten. Cobb was born in 1885 in southeastern Alabama to former slaves. As a boy, Cobb was hired out by his father, who kept his earnings. At twenty-one, he married, left home, and began sharecropping. He managed to save money in spurts, acquiring one mule, then a second. His unsteady climb up the agricultural ladder was variously impeded by white landowners who resented his limited success, by fluctuating cotton prices, and by the boll weevil, which taught him that "all god's dangers ain't a white man." He joined the Communist-led Sharecropper's Union as the Depression began. The pivotal moment in his life, and of *All God's Dangers*, came in 1932, when police tried to evict a neighbor and fellow union member from his land. The attempted eviction led to a shoot-out with police, and Cobb was eventually jailed for his role. After serving a ten-year sentence he moved home and returned to farming, though, as Rosengarten points out, by the time he was released he had become a "mule farmer in a tractor world." He died in 1973, several months before the publication of *All God's Dangers*. After his death, Cobb's family, fearing repercussions from the white community if his true identity was revealed, asked that Rosengarten use a pseudonym. The historian alone chose the name "Nate Shaw," though he and Cobb had worked together to create the historical character to which the name refers. Having recorded over 160 hours of Cobb's testimony in the final years of his life, Rosengarten transcribed Cobb's words, edited them, and arranged them as *All God's Dangers*. His role in this creation of Nate Shaw is integral to understanding why the book has been so durable and engendered wide-ranging interpretations.[2]

Cobb's life is on one hand a story of economic struggle, resistance to racial oppression, and enduring familial bonds, representative of thousands of other southern lives of the same period. On the other, it is a unique account of political agitation, labor organizing, and armed resistance to a racist economic and political system. *All God's Dangers* is, as a result, a book told from the perspective of an impoverished, disenfranchised black sharecropper, which offers unequaled insight into the major themes of southern history. And although observations of the larger historical forces at work in his life—most notably class, race, and gender—necessarily frame the book, it is Cobb's detailed descriptions of daily work routines, family relationships, and nonhuman actors like the boll weevil that make this book an uncommon document of interconnected historical forces.

Upon *All God's Dangers*' publication in 1974, reviewers raved. The London *Sunday Times* called it a "Deep South classic"; the *Chicago Tribune*, "a unique triumph"; *Newsweek*, "extraordinarily eloquent." Historians liked the book, too. In a critique in *Reviews in American History*, David Brion Davis said *All God's Dangers* was "not only a great book" but that it was "certain to emerge as one of the literary monuments of our era." Davis's prediction was a good one. Historical accounts of the South from the end of the Civil War through the 1960s have used Cobb's voice to explain not only sharecropping but a variety of issues. Litwack, for example, quotes Cobb to speak about topics as varied as tenancy, domestic violence, the judicial system, migration, prison, schools, women's labor, and black opinions of Booker T. Washington. Other scholars have used *All God's Dangers* more sparingly but have clearly formed much of their thinking about sharecropping from Cobb's life. Jay R. Mandle, for example, uses Cobb's words to claim that poor black southerners rejected "the paternalistic ethos of the South," a rejection that sowed the seeds for the civil rights movement. Still others cite Cobb's memories to elucidate minor arguments. In *Nothing But Freedom*, Eric Foner relies on Cobb's recollections of his father hunting for food after the Civil War to illustrate a point about freedmen's resourcefulness. In *New South, Old South*, Gavin Wright extracts a line from *All God's Dangers* to support his argument that sharecropping was not a static arrangement. Indeed, thirty years after its publication, historians continue to use *All God's Dangers* for hard evidence about early twentieth century life and to conclude differing, even oppositional, interpretations of the rural South. It is because historians rely on *All God's Dangers* for hard evidence about early-twentieth-century life thirty years after its publication that it is important to look back and examine not only the forces that went into creating the book but also how its creation shaped the lasting image of Nate Shaw.[3]

The timing of its publication has a good bit to do with the book's enduring relevance. When *All God's Dangers* was published in 1974, it was among the first sharecropper accounts from the interwar period to be widely available, and very few had the spirit and tenor of Cobb's narrative. Not only was his story rare, it was one audiences desperately sought. In the 1960s, new thinking on race and on class structure irrevocably altered historians' analysis of the past, resulting in a shift in perspective. Scholars as well as the wider public were looking for stories "from below" in which hard-working Americans survived despite racism and economic oppression. Readers did not want an institutional analysis of sharecropping or poverty; they wanted to hear the story from someone who had lived it. *All God's Dangers* fit the bill perfectly and immediately gained a wide audience. Reviews in every major newspaper and magazine fueled the book's sale to the general public, while it also enjoyed laudatory critiques in academic journals.

Much of *All God's Dangers'* success was due to what readers perceived as Cobb's authenticity. To many, he represented—and continues to represent—the archetypical southern black man. His stories seemed to spring straight from the red Alabama clay. He talked like a sharecropper. He told stories as intellectuals imagined an old sharecropper would. His language and expressions were perfectly ungrammatical. As for his politics, it seemed to readers on the left (new left or old) that Rosengarten had uncovered a homegrown radical. Cobb did not learn his politics, he lived them; his beliefs on property, race, and class were formed not with the aid of Marx but with that of mules. Throughout the book he expresses distrust of landowners and an unshakable faith in his poorer neighbors, white and black.

Despite popular opinion, the book's 1974 publication was not the beginning of Cobb's life as a literary character. Though Rosengarten writes that he went to Alabama "to study a union and . . . stumbled on a storyteller," he actually stumbled on a man already known to thousands of Americans: Cobb had been the subject of a scholarly essay in an academic journal, of several newspaper articles, and of a popular poem.

Almost thirty years before Rosengarten went to Alabama, John Beecher, then a little-known southern scholar and poet, mentioned Cobb by name in both an article in *Social Forces* about the Alabama Sharecropper's Union and in a widely read poem. Beecher, the great-great grandson of Lyman Beecher and a great-grand nephew of Harriet Beecher Stowe, traveled to southeast Alabama to research the union while working toward a doctorate degree in sociology under Howard Odum at the University of North Carolina in Chapel Hill. This research on the Sharecropper's Union provided Beecher's introduction to Cobb, but by 1940, he abandoned his sociology training for work as a poet. That year he wrote "In Egypt Land," a long narrative poem describing Cobb, fellow union member Cliff James, and their 1932 shoot-out with police.[4]

Although Beecher's *Social Forces* article found a scholarly audience, it took thirty years for the poem to be published. As Beecher's body of poetry grew, so too did resistance to its radical subject matter. His poems were concerned chiefly with labor activists: sharecroppers, Italian steel workers, and "Negroes from the slag hole." Beecher found that his work was "too subversive" to be published. "In Egypt Land" heralded armed resistance to racism, a topic that in Beecher's view, "Even the so-called Left wouldn't touch . . . while they were on the non-violence kick." In the late 1960s, he published a collection of poems himself. "In Egypt Land" appeared as the opening poem in the collection *To Live and Die in Dixie*. For a self-published collection, the book did respectably well, especially in the South. Nationwide, it sold eight thousand copies and became popular in leftist circles and among civil rights activists. Late-sixties leftists and artists like Myles Horton, Virginia Durr, Pete Seeger, and Studs Terkel publicly praised Beecher's work. Flooded with requests, Beecher granted public readings throughout the South and Midwest. Beecher read "In Egypt Land" to audiences at Tulane University, the University of Alabama, Tougaloo College and even the Alabama Arts Festival, held within a few miles of Cobb's home (and of his shoot-out with police). Terkel invited Beecher to read the poem on his radio show in Chicago, which he did in early 1967. The result of the poem's publication in *To Live and Die in Dixie* and of Beecher's numerous public readings was that at the very least several thousand people read about or heard of Ned Cobb. Thus Rosengarten cannot be said to have "discovered" him. Perhaps Beecher and Cobb's ties to Communism and the Left explain why Cobb's story was "forgotten" by the public for a period before Rosengarten brought it back to light.[5]

Nonetheless, for the vast majority of readers, *All God's Dangers* was their first exposure not only to the life of Ned Cobb but to the voice of a sharecropper.

But just as Beecher's version of Cobb was filtered through his own poetic, leftist lens, Rosengarten too played a crucial role in the Nate Shaw that emerges from *All God's Dangers*. The young historian asked questions, listened, transcribed, edited, and ultimately compiled Cobb's words in book form. He absorbed Cobb's voice. Consequently, what Nate Shaw was to become for historians is undeniably linked to Rosengarten's own conception of what Cobb told him and what Rosengarten believed was important in the sharecropper's life history.

The historian's own role in the book's creation, while downplayed, is the first thing a reader encounters in *All God's Dangers*. Though Rosengarten includes only thirteen pages of his own writing as a preface, those pages establish the context for Cobb's words and introduce the reader to Rosengarten's own role. Surprisingly, nearly every review of the book excerpted this short preface; critics suggested that, without appreciating Rosengarten's role, a reader would not understand the story itself. Though his introductory comments are brief, Rosengarten revealed additional information about the creation of *All God's Dangers* after its publication. Contacted by a reporter from the *New York Times* two months after the book's release, he added additional details about the number of interviews he conducted with Cobb and the process of how the interview transcripts eventually became the book. In a 1980 interview with George Abbott White, Rosengarten revealed still more about his journey south, his preparation for the sessions with Cobb, and the influences his personal politics had on the manuscript. The most complete—and indeed fascinating—disclosure about the creation of *All God's Dangers* came in an essay Rosengarten contributed to a 1979 collection titled *Telling Lives: The Biographer's Art*. From these sources we can compile a much more complete and informative introduction to *All God's Dangers*, capable of shedding light on the book's creation and influence.[6]

Rosengarten, by his own admission, was lucky to meet Ned Cobb. In the winter of 1968, Rosengarten was a self-described "graduate student in American Civilization going nowhere fast" when he offered to help Dale Rosen, a senior undergraduate at Harvard-Radcliffe, with her thesis on the Alabama Sharecroppers Union. On an "impulse," the two traveled together to the dusty basement of the Dadeville, Alabama, courthouse, where Rosen began sifting through trial transcripts and newspaper accounts related to the union. Rosengarten's role was "the same [as Rosen's] but with much less energy." Near the end of their research trip, having worked only with the documents left by white Alabamans who had fought the labor union, Rosen and Rosengarten "got out of the courthouse basement" and began talking to local people. They were told that a former union member was still living nearby, and they drove off in search of him.[7]

After getting directions from the town's post office, the two students drove their car through winding woods, over the "asphalt by-roads" until they arrived at a small metal-roofed house where the mailbox read "COBB" in bold letters. They stopped. "We became very frightened, very self-conscious," Rosengarten later remembered, until a woman walked out onto the porch and waved for them to come in. The cabin turned out to be the home of Ned Cobb's brother, though as soon as the students said they were from Massachusetts, the family knew they were there to see Ned. When Cobb arrived, Rosengarten remembers, "He walked in, a big man even in his mid-eighties, slapped his knee, raised his right hand, said '*I always recognize my people when I see them. I love you folks. Do you want to come to my home or stay and talk here?*' " As Rosen and Rosengarten left after a long day, trying desperately not to forget the details of Cobb's stories, Rosengarten promised to return to Cobb later. He commented that, at the end of the day, "we went back North, and we went back stunned."[8]

In Massachusetts, Rosengarten pored over the literature on southern black culture that he thought would prepare him for future interviews with Cobb. He studied Alabama politics, sociology, black family life, churches, music, and agriculture. He tried to learn the context of what he presumed was Cobb's life story so he could, in his words, "go South and collect some 'data' and 'analyze' it" himself. His prediction, and therefore his preparation, proved to be misguided. At this stage, Rosengarten did not know what his role as interviewer would entail or necessarily what final form his oral history would take.[9]

Rosengarten returned to Tallapoosa County twice in the next two years. On his third trip, in March 1971, he proposed a formal plan to document Cobb's life. That June, the Harvard graduate student climbed behind the wheel of a decaying Mercedes-Benz and pointed it for the Heart of Dixie. Once in Alabama, he solicited the help of Ned Cobb's half-brother, L. G. Cobb, in finding a place to live. Dissuaded from living in any remote areas, Rosengarten found a home in an old Pullman car that sat on an unused stretch of rail in the small community of Jackson's Gap. He soon found himself bringing buckets of ice to railroad men in return for their spreading word down the line that he was to be left alone. Over the course of the next several months, Rosengarten lived in the railroad car and traveled to Cobb's farm to interview him.[10]

Once the interviews began, the young scholar did not spend all his time with Cobb. Downtime allowed his mind to wander, and he soon began to question the ease with which he had moved into this rural Alabama community. "My mind fell prey to its own demons," he remembered. "No one seemed to feel threatened by my presence—at least not the people I thought *should* feel threatened." Rosengarten wondered if his seeming invisibility indicated the town's willingness to tell its own history and to accept Rosengarten's analysis of their lives. He internally questioned if the townspeople thought "the sight of a disheveled young man hiking around with a tape recorder in the morning and a fishing rod in the afternoon [was] merely laughable" or if their lack of interest was more pointedly a judgment of him. He eventually found that neither was the case. [11]

Bigger historical events were in play in this section of Alabama than a graduate student's interview of an old sharecropper. The dispassion that white middle-class people had for Rosengarten's appearance was less a reflection on his purpose there, or on Cobb, than of their attention to more important matters. In Rosengarten's words, the locals were obsessed "with their own sad concern: their children were being 'niggarized' . . . [by] dope, flashy clothes and Rolling Stones albums." In addition to the penetration of hippie culture to rural Alabama, local whites were disturbed by the distribution of union leaflets at the town's mill. Most townspeople recognized labor organizers as a greater threat to the status quo than one Yankee graduate student. Rosengarten shrewdly observed, "this demonstrated to me the difference in risk for those who come to give the word and one who comes to take it." [12]

During the first interviews with Cobb, Rosengarten realized that his plan to collect "data" from Cobb and to analyze it later was misguided. His prepared questions were worthless because Cobb required no prompting. Rosengarten recalled "there was no need to tell him what we wanted to know." Not only did Cobb decide which events to detail for Rosengarten, he also provided the analysis. Once the young researcher realized that Cobb was in full control of the narrative *and* its analysis, he discarded the hundred pages of questions he had prepared. "He already figured out what was significant about his life," Rosengarten said. "Or, more specifically, what stories raised the significant issues of the time we would want to know as historians." Rosengarten seemingly took Cobb's word and his analysis without alteration or direction. However, the interviewer's confidence as to his subject's knowledge of the historically "significant issues" fluctuated. Rosengarten told George Abbott White that Cobb asked him once what "soviet" meant, and that when Rosengarten explained the Russian Revolution to him, Cobb's response "was to flip almost over in his chair. He slapped his knee and said, 'I knew that poor people fighting against landlords would win somewhere.'" Rosengarten's recollection of that discussion, down to Cobb's exact wording, suggests both the power of the story and the limits of the sharecropper's world. And it suggests that Rosengarten did more than simply listen. Despite his claim that Cobb knew what he wanted to hear, Rosengarten provided Cobb with the historical context for this story, and it is unstated in *All God's Dangers* which additional elements of the narrative received Rosengarten's encouragement. Rosengarten has always claimed that his role as interviewer was simply to record Cobb's words. "The man already *had* an analysis," he later said, "he needed me only as a listener!" [13]

As the interview sessions continued, the graduate student began to question not only his role as interviewer, but his formal education as well. "My training in analytic methodologies was irrelevant to Nate's understanding his experience," Rosengarten said, "He understood the forces behind the actors who played roles in his life, in the lives of his children and his people." Not only was his scholarly preparation failing, he found himself learning through the interview process: "In an important sense, though, I learned to interview by interviewing. Entirely. The interviews with Nate Shaw were not the movie stereotypes of a young man coming to see an old man and the old man 'imparting' what he knew . . . it was a matter of education. It was a joint venture. I suppose I would have to add, however, that it was Nate Shaw educating me and less me educating him." After each interview session, Rosengarten listened to his recordings and created follow-up questions, which might elicit more details or fill in certain gaps. He then returned to Cobb and tried to build on the detail of the stories. [14]

The result of these interviews was Cobb's life story, recorded onto 160 hours of tape. When transcribed, Cobb's words filled 1,500 pages of text, an unpublishable amount. Cobb's retention of detail was such that he mentioned over four hundred people by name. Though Rosengarten admitted to playing a limited role as collaborator in the interview process, once he was alone with the tapes and transcripts he made the project his own. Rosengarten thus began that segment of the book's production that has most directly shaped the book's legacy. Prior to this point, the young doctoral student had followed the basic procedures for oral interviews and background research: he had "found" his subject, interviewed him, recorded, and transcribed. At this crucial editing stage, however, Rosengarten made decisions that fell outside the purview of traditional autobiography, biography, or oral history. Rosengarten necessarily had to trim the material, but whereas a biographer would choose evidence to support his or her own analysis, Rosengarten's choices were based on *his* perception of Cobb's analysis. In short, Rosengarten framed the important issues of Cobb's life in Cobb's words. In so doing, he combined some of Cobb's repetitious stories, taking colorful language from one version and adding it to another. This process not only crafted the framework of the book (its chronology, characters, and topics), it ultimately shaped the overall argument. Though Rosengarten assured White that there was "very, very little shifting of words," he was less straightforward about the decision to omit certain stories completely. Admitting in the preface that at the interview stage he "had no idea what shape it would take," Rosengarten sat down with Cobb's words and made Nate Shaw's life story. This crucial decision to opt for a nontraditional kind of editor-constructed autobiography was also integral to its reception and explains why the book has elicited such wide-ranging critical reactions.[15]

The outcome of Rosengarten's editing we know as *All God's Dangers: The Life of Nate Shaw*. But what exactly is this book? It is most certainly not a biography of Cobb, though Rosengarten is listed as author. Rosengarten contributed an essay to a collection subtitled "The Biographer's Art" about his experience putting the book together, but it is not a biography. The book cannot be called an autobiography, either, because Cobb did not establish the structure or content of the final product. Neither is it simply the unabridged and undigested recollections of a historical actor. With Rosengarten setting the book's chronology and choosing which people and stories were most important, he eased the book away from its subject. To be more exact, Rosengarten created a text that falls outside the borders of academic historical writing and so escapes the rubrics governing such scholarship. As a result, readers of *All God's Dangers* did not treat it as they would a biography, autobiography, or monograph.[16]

Though critics argued over the exact form of the book, most agreed that its description of southern poverty was unlike anything previously published. David Brion Davis's confusion over form is apparent: "In short, we are dealing with a book, a 'documentary,' a genre of literature." That *All God's Dangers* consists of a written testimony from an illiterate subject has also confused and attracted historians. Readers realized that Cobb had help in telling his story, though the ambiguity of Rosengarten's role did not seem to bother the critics. For most readers, Cobb was a sole southern voice the likes of which they had not previously heard in nonfiction. Ironically, befuddled critics found immediate comparisons to Cobb not in historical literature or autobiography, but in fiction. Davis said Cobb's "cadence and diction are pure Huckleberry Finn." In a front-page review for the *New York Times Book Review*, H. Jack Geiger explained that Rosengarten "had found a black Homer, bursting with his black Odyssey and able to tell it with awesome intellectual power." It is impossible to imagine that reviews of an autobiography released today would call a 1930s sharecropper "Huckleberry Finn," nor is it likely that the same comparisons would have been made in the 1970s if the book had been strictly a biography or an autobiography. The book's ambiguous form allowed critics to think of the book and of Cobb himself as something apart from history.[17]

Some reviewers found the hints of fiction troublesome, but Rosengarten himself was the first to make the comparison. In the preface, he compares Cobb's life to that of William Faulkner's Snopes family: "Faulkner writes about the white south; Shaw speaks about the black." The observation is shortsighted, as Wendell Berry pointed out in his review of the book. To claim that Faulkner wrote about white southerners and Cobb black, while doing scant justice to

Faulkner, effectively implies that black and white in the South were not code-pendent—a notion that even by the 1970s had long lacked currency. Rosen-garten was not the only one to make that observation, however. Geiger picked up the cue in his review. "We have a black Faulkner," he wrote, adding par-enthetically "and what an appropriate irony it is that Faulkner's black coun-terpart should prove, if only in the merest technical sense of the world to be illiterate—about as illiterate as Homer!" Playing with the comparisons more, Geiger added, "It's all there: the dizzying genealogies, the careful inventories, the richness and variety of characters and the complexities of purpose, white and black." The dichotomy that these comparisons to Faulkner's writing assume does a disservice to the stories of both men.[18]

Critics interpreted Nate Shaw not only as a Faulknerian, mythological Jesus, but also as a genuine political character. In *Esquire*, Malcolm Muggeridge com-pared *All God's Dangers* to *Uncle Tom's Cabin*. Though he stopped short of com-paring the protagonists directly, he did suggest that the new book could rival its predecessor in political influence. Apparently, Rosengarten had given voice to the voiceless, and just as reading *Uncle Tom's Cabin* awakened Americans to the realities of slavery, many reviewers thought that *All God's Dangers* would shed light on the more recent plight of African Americans in the rural South. David Brion Davis claimed the entry of Cobb's story into the historical canon resolved scholars' search for a "mute, inglorious Milton." Liberals and leftists seemed to have found not only a historical character who might personify their politics, but also a political mouthpiece. Not all reviewers, however, rushed to claim that Cobb's story finally supplied a poor, noble, black voice with literary credentials. Wendell Berry offered a dire appraisal of the political motivations behind exalting Cobb's story: "The idea seems to be that until the blacks have *their* Faulkner they won't be 'equal.'" Berry wrote, "Rosengarten's sentences fairly sigh with relief" over this discovery of this black Faulkner. "As I see it," Berry added, "Shaw is valuable to us precisely because he is not like Faulkner. He is richly different." Among popular and scholarly reviews, observations that set Cobb's life apart from familiar fictional or historical characters were rare.[19]

Crucial to the politicization and fictionalization of Cobb were readers' claims of the story's authenticity. Ironically, despite constant comparisons to fictional characters, Cobb was concurrently portrayed as the supremely authentic poor black southerner. Critics' simultaneous expressions of surprise over and praise for Cobb's illiteracy ratified these claims of authenticity. Berry exclaimed, "Here is a superior man who never went to school!" For reviewer Geiger, Cobb was not merely the black Homer and the black Faulkner, he was also a kind of unprece-dented super-southerner: Cobb was "the strong, tough, autonomous, powerful, rural Southern black man, self-possessed, ego intact, a whole man, unbroken by a system whose every purpose was to exploit shatter and destroy him" and his story was no less than that of "a million other black lives . . . the very fiber of the nation's history." Indeed, for most reviewers Cobb's poverty and illiteracy, and his resistance to both, were characteristically southern. For one reviewer, even Cobb's ability to recall genealogical minutiae had a "particularly southern" flavor. [20]

For other reviewers, the key to understanding *All God's Dangers* was the resonance of Cobb's voice and his organic language. Cobb's linguistic facility seemed to both surprise and intoxicate intellectuals, who expected not to be able to understand the sharecropper. Berry wrote that "Shaw's vocabulary and usage will sometimes seem strange to readers not familiar with his region or way of life," but added "it will never seem empty or inert." Rosengarten himself felt compelled to explain that he did not need to translate Cobb's language, for "Nate Shaw speaks as clearly as you or I. Once you adjust to the regional inflection it's easily understood." Getting past the imagined hurdle of understanding the language of this foreign creature, reviewers found themselves enraptured by the rhythms of Cobb's voice. Geiger suggested that "one does not read this book— one listens to it, and gasps, and nods in agreement, or laughs, or frowns, as one does in conversation." Reviewer Mark Naison admits that no amount of Rosengarten's editing could have created the "power and grandeur" of the story that Cobb's attachment to the "Black oral tradition" necessarily produced. Again, this is Ned Cobb as authentic southern black man. His language ties him to the somewhat mysterious southern past and to the legacy of oppression and violence inherent in that history. For Berry, Cobb's language is experiential, interacting with his world; it does not derive from "the discipline of ideas or rules." Cobb and his language are organic, tying the speaker to nature and so to authenticity. Reviewers even applauded the pre–civil rights characteristics of Cobb's language, approving the absence of phrases like "Power to the people" or "Black is beautiful." Although Cobb's folksy language is undeniably political, for some reviewers, it is not self-consciously so. For intellectuals in the early 1970s who identified themselves with the civil rights movement and the New History, Cobb was a godsend: an austere, poor, radical who was fluent in the language of revolution, but who did not realize it. [21]

Though putting great stock in the perceived political implications of Cobb's language, many critics failed to listen to its substance. While reviewers often noted the representativeness of Cobb's life story, they were also quick to point out the uniqueness of his involvement in a radical union. For many readers, the evidence of his involvement with the Communist-led union overshadowed the evidence of his day-to-day engagement in the capitalist system. Despite Cobb's constant explanations of how he worked to improve his own economic standing by extricating labor from himself and his family, by producing more, and by bargaining with buyers for a greater profit, readers focused mostly on his radicalism. The sole exception is a review written by James M. Youngdale. Youngdale makes the point that Cobb was "an expectant petty capitalist" who partially succeeded in his attempt to acquire increasing amounts of property.[22]

Not only were critical appraisals wide ranging, they were frequently self-contradictory. Descriptions of Cobb as the black Faulkner or black Homer contradict the portrayals of Cobb as a sharecropper everyman or political radical. One explanation for the wide-ranging interpretations of *All God's Dangers* might simply be the malleability of primary source interpretation. The notion that opinions of a text change over time or that different people read and analyze things differently does not, however, fully explain the impact of the book and its lasting but varied legacy. From the moment Rosengarten began on his own to sort through Cobb's words to compile *The Life of Nate Shaw*, both figuratively and literally, Rosengarten was making decisions that would influence the book's form and reception. That final form—the selected quasiautobiography of Ned Cobb—licensed reviewers and historians to conceive of it outside of traditional rules. Rosengarten chose not to provide an historical context for Cobb's narrative within the text, though he provided historical pointers when interviewed after publication. He also chose not to explain in the preface exactly how he edited Cobb's words. Arguably, therefore, Rosengarten created the ambiguity of "his" book that primed the diversity of response that sustains it.

What began with a Harvard graduate student going to Alabama to aid a friend's research of a union resulted in a critically and popularly successful book. Publishers have reprinted the volume numerous times and critics continue to praise the book years after its publication. In 1984, ten years after its first appearance, the *New York Times* recommended this story of poverty and radicalism as "vacation reading." The book even generated media spin-offs. A 1980s stage adaptation starred actor Cleavon Little, and in 1990, public television filmed and broadcast a movie version. In academic circles, historians continue to pull *All God's Dangers* off their shelves seemingly every time they need to embroider an argument with a sharecropper's voice. Though other sharecropper narratives have been published, and hundreds more lie in archives across the country, scholars still seem to gravitate toward Nate Shaw. The book's legacy shows no signs of weakening despite—or perhaps because—readers know little about its creation. The book's permanence does raise the question of what scholars might learn about sharecropping or African American life in the rural South and how our interpretations might change if we turned away from the single interpretation of Nate Shaw and toward the multitude of oral histories that lie dormant in archives across the country.[23]

NOTES

1. Leon Litwack, *Trouble in Mind: Black Southerners in the Age of Jim Crow* (New York: Knopf, 1998); "A Statistical Summary of Survey Results," *The Journal of American History* 81 (Dec. 1994): 1,205; Theodore Rosengarten, *All God's Dangers: The Life of Nate Shaw* (New York: Alfred A. Knopf, 1974).

2. Rosengarten, *All God's Dangers*, 223, xxii.

3. Donald McRae, "Deep South classic," London *Sunday Times*, 11 Jan. 1976, 37. Alfred C. Ames, "The Alabama Nate knew," *Chicago Tribune*, 20 Oct. 1974, sec. 7, p. 7; Walter Clemons, "The Unvanquished," *Newsweek*, 21 Oct. 1974, 102. David Brion Davis, " 'Some Mute Inglorious Milton': History by the Illiterate," *Reviews in American History* 3 (Sept. 1975): 278; Litwack, *Trouble in Mind*; Jay R. Mandle, *The Roots of Black Poverty: The Southern Plantation Economy After the Civil War* (Durham: Duke Univ. Press, 1978), 82; Eric Foner, *Nothing But Freedom: Emancipation and Its Legacy* (Baton Rouge: Louisiana State Univ. Press, 1983), 64; Gavin Wright, *Old South, New South: Revolutions in the Southern Economy Since the Civil War* (New York: Basic, 1986), 100.

4. Rosengarten, *All God's Dangers*, xv; John Beecher, "The Share Croppers' Union in Alabama," *Social Forces* 13 (Oct. 1934): 124–32; "Biography," in *John Beecher Papers, 1899–1972*, microfilm edition (Glen Rock NJ: Microfilming Corp. of America, 1973); Beecher, "In Egypt Land," in *To Live and Die in Dixie* (Birmingham: Red Mountain, 1966).

5. Beecher, "Like Judas, Wasn't It?" in *Collected Poems, 1924–1974* (New York: Macmillan, 1974), 23; Beecher to Todd Gitlin, 20 Jan. 1970, in *Papers of John Beecher, 1899–1972*, microfilm edition; James Alfred Helton, "Do What the Spirit Say Do: John Beecher and His Poetry," Ph.D. diss., University of North Dakota, 1985, 231; Beecher to Studs Terkel, 28 Dec. 1966, in *Papers of John Beecher, 1899–1972*, microfilm edition. Beecher to Max Geismar, 1 March 1967, *Papers of John Beecher, 1899–1972*, microfilm edition. The first formal publication of "In Egypt Land" was by Beecher's Rampart Press (Scottsdale, Arizona) in 1960. It was in the form of a twenty-seven-page pamphlet that contained only that poem and was printed in a small quantity.

There is no direct evidence that Rosengarten had read Beecher's work before he met Cobb personally. Frank Adams, a Highlander Folk School administrator and friend of Beecher, wrote in *Southern Exposures* that Beecher had in fact told Rosengarten about Cobb's existence. Rosengarten made no mention of Beecher in the first printing of *All God's Dangers*, but in subsequent editions he acknowledged Beecher for "leading the way almost forty years ago." Frank Adams, *Southern Exposures* (1981); Rosengarten, *All God's Dangers*, xxiv–xxv.

6. Theodore Rosengarten, *All God's Dangers*, xiii–xxv; Ray Jenkins, "Rural Black Activist Becomes Folk Hero," *New York Times*, 28 Nov. 1974, sec. A, p. 26; George Abbott White, "The Hem of My Garment: An Interview with Theodore Rosengarten About the Making of *Nate Shaw*," *Massachusetts Review* 21 (1980): 787–800; Theodore Rosengarten, "Stepping Over Cockleburs: Conversations with Ned Cobb," in Marc Pachter, ed., *Telling Lives: The Biographer's Art* (Washington DC: New Republic, 1979), 104–31. Dale Rosen and Rosengarten also cowrote an article about Cobb which appeared prior to the pub-

lication of *All God's Dangers*. That piece concentrated solely on Cobb's altercation with police which led to his prison sentence. It refers to Cobb not as "Nate Shaw" but by another pseudonym, "Jess Hull." See Dale Rosen and Theodore Rosengarten, "Shoot-Out at Reeltown: The Narrative of Jess Hull, Alabama Tenant Farmer," *Radical America* 6 (Nov.–Dec. 1972): 75–84.

7. White, "Hem of My Garment," 788; Rosengarten, *All God's Dangers*, xiiv; Jenkins, "Rural Black Activist Becomes Folk Hero," 26.

8. Rosengarten, *All God's Dangers*, xiv, xv; White, "Hem of My Garment," 789, 790 (original emphasis).

9. Rosengarten, *All God's Dangers*, xv; White, "Hem of My Garment," 790.

10. Rosengarten, *All God's Dangers*, xv, xvi, xviii; Rosengarten, "Stepping Over Cockleburs," 105–7; Jenkins, "Rural Black Activist Becomes Folk Hero," 26.

11. Rosengarten, "Stepping Over Cockleburs," 107–8 (original emphasis).

12. Rosengarten, "Stepping Over Cockleburs," 107–8.

13. White, "Hem of My Garment," 789, 790, 794; Rosengarten, *All God's Dangers*, xviii.

14. White, "Hem of My Garment," 789, 790.

15. Jenkins, "Rural Black Activist Becomes Folk Hero," 26; White, "Hem of My Garment," 791.

16. Rosengarten, *All God's Dangers*, xviii; Rosengarten, "Stepping Over Cockleburs," in Pachter, *Telling Lives*, 104–31.

17. Davis, " 'Some Mute Inglorious Milton,' " 277, 278; H. Jack Geiger, "All God's Dangers," *New York Times Book Review*, 20 Oct. 1974, sec. 7, p. 1.

18. Rosengarten, *All God's Dangers*, xviii; Wendell Berry, "Nate Shaw: The Burden of His Book," *Nation*, 1 March 1975, p. 246; Geiger review, "All God's Dangers."

19. Malcolm Muggeridge, "Books," *Esquire*, March 1975, 34; Davis, " 'Some Mute Inglorious Milton,' " 278; Berry, "Nate Shaw," 246.

20. Berry, "Nate Shaw," 248; Geiger review, "All God's Dangers."

21. Berry, "Nate Shaw," 246, 247; White, "Hem of My Garment," 791. Geiger review, "All God's Dangers"; Naison, "All God's Dangers and Oral History," *Journal of Ethnic Studies* 4 (winter 1977): 105. Not all critics liked Cobb's language. In *Esquire*, critic Malcolm Muggeridge wrote that he was glad to finish *All God's Dangers* and move on to the next book he was to review, Eugene Genovese's *Roll, Jordan, Roll*, because he found that "after a surfeit of Nate's deep, droning voice, [Genovese's writing] came as something of a relief." Muggeridge, "Books," *Esquire*, March 1975, 34.

22. James M. Youngdale, review of *All God's Dangers*, *Agricultural History* 50 (Jan. 1976): 322.

23. "Vacation Reading," *New York Times*, 3 June 1984, sec. 7, p. 48. For yet another recent example of the enduring legacy of the book, see Jacqueline Jones, "Ned Cobb: He Stood His Ground," in Susan Ware, ed., *Forgotten Heroes: American Portraits from Our Leading Historians* (New York: Free Press, 1998), 203–10. Directed by William Partlan, the stage adaptation of *All God's Dangers* opened on 13 Oct. 1989. A PBS version of the same title and also directed by Partlan aired in 1990 in the American Playhouse series.

Poetics in a Poor Place

A Southern Writer and Class War

in the Mountains

Grace Lumpkin's To Make My Bread

RICHARD GRAY

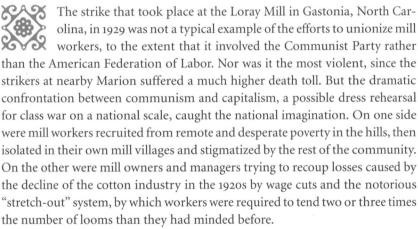 The strike that took place at the Loray Mill in Gastonia, North Carolina, in 1929 was not a typical example of the efforts to unionize mill workers, to the extent that it involved the Communist Party rather than the American Federation of Labor. Nor was it the most violent, since the strikers at nearby Marion suffered a much higher death toll. But the dramatic confrontation between communism and capitalism, a possible dress rehearsal for class war on a national scale, caught the national imagination. On one side were mill workers recruited from remote and desperate poverty in the hills, then isolated in their own mill villages and stigmatized by the rest of the community. On the other were mill owners and managers trying to recoup losses caused by the decline of the cotton industry in the 1920s by wage cuts and the notorious "stretch-out" system, by which workers were required to tend two or three times the number of looms than they had minded before.

Into this combustible atmosphere in March 1929 came Fred Beal, a seasoned Communist leader, who was aiming to organize a branch of the National Textile Workers Union at the Loray Mill. The outcome of his efforts is a long and frequently bloody story, only briefly summarized here: There was a strike. The National Guard was called in. The mill owners imposed draconian punishment on those who refused to go back to work, including eviction and beatings. And when a tent colony of those evicted was organized by the union, it was invaded by the Gastonia police. During the police attack, several lives were lost, including that of the police chief. Beal and fourteen others were promptly arrested and charged with conspiracy to murder. The trial attracted national attention. And, as soon as it began, it became clear that Beal and his co-accused had little chance of a fair hearing locally. The presiding judge, accordingly, agreed to move the proceedings to Charlotte. He also ruled that the defendants should not be questioned about their social and political beliefs. The chief prosecutor, deprived by this ruling of what he clearly saw as his most fruitful line of attack, resorted to a grim final maneuver in an effort to shift the sympathies of the court (which, despite the local press, seemed not unsympathetic to the defendants). He had a wax replica of the murdered police chief made. Clad in the chief's bloodstained clothes, this effigy was wheeled into the courtroom. The chief's wife and daughter, understandably, wept. But the prosecutor's strategy misfired: one juror, whose mental stability had already given rise to questions, had a mental breakdown on the spot. And the judge was forced to declare a mistrial.

A poll of jurors after the initial trial suggested that the majority were in favor of acquittal. However, this was of little comfort to Beal or to at least some of the accused. There had been mob violence during the proceedings, and the publication of this poll provoked something little short of a riot. Three of the union leaders were kidnapped and beaten. Worse still, Ella May Wiggins, a writer and singer of strike ballads, was murdered by mill gangsters who, despite the presence of fifty witnesses, were never brought to court. Beal and his fellow accused were vilified in the local newspapers. When a new trial was quickly convened, the prosecution dropped charges against eight of the defendants, including all the women on the pretext of chivalry—though it was clear that the main motive was to make a conviction of the rest more likely. Unlike its predecessor, the second trial quickly turned into an inquisition, in the sense that the judge did permit cross-questioning on beliefs. Given the chance, the prosecutor then played on the prejudices of some of the locals. He characterized Beal and the other defendants as "creeping like the hellish serpent into the garden of Eden, fiends incarnate, stripped of their hoofs and horns, bearing guns instead of pitchforks, sweeping like a tornado to sink damnable fangs into the heart and lifeblood of the community." Just in case that was not enough to guarantee conviction, the prosecutor also characterized Gastonia, the "community" into which the accused had allegedly crept, as a pastoral haven, offering a rich yield of cotton yarn to the world. "Why," he declaimed, "you could wrap it [the yarn] around the sun sixteen times, around the moon thirteen times, around Mercury, Venus, and Saturn, stretch it to San Francisco to southernmost Africa and right back to Gastonia."[1] Inspired by such rhetoric, it was perhaps hardly surprising that the jury this time took less than an hour to find the accused guilty. All were given heavy sentences—the heaviest going to northern organizers, against whom the evidence was flimsiest. Freed on bail while an appeal was pending, Beal and all the others took the opportunity to flee the locality and country, for Russia.

The strike and the trial attracted national attention. What is more, it inspired a brief experiment in southern proletarian literature. No less than six novels based on events at Gastonia appeared between 1930 and 1934: *Strike!* by Mary Heaton Vorse; *Call Home the Heart* by Fielding Burke; *Gathering Storm* by Myra Page; *Beyond Desire* by Sherwood Anderson; *The Shadow Before* by William Rollins Jr.; and the best, in my opinion, *To Make My Bread* by Grace Lumpkin.[2]

To Make My Bread has been described by critic Walter Rideout as "local color fiction performed with a radical purpose."[3] There is an element of truth to this, although the description does not do justice to the power of Lumpkin's portrait of mountain community disrupted by change. Nor does it catch just how much the novel is fired into life by the writer's sense of both the conflicts and the connections between the old culture and the new—as her characters struggle to come to terms with ways of life that are not only oppressive but unfamiliar, and move hesitantly toward new forms of belief.

Centered on one mountain family called the McClures, Lumpkin's *To Make My Bread* is connected with two other Gastonia novels, in particular, Burke's *Call Home the Heart*, and Page's *Gathering Storm*, in the sense that it focuses on the experience of mountain women as they struggle to reconcile their traditional status as matriarchal keepers of the house with new demands made on them by an oppressive system of wage labor and the poverty and deprivation attendant upon it. The conflicted role of the woman in the emergent culture of town and factory offered Lumpkin, as it did Burke and Page (or, for that matter, novelists who did not draw their inspiration from the Gastonia strike, like Anne W. Armstrong and Harriette S. Arnow[4]), the chance to measure social alterations as alterations of consciousness—to register a material change as, in addition, an ideological one. To this extent, a telling link exists between what the author of *To Make My Bread* was doing and what she was dramatizing. Both Lumpkin and her women characters were caught in the crossfire between old and new, and trying to make sense of it. For Lumpkin's women, this meant struggling to meet the challenge of an altered world while not entirely forfeiting traditional beliefs; for Lumpkin herself, it meant finding some way of achieving a rapprochement between inherited literary forms and a radical agenda. Just how successful she was is a matter for debate: A. B. Magil, the *New Masses* reviewer, for instance, thought that there was too little class consciousness in either the characters or the narrative approach—too much rural portraiture and romantic pity and not enough revolutionary fervor.[5] The novel is remarkable, however, precisely because Lumpkin does not take the easy way out, either by jettisoning the old ways (her inherited southern tradition) or by ignoring the new ones (her allegiance to the Communist party); the novelist tries, in terms both of creative practice and of imaginative analysis, to see even violent transformation, and the pain and sense of promise it engenders, as a product of necessity—part of a vital, evolutionary pattern.

To Make My Bread begins in the mountains. The McClure family are living on a small farm that belonged to the husband of Emma McClure. Emma, a widow, lives with her father, "Grandpap," and her children, among them a son named John and a daughter, Bonnie; and the family scrape a living from farming, hunting, and brewing moonshine. Mostly, they depend on credit from the local store. Lumpkin is particularly adept here in sketching out the peculiar impact of religion on hill folk. The attitude of people like the McClures to the admonitions of the local Baptist preacher is one of wary belief. When the preacher condemns music and dancing, for example, Grandpap, a skilful fiddle player, marches out of the church in protest, and the entire McClure clan follow him. Nevertheless, the McClures then feel that they must make a sacrifice to God, just in case, as they put it, "Grandpap's made the Lord mad" (49). Religious events, like the baptizing day, in any case supply moments of sociability and community: they are, as the narrator puts it, "an occasion for neighbors and kin who had not seen each other for a year or more to meet. People came from miles around" (55). And, at such moments, the cathartic rituals of the Baptist church, with their emphasis on both suffering and release, offer a handy insight into the mountain character. Normally stolid and stoic people like the McClures are carried away on a tide of feeling, singing songs about immersion "In the blood, in the blood of the Lamb," while their half-naked children are plunged into the chill mountain streams. Lumpkin is concerned to identify, here (and later), the fundamental rhythm of feeling and personality in the hills: pious endurance punctuated by startling moments of release like baptism day. Contemporary observers of the Gastonia strike, and especially those from outside the area, were sometimes baffled by strikers' vacillation between apathy and violence, mute acceptance of their lot attended by sudden eruptions of political awareness and action. Already, in her sketch of hill religion, Lumpkin is disclosing a possible reason for what outsiders seemed to find so strange; in this sense, she suggests, the striking mill workers from the hills were translating into political terms an emotional language they had first learned from their religion.

The other aspects of life in the hills that receive special attention in *To Make My Bread* are scarcity and the sufferings of women. Communal life is sustained at church gatherings, dances, or the local store, but whenever "food became scarce," we are told, "neighbors kept away from neighbors as if they were afraid or ashamed to show each other their misery" (13). Emma McClure is described as "a strong young woman" (x), but at such times her strength is sorely tested, as she struggles to make meals without much food to make them with, or is forced to "tell the others the last potato had been eaten" (28). On occasion, there is a primeval quality to her troubles and pain. As Emma gives birth to a child, for example, Grandpap bending over her bed is compared to "a man bending over a slaughtering," while "Emma's last cries were those of a pig with the knife at its throat" (29). So when strangers arrive talking about a "promised land" (29) in the mill towns, she is torn between confused skepticism and a kind of desperate faith, the belief that there must be some kind of deliverance beckoning somewhere. "[H]it's hard t'know what to believe and what not, these days. Everything's changin' so," she says, but then begins to dream of working in the mills as, quite probably, "a very neighborly arrangement" (136). Maybe, she tells herself, it will be pleasant working in a "quiet" factory "at a leisurely pace" in the company of others—"as if neighbors had gathered to sit round and talk at a quilting . . . bright shining dollars would pour into her lap" (137). "With the money," she fancies, "she would buy new clothes for the young ones, and books for school, a fiddle for Grandpa, and perhaps for herself a new waist or a scarf for her head" (140). In effect, her wandering imagination transforms the mills into both a refuge from mountain scarcity and a place where the old pieties of mountain life can be resurrected. For her, the pastoral dream of quiet surroundings, gentle labor, good company, and a modest sufficiency is relocated in the town.

The process by which Lumpkin strips Emma and her family of all their illusions about the new methods of labor is a detailed and, in many ways, a familiar one. The mill village, far from supplying release and neighborliness, offers only imprisonment and anonymity. "The rows of houses . . . were silent as if all the people had deserted their homes" (156). "Only smoke coming from some of the chimneys showed that life was going on inside" (157). Grandpap is humiliated by being told he is too old to be given a job—"Grandpap is changed if he can stand that kind of talk" (160), Emma reflects—and Bonnie, treated as a "unit" in the cotton mill, begins to think of herself as Bonnie Thirteen instead of Bonnie McClure. The achievement of the novel does not really lie in its material portrait of life in the mill town, stark and powerful though that portrait is, but elsewhere: in the carefully graduated account of the different responses among the hill folk to the new forms of labor and affliction. Some, like Grandpap McClure, just give up and try to retreat into the past. At first the retreat is purely an emotional one. Grandpap attends a Confederate rally, for instance, at which the main speaker is one of the mill owners, who sings the praises of what he calls "Race Domination." "The Creator in his wisdom made the Caucasian race of finer clay than he made any of the colored people," the mill owner declaims, adding to his all-white audience, "here in the mills . . . you have made a New South, a South . . . of smooth-running factories . . . where you possess peaceful homes, and the freedom to work" (187). His phrasing ironically echoes Emma McClure's dream of a promised land in the mill town. Deeper irony, however, lies in the cultural work performed by the speech: old habits of division are made to serve the purposes of new kinds of subjection. Although Grandpap does not realize it, and the speaker would certainly not acknowledge it, the Confederate flag is being waved over the factories to legitimize their oppressive system—to give them a peculiarly southern stamp of approval.

Eventually, the purely emotional withdrawal from the present afforded by occasions like a Confederate rally is not enough for Grandpap. He goes back to the hills, in what turns out to be an unsuccessful attempt to live off the land. His daughter is attracted to this herself: "sometimes," we learn, "Emma talked of going back" (213). Most of the time, however, she is caught as most of her generation are in these novels of exodus between bewilderment, anger, and resignation. "There's no use getting mad," she tells herself. "Hit's the way the Lord made things to be." "I get that way sometimes," she adds, "mad at something I don't know what. Then I have to remember whatever happens is the Lord's Will" (227). Here again is that fluctuating rhythm between apathy or weary acceptance and sudden moments of emotional violence. The only trouble now is that, for Emma, the rhythm leads only to exhaustion, emotional and physical, and eventually, to death. One reason for this, Lumpkin intimates, is that the churches in mill towns do not even offer the chance of group emotional exorcism, the ritualized catharsis afforded by those in the hills. The urban services are too restrained, ordered; Emma can hardly share her pain and confusion with anyone else, save one or two friends. So Emma's feelings have to go elsewhere for release and expression; not into religion but into politics. Although the church can give no satisfaction, Lumpkin suggests, activism can and indeed should, answering emotional as well as material need. In establishing connection between the emotional rhythms of the hill people as strikers and as churchgoers, Lumpkin at once records a fact of the time that puzzled many observers (those who wondered how mountain folk–turned–workers could alternate between quiescence and rebellion)—and register a hope, a possibility. Properly channeled, the implication is, the impulses shaped by the emotional drama of highland religion could give birth to a new kind of activism. Those impulses were not necessarily at odds with organized union action, as both union and church leaders of the time tended to believe: on the contrary, they could enable and energize such action. The motives and drives associated with hill faith might find proper articulation in a language that was, in the last analysis, political.

The transvaluation of religious values into political ones is particularly noticeable among the younger generation of the McClure family. Bonnie McClure reveals a talent for writing and singing songs: not songs about "the blood of the Lamb," that is, but about the blood and sacrifice of the striking workers. She becomes the ballad singer for the strike, deploying skills that once would have been used to praise the Lord in celebration of the mill workers, and in a language that still recalls the hymns and religious rituals of the hills. Bonnie, like Ella Mae Wiggins, is killed during the strike, and the speech given at her funeral tellingly mixes politics and religion. As one critic, Sylvia Jenkins Cook, has observed of the speech, "the cadences of it are biblical, but the message is to remember in bitterness the evil that must be purged from the face of the earth."[6] A similar crossover between related kinds of faith is witnessed when a union colleague of Bonnie's brother, John, tells him:

> We must go beyond the strike to the message . . . that we must join with all others like us and take what is ours. For it is our hands that dig the coal and keep the furnaces going; and our hands that bring in the wheat for the flour. . . . It is for us who know to make a world in which there will be no masters, and no slaves except the machines: but all will work together and will enjoy the good things of life together. (328)

The millennial vision, heightened by biblical rhythms, picks up on John Mc-Clure's own story, as it happens, as well as Bonnie's. John is one of the organizers of the strike, and his eventual commitment to union activism issues out of a memorable slippage between political and religious feeling. He is aroused by the story of Sacco and Vanzetti and then finds something in the Bible that seems to him to endorse his growing suspicion that injustice and privilege must and will be abolished. "Go to now, ye rich," he reads, "weep and howl for your miseries that are coming upon you" (295). In this novel, it is the inherently skeptical and irreligious among the younger generations of hill folk who are without hope of any kind. One character, for instance, alternates attacks on religious belief with a critique of the idea of progress. "There is . . . no purpose, no progress for the human race," he tells John, "history repeats itself over and over" (325). Those with religious origins and inclinations, on the other hand, like Bonnie and John, are moving steadily and by no means slowly toward the idea of material redemption, salvation here and now in the world.

The remarkable feature of *To Make My Bread*, and of Grace Lumpkin's other works, is that she does not underestimate the power of residual belief, the undertow of feelings that tugs at mountain people in the towns, for ill sometimes as much as for good. The ill is certainly there. Emma McClure, for instance, is blinded by such feeling to the origins and reality of her oppression. She cannot see the factory for what it is: an engine and agent of a particular system of labor. For her, it can only be understood in terms of old hill myths and fairy tales, as a monster whose machinery is constantly murmuring, "I'll grind your bones to make my bread," and as such, invulnerable, irresistible (219). She is in a similar position to a black housekeeper, a "mammy" figure in Lumpkin's

A Sign for Cain, who is genuinely shocked when her activist son tells her, "my people are white people too. They are working people, white and colored." "You mean po' white people," she exclaims with a mixture of disbelief and affronted dignity, "white trash is *your* people?" (53). In such cases, past beliefs cripple the present; and, when the experience of mountain exodus is involved, they usually involve the first generation of immigrants. The next generation, Bonnie and John McClure and their kind, are different; as for that matter, are many of the younger generation of Lumpkin's black characters—like the son of the outraged housekeeper, called Denis. They seem to be overpowered by the past, rather than disabled by it; it enables them to construct a viable language for dealing with the present, as well as a set of practices that opens up the chance of building a more tolerable and more decent future. "We are the new pioneers, cleaning out the world, making a new world" (233), declares Denis (*A Sign for Cain*), in a familiar but still effective harnessing of the myths of yesterday in the service of today and tomorrow. "Because we have worked and suffered," insists a young union member in *To Make My Bread*, "we will understand that all should work and all should enjoy the good things of life" (328). Note how the rhythms of this insistence, his idiom and cadences, recollect old pieties, making aspects of hill religion the tools of social transformation. *To Make My Bread* contains no dispassionate analysis of the plight of the poor, no carefully articulated, pro-grammatic solution: something that incurred the displeasure of Magil at *New Masses*, among others.[7] What there is, however, is something subtler and, in effect, more in touch with other writing from the South: the intimation that the past can work in the present to alter the material conditions, by altering consciousness of them—the sense that tradition can and perhaps should be an agent of change.

This necessarily brief look at one book by one writer is not intended sim-ply to resurrect a forgotten masterpiece. Masterpiece is, in any event, too con-tentious a word to describe *To Make My Bread*—even though I myself believe it deserves a place in any serious history of twentieth-century southern writ-ing. I wanted to draw attention to this book. But I also wanted to suggest just how many good books about the southern rural poor have either been under-estimated or altogether neglected. Books like *Weeds* by Edith Summers Kelley, *Jacob's Ladder* by Marjorie Kinnan Rawlings, *The Hawk's Done Gone* by Mildred Haun—and better known but still severely undervalued, the novels of Erskine Caldwell and Harriette S. Arnow. Beyond that, I want to intimate just how much we are perhaps still trapped in a version of southern literary history that was first sketched out by the Vanderbilt Agrarians and then given substance in those two groundbreaking accounts of southern literature edited by Louis D. Rubin Jr. and Robert D. Jacobs, *Southern Renascence* (published in 1953) and *South: Modern*

Southern Literature in Its Cultural Setting (which first appeared in 1961). This version tends to exclude or marginalize the kind of writing that Lumpkin favored and *To Make My Bread* typifies: because, the argument—or, more usually, the assumption—goes, such writing is "protest" literature, or "propaganda."[8]

In 1935, for example, only three years after *To Make My Bread* was published, Donald Davidson contributed an essay, "The Trend of Literature," to the anthology, *Culture in the South*, in which he explained that he had decided to exclude all books dealing with poor whites because they betrayed the habits of mind that were—as he put it—"not quite healthy." Writers who write about poor people, Davidson insisted, like those whose subject was "Negro life," were turning away from what he called "southern life in broader aspects." For Davidson, the choice was simple. The southern writer could either observe what he termed "fidelity as an artist to his subject-matter" or he could surrender to "the social programs that emanate from the metropolis." And, evidently, if he directed his attention to the poor, black or white, he was doing the latter. By an adroit, if not untypical or even intended, twist of irony, those who opted for writing about the rural poor were accused of yielding to the pressures of the city and to what Davidson dismissed as "the little Russians of the *New Republic*." "As a student of farm tenancy in the South," Davidson observed in a review of one of Erskine Caldwell's books, "Mr Caldwell would make a splendid Curator of a Soviet Park of Recreation and Culture."[9]

Davidson's position was extreme, or at least extremely stated. Still, his fellow Agrarians arrived, if rather more circuitously, at similar conclusions. For Robert Penn Warren, for example, what Warren called the "tragic contradiction" that confronted the southern writer had its source in the absolute and necessary opposition between the regional and the political. John Donald Wade and Cleanth Brooks both criticized books by Caldwell and by other writers of the period for what Brooks termed "propaganda for various causes with a resulting confusion of attitude toward . . . the material." Wade's comments on Caldwell are instructive here and, besides, echo Davidson's. Caldwell's books, Wade suggested, "Would be more impressive if—a good Southerner still—he were not as plaintively anxious as he is to please the kind and class of people that he has come to be affiliated with—the detached, nervous, thrill-goaded metro-cosmopolitans of his own day."[10] The message from all such critics and reviewers was clear. To write of the poor was to write as a sensationalist catering to the jaded appetites of the metropolis. And/or it was to write of the political. Either way, or both, it was not to write as regionalist.

This exclusion of fictions concerning poverty from the regional canon has not, of course, continued with quite the same degree of intensity. There have been some powerful accounts of the writing Davidson casually dismissed. But the general habit of segregating or sidelining such writers has not abated. As late as 1981, for instance, one critic, Scott MacDonald, could point out that Erskine Caldwell has been "the subject of less . . . critical discussion than . . . any American writer of comparable stature." Although they are represented in 1985's *The History of Southern Literature*, most writers who wrote about the rural poor between the wars, including Lumpkin, are briefly considered under the heading, "The Fiction of Social Commitment"—as if, somehow, such commitment were their exclusive preserve and determining characteristic.[11]

Writers like Grace Lumpkin were faced with a difficult critical situation. A bias toward misunderstanding, and a tendency to deny the literary value and the regional centrality of what they were doing, were the conditions under which they wrote. They were faced with a local audience that, for the most part, regarded their work as failing on both aesthetic and regional grounds and, as such, hardly to be described as southern literature. To make matters worse, they were also challenged by a reception outside the South that was at once the opposite and the mirror of the local response. For those many critics of the period between the wars for whom writing was an agent of social change, literary accounts of the rural poor folk *had* to be openly political and programmatic. And a common charge leveled at writers like Lumpkin was that their fictions were not political and programmatic, or at least not sufficiently so. In his *New Masses* review of *To Make My Bread*, for instance, Magil comprehensively dismissed Lumpkin's novel because of what he saw as the author's failure to offer revolutionary optimism, sardonic class portraiture, and a broader perspective on the local struggle that might place it, openly, as part of an international movement. This was typical. Erskine Caldwell was similarly attacked, in *New Masses* and related publications, for what was seen as his failure to follow an openly political agenda. "He lacks social understanding which is the life of revolutionary prose," the proletarian novelist Jack Conroy said of Caldwell in one review; "he should go left," another commentator in *New Masses* recommended; while a third, also in *New Masses*, declared that "he must go into the higher sphere of dialectical development of characters placed in situations that clamor for treatment today."[12] At the back of such advice were assumptions curiously like those of the Agrarian critics. Writing about the poor people of the South was necessarily political, the Agrarians either claimed or assumed. The critics on the metropolitan left simply turned this formal imperative into a moral or ideological one: writing about such people need not be political, they argued, but it should be. The writer had a social obligation, a duty to approach a subject like the southern rural poor with the correct degree of "social awareness." As a citizen and a writer, an analyst of the current crisis as well as an inventor of narrative, he needed to write in such a way as to insist on political understanding and to implement social change.

The arguments of the *New Masses* critics were, of course, at odds with those of the Vanderbilt Agrarians, as far as measuring where fictional portraits of the rural South went wrong. On one fundamental level, however, they reflected the Agrarian belief that viably to represent the rural poor was to be political. For the Agrarians, that representation was anathema, for the urban critics of the left it was the ideal. But for both groups there was only one way. The pity of it, for the Agrarians, was that this way had to be followed—it went somehow with the territory—and, for the leftist critics, that it ought to be followed but, on the whole, was not. Either way, the model for writing about the rural folk of the region was singular, prescriptive, and unalterable; and either way, that model was wrong—in that it did justice neither to the plurality nor to the power of the books about such folk being produced in the South. The net effect as far as the story of southern writing is concerned, has been to sideline or exclude writers like Lumpkin.

Allen Tate, as usual, was franker than most regarding the arguments and assumptions at work in the making of a southern canon. "One of the faults of the liberals and communists," Tate wrote to his friend and compatriot in the cultural wars, John Peale Bishop, in 1933, "is that their art has not gone beyond the most naïve propaganda." After talking it over and over, Tate explained, the Agrarians had come to another view: "that the most powerful propaganda that any social movement could have is a mature literature which is superior to propaganda." Quite how a literary work could both be "the most powerful propaganda" and "superior to propaganda," Tate did not go on to say, beyond citing the formulation "a mature literature." But in a way, he did not have to spell it out. The whole nature of the project on which he, and other Agrarians, were embarked started from the premise that a mature literature offered (as Tate put it once) "complete knowledge of man's experience"; and complete knowledge was what the traditionalist writer first saw and then transposed into the mythical order. Mature literature was "propaganda" only in the sense that it propagated the truth, what Tate called the "completeness . . . not of the experimental . . . but of the experienced order"; other "propaganda" was just that, propaganda, its "sense of the natural world . . . blunted," Tate argued, "by a too rigid system of ideas."[13] The ground on which Tate and his brothers in literary arms took their stand was slippery. Nonetheless, it became the base on which the canon of modern southern literature was erected. That canon has been challenged, of course. And not many people would now see the foundations on which it was built as entirely stable. But, ironically, those who wrote about the poor, like Lumpkin, those whom Tate stigmatized as "the liberals and communists," still get much less than their due. The neglect of a book like *To Make My Bread* suggests that we still tend to see southern writing through Agrarian eyes.

NOTES

1. Quoted in Paul Blanshard, "One-Hundred Per Cent Americans on Strike," *Nation* 128 (24 April), 501, 556. The account of the Gastonia Strike is taken from Liston Pope, *Millhands and Preachers: A Study of Gastonia* (New Haven: Yale Univ. Press, 1942), and Fred E. Beal, *Proletarian Journey: New England, Gastonia, Moscow* (New York: Hillman-Curl, 1937).

2. Grace Lumpkin, *To Make My Bread* (Urbana: Univ. of Illinois Press, 1995 [1932]), page citations appear in text; William Rollins Jr., *The Shadow Before* (New York: R. M. McBride, 1934); Sherwood Anderson, *Beyond Desire* (New York: Liveright, 1961 [1932]); Myra Page, *Gathering Storm: A Story of the Black Belt* (New York: International, 1932); Fielding Burke, *Call Home the Heart: A Novel of* the *Thirties* (Old Westbury NY: Feminist Press, 1983 [1932]); Mary Heaton Vorse, *Strike!* (Urbana: Univ. of Illinois Press, 1991 [1930]).

3. Walter B. Rideout, *The Radical Novel in the United States, 1900–1954: Some Interrelations of Literature and Society* (Cambridge: Harvard Univ. Press, 1956), 174.

4. See Anne Armstrong, *This Day and Time* (New York: Lee Furman, 1932); Harriette S. Arnow, *The Dollmaker* (New York: Avon, 1972 [1954]). The comment by Walter Rideout is in *The Radical Novel in the United States 1900–1954* (Cambridge: Harvard Univ. Press, 1956), 174.

5. A. B. Magil review, "*To Make My Bread*," *New Masses* 8–9 (Feb. 1933): 19–20.

6. Sylvia Jenkins Cook, *From Tobacco Road to Route 66: The Southern Poor White in Fiction* (Chapel Hill: Univ. of North Carolina Press, 1976), 115.

7. Grace Lumpkin, *A Sign for Cain* (New York: Lee Furman, 1935), page citations appear in text; Magil review, "*To Make My Bread*."

8. Edith Summers Kelley, *Weeds* (New York: Feminist Press, 1996 [1923]); Marjorie Kinnan Rawlings, *Jacob's Ladder* (Coral Gables: Univ. of Miami Press, 1950 [1940]); Mildred Haun, *The Hawk's Done Gone, and Other Stories*, ed. Herschel Gower (Nashville: Vanderbilt Univ. Press, 1968 [1940]); Harriette S. Arnow, especially *Hunter's Horn* (New York: Macmillan, 1949) and *The Dollmaker* (New York, Macmillan, 1954). See also Louis D. Rubin Jr. and Robert D. Jacobs, eds., *Southern Renascence: The Literature of the Modern South* (Baltimore: Johns Hopkins Press, 1953) and *South: Modern Southern Literature in its Cultural Setting* (Westport CT: Greenwood Press, 1974 [1961]).

9. Donald Davidson, "Erskine Caldwell's Picture Book," *Southern Review* 4 (1938–39): 18. See also Donald Davidson, "The Trend of Literature: A Partisan View," in W. T. Crouch, ed., *Culture in the South* (Chapel Hill: Univ. of North Carolina Press, 1935), 185, 199, 204.

10. Robert Penn Warren, "Some Recent Novels," *Southern Review* 1 (1935–36): 624; Cleanth Brooks, "What Deep South Literature Needs," *Saturday Review of Literature* (19 Sept. 1942): 8–9; John Donald Wade, "Sweet Are the Uses of Degeneracy," *Southern Review* 1 (1935–36): 466.

11. Scott MacDonald, "Introduction," *Critical Essays on Erskine Caldwell* (Boston: G. K. Hall, 1981), xi; James Mellard, "The Fiction of Social Commitment," *The History*

of Southern Literature (Baton Rouge: Louisiana State Univ. Press, 1985), 351–55. On the other hand, the more recent work of, among others, Barbara Foley, Jacquelyn Hall, and Alan Wald has begun to redress the critical imbalance. Among other things, this work enables us to know more about Lumpkin's politics, in particular her communism and later repudiation of communism and the degree to which her female characters' experiences are vitally connected to the realities of contemporary historical experience—and, in particular, the experience of rural women. These issues fall outside the scope of this chapter. So does the equally central issue of just how Lumpkin's portraiture of the rural poor—like, say, Erskine Caldwell's dedication in both his fictional and nonfictional prose to what he called "the unknown people" of the South (*New York Post*, 18 Feb. 1935, sec. 1, p. 1)—connects with a larger regional, national, and international movement of poor people campaigning against invisibility. I have addressed some of these larger issues, as well as the intricate links and conflicts between literary criticism, political ideology, and writing in and of the rural South between the world wars, in *Southern Aberrations: Writers of the American South and the Problems of Regionalism* (Baton Rouge: Louisiana State Univ. Press, 2000), chapters 4 and 5.

12. Edwin Rolfe, "God's Little Acre," *New Masses* 7 (April 1932): 24–25; Norman MacLeod, "A Hardboiled Idealist," *New Masses* 7 (July 1931): 18.

13. Tate to Bishop, 7 April 1933, in John Tyree Fain and Thomas D. Young, eds., *The Literary Correspondence of John Peale Bishop and Allen Tate* (Athens: Univ. of Georgia Press, 1974), 78; Allen Tate, preface, *Reason in Madness: Critical Essays* (New York: G. P. Putnam's Sons, 1941), 19; Tate, "Literature as Knowledge," *Reason in Madness*, 60.

Rural Poverty and the Heroics of Farming

Elizabeth Madox Roberts's The Time of Man *and Ellen Glasgow's* Barren Ground

PETER NICOLAISEN

Published within a year of each other, Elizabeth Madox Roberts's *The Time of Man* (1926) and Ellen Glasgow's *Barren Ground* (1925) seem to anticipate the wave of social protest that was to follow in the fiction of the 1930s, yet neither of them is in itself committed to the cause of social reform. Focusing on the role of women who try to extract a living from the soil, both novels waver between admiration and pity for the lives their heroines lead. They pay them respect and give them dignity but deny them fulfillment. Questions of gender loom as large as those of the economics of farming, and in both novels what one may call "the ideology of the soil" figures prominently. The spirit in which the two authors approach the plight of their protagonists differs considerably, however, as do their strategies to give their characters literary substance. By choosing a very private, closely circumscribed perspective that "keeps starkly within one consciousness"—a consciousness that lacks the "analytical nature of a 'conscious' consciousness"—Roberts, as she said in a note about her novel, deliberately eschews "an analysis of society or of a social stratum." Glasgow, on the other hand, is clearly interested in the social and economic conditions she describes in *Barren Ground*; the attempt to change these conditions is at the core of the novel. Nonetheless, Glasgow is anything but a social reformer.[1]

Examining the two novels together, as we do here, both illuminates the differences in the ideological stand the two authors took on the issue of rural poverty and also suggests their place within the more general context of rural fiction in the 1920s and 1930s. They were published almost simultaneously with the English translation of the first volume of Oswald Spengler's *Untergang des Abendlandes* (*The Decline of the West*). Spengler praised the farmer as "the eternal man" who is independent of all culture "that ensconces itself in the cities."

The farmer "roots in the earth that he tends," he wrote; "earth becomes *Mother Earth*. Between sowing and begetting, harvest and death, the child and the grain, a profound affinity is set up."[2] Although Spengler's impact was probably more strongly felt in Europe than in the United States, he was widely read here, too. He especially helped to shape the thinking of the southern or Vanderbilt Agrarians, whose volume *I'll Take My Stand* was enthusiastically welcomed by Elizabeth Madox Roberts.[3] Ellen Glasgow was more subdued in her praise. In 1933, she wrote to Allen Tate that she, too, found herself "turning definitely away from the raucous voice of the modern industrial South."[4] The system of agriculture she espoused in *Barren Ground*, however, would have found little favor with her fellow southerners at Vanderbilt University.

Although *The Time of Man* and *Barren Ground* share in the glorification of agriculture and a life close to the soil current in the early decades of the twentieth century, they do so in different ways. For Elizabeth Madox Roberts, agriculture is a timeless endeavor, transcending the economic and social barriers that separate the people who work in the fields from those who own them. Although she acknowledges poverty as an integral part of her characters' lives, she does not foreground it or emphasize the limitations it imposes on people; for her, rural poverty, it seems, is something to be taken for granted. Ellen Glasgow, too, sings the praise of the farmer's life, but in contrast to Roberts is acutely aware of the changing social and economic conditions within which her farmers operate. Far from being timeless, these conditions can and must be altered. In *Barren Ground* poverty is triumphantly overcome, not by social protest but by hard work and the shrewd use of capital. While Roberts renders the poor farmer heroic, for Glasgow he represents a state of affairs (and of mind) that needs to be changed. Despite her trust in modern, market-oriented methods of farming, however, Glasgow, too, resorts to the rhetoric of the soil so frequent in rural novels of the 1920s and 1930s—in the end, her heroine is saved from despair not by her material success, but by her belief in the healing powers of a Spenglerian "Mother Earth."

IN *THE TIME OF MAN*, Elizabeth Madox Roberts explores the consciousness of a poor tenant farmer's daughter, giving her a sense of beauty, dignity, and emotional depth. This characterization is a literary tribute to poor whites, who had most often been the object of ridicule.[5] Roberts deliberately grants Ellen stature, portraying her as something of a fertility goddess. "Out of me come people forever, forever," Ellen muses at one point.[6] In the way she dispenses food to her children, she resembles the type of earth mother Spengler might have had in mind: "Sun-stained and hearty, her body deep and broad, she tried to give each one the vegetable he liked best in ample profusion" (345). "Her body was strong now," we learn, "and the blood ran high in her cheeks and in her warm strong hands" (324). As she works the soil, she becomes one with it, so that each serves to cast the other in a heroic mold: "Her body and mind were of the earth, clodded with the clods; the strength of her arms and her back and her thighs arose out of the soil, the clods turned upon themselves to work back into their own substance endlessly" (263, cf. also 258, 259). The monumental quality of such descriptions recalls the "blood-and-soil" movement in Germany; when *The Time of Man* came out in German translation in 1928, readers might well have felt at home with it.[7] Sentences like "She would sink down into the land" (238) or "her mind [was] one with the wants of the fields, with the beasts and the plowed trenches" (258) work toward imagining that the farming woman has no will or corpus of her own. Instead, she identifies with the land she works, with nature and the seasons and the eternal order they represent: "The design of the grass roots matted with the soil lay under her eyes, complete forever, varying in every detail but forever the same" (259). The monumentalization Roberts seems to be after is underscored by Clara Leighton's wood engravings in the 1945 Viking edition. Leighton's illustrations could have appeared in any number of German *Bauernromane* of the period and support a tendency noticeable throughout the book—they elevate the simple farming folk to a higher plane, removing them from their specific historical context so that their timeless, eternal traits shine through the events portrayed. Even when Roberts describes ongoing events such as the courtship of Ellen and Jonas (who deserts her), the sentiments felt by the young people are expressed in a highly stylized manner meant to give them significance beyond that of a day-to-day occurrence: "She felt his gaze and his hands searching her for her beauty and she felt her beauty grow more full and rich when he called to it, and it became something which they held and owned together" (187). The title *The Time of Man*, explained at length and then often alluded to, likewise suggests that we are to understand the novel within a generic, trans-historical time frame within which, it appears, the events attain their true and universal meaning.

Given Roberts's efforts to transcend the mundane, it is easy to forget that *The Time of Man* deals with twentieth-century Kentucky sharecroppers and tenant farmers. But as Richard Gray pointed out many years ago, against the idealized vision of a life close to the soil, Roberts often posits a rather more sober picture of "rural reality." As we follow the course of Ellen Chesser's life, we cannot help but become aware of some of the sordid aspects of the sharecropping system. A list of these would include much of the data later assembled by sociologists Margaret Hagood and others—the dilapidated cabins assigned to the tenants or "croppers," the scarcity of furniture and clothing, the lack of cash, the constant threat of malnutrition, the endless toil in the tobacco fields, the whimsies of landlords, the frequent pregnancies—in sum, the general drabness of the share-cropper's existence.[8] "When the cow was without milk," the novel observes, "Joe and Nannie became hollow-eyed and thin, their beings waiting upon the hazards of the seasons. The hazards of the seasons followed them into the cabin in long rainy periods, the leaking roof scarcely leaving them one dry corner for their play" (331). Roberts usually introduces such details almost casually—often Ellen seems hardly to be aware of them or to be preoccupied with other matters. "The cold of the autumn found the children unprepared, their garments thin and ragged," the narrator states laconically (359). Nor does Roberts go beyond the kind of personification she employs here and elsewhere, thereby minimizing the responsibility of the landowners for leaking roofs and other hardships.

How, then, are we to respond to the references to Ellen's poverty? Most critics pay little attention to them, focusing instead on Ellen Chesser's "identity" and her awareness of herself, topics Roberts indeed foregrounds.[9] Only when we read the novel against the grain, so to speak, does the general plight of the tenant farmer's existence begin to reveal its significance. Ellen's poverty works against her self-realization and, in the end, destroys the strong sense of self with which she sets out at the beginning of the novel. As an adolescent and, later, a young woman, Ellen is imbued with a keen wish to find her place in the world, to learn about her environment and, most of all, to assert her triumphalist sense of being alive. As the novel opens, she metaphorically writes herself into existence: "Ellen wrote her name in the air with her finger, Ellen Chesser" (9); similar gestures abound in the text. The mere fact that she is alive makes her believe that she is "better" than those who are dead, no matter what the dead persons' rank or standing may have been. Accidentally coming across a small graveyard, she muses aloud: "He's Judge Gowan in court, a-sitting big, but I'm better'n he is. I'm a-liven and he's dead. I'm Ellen Chesser and I'm a-liven and you're Judge James Bartholomew Gowan, but all the same I'm better. I'm a liven. . . . I'm a-liven and you're dead. *I'm better.* I'm a-liven. I'm a-liven" (102, emphasis added). Her claim that she is better than a dead judge is based on the observation that being alive is somehow preferable to being dead. Her self-assertion rings as social defiance once we remind ourselves that the girl who proudly insists on her superiority over a judge is the daughter of a Southern poor white, a tenant farmer and sharecropper.

On occasion Ellen is painfully aware of the implications of her social status and angrily defends herself against such implications. When she imagines that a young man she admires will shrink back from her touch—"Lousy Brat! I'd be afraid to touch your lousy rags" (75), she is deeply embarrassed.[10] Against the shame she suffers, both real and imagined, she asserts her loveliness: "And in myself I know I'm lovely. It's unknowen how beautiful I am. I'm Ellen Chesser and I'm lovely" (3). Often Roberts may have had no more in mind than the self-doubts of a young girl who is as yet unsure of herself; these doubts gather weight, however, when they are held against Ellen's background:

> She had hung her wardrobe on the nails of the east wall, her skirt of black wool, her dark waists, and her nightdress. . . . The morning sun with its hard light searched out every meagerness of the apartment. . . . "I'm ugly," she said, "and I might as well know it and remember. My hands are big and coarse and my skin is browned and redded in the wind. . . . My face looks like the ground and my back looks like the ground with my old cloak pulled over it. I'm ugly. My hands, they're ugly and my feet have got on big old shoes. . . . No use for you to think of something pink to wear or something blue or yellow. No use to think of soft colors. You might as well wear one kind as another. Drab. Brown. Faded dark old shrunk-up anything is good enough. Why don't you just give up and be ugly? That's what you are. Ugly. That's all." (91)

Ellen's sentiments are echoed a decade later in Hagood's observations in *Mothers of the South* of the bare interiors of tenant farmers' houses characterized by "a lack of color and by drabness" that demonstrate the "sensory deprivation in the lives of developing children" and "the general cultural lacks in their environment."[11] Yet unlike her mother, whose "broken hair" hangs "in oily strings around her forehead" and whose few words edge "their way out from her mouth between the lips and the pipestem from time to time" (27), Ellen in *The Time of Man* does not give in. For a while at least she retains her hopes for "a room to sleep in where there would be pink and blue, herself reading a book by the window. Things to put in drawers and drawers to put things in, she would like. . . . Her mother would sit in a gay chair on a gallery sewing a seam . . . saying gentle things" (47). Her vision of a life filled with color haunts her for a long time: "Blue cloth would go trailing over wide stairs, down white steps . . . herself spreading and trailing through blue cloth, gentle and sweet-scented . . . all her enduring life" (72).

Roberts's awareness of the real conditions in the South gains in poignancy when we realize that she not only portrays her protagonist as a highly sensitive being, but at times gives her an almost artistic sensibility. As a child Ellen has attended school (thence her ability to write her name) and early on comes into contact with books. In her imagination she transforms her experiences into stories to tell her friends—the opening gesture of "authoring" herself is probably not accidental. Moreover, she often muses about words, trying to articulate her feelings and her impressions of the world around her: "Feeling could not take words, so melted in and merged it was with the flowers of the grass" (73).[12] Her sense of beauty (or its lack) is acute, and she judges her environment— including her friends—accordingly. Thus she muses that her friend Sebe "gave her no beauty" (134). At times she is given to a kind of painterly appreciation of the world around her, perceiving the land from different angles and in planes of color much as a painter would: "She retraced her way to the tobacco field again, climbing on fences to peer out over the land, but later she went down the wooded hill again, drawn by the strange vistas seen through the trees, framed by the trees, and climbed a stone wall which ran up on one side of a cut grain field. . . . The angles of the hills turned in strange ways and the white stones lay wide in the sun" (98). As she learns about the names and faces around her, she appropriates the land, "gathering it into her knowledge incessantly" (115).

In a key scene Roberts foreshadows Ellen's fate as a mature woman. A group of women—functioning like a Greek chorus—are gathered at a country dance and discuss the institution of marriage. Their views are deeply pessimistic; in their eyes, the only purpose of a "good" marriage is to find a provider, a "man that's got it in head to own a place and some property" (157). They wonder why girls want to get married as quickly as they can when the only fate awaiting them is hard work and an endless series of childbirths. They will lose their good looks and their health, only to discover that "under their shirts [men] are all just alike" (57). Ellen, who overhears these remarks, soon finds out that to a large extent they are true. She becomes like the women around her, praising her husband in public despite his unfaithfulness and making up stories of his generosity. Although occasionally she still feels "the vigor of her being" (349), especially when she is admired by other men, at the end she is worn out by her work and her pregnancies. "It mattered much less to her now what country she lived in, here or there, or whether there was a tree in the yard or a spring or a well for water, a stove for heat or a fireplace. A year on Robinson's place, a year on McKnight's, it was all one, or if there was a hoe to dig the garden or a mattock, a fork or a spade. If there was vermin in the hencoops, her work was doubled; it was all one" (363). After her father's death, Ellen's thoughts focus on her mother. "Ellen would merge with Nellie in the long memory she had of her from the time when she had called from the fence with so much prettiness, through the numberless places she had lived or stayed and the pains she had known, until her mother's life merged into her own and she could scarcely divide the one from the other" (383). At the end of the novel, after a violent quarrel with their neighbors, the Chessers leave the farm they have stayed on, again moving somewhere else. Their dream of owning a place—"our trees in the orchard. Our own land sometime. Our place to keep" (396)—never vanishes, but the chance that it will be realized is slim.

The change that has come over Ellen is substantial. If she now finds her life indistinguishable from that of her mother, the implication is not only that the once spirited, joyful, self-assured girl full of zest for life has turned into a hard and bitter woman. Even worse, her identity as Ellen Chesser has dissolved and she will soon fade into the anonymous mass of women who grumble about the futility of their lives. But even at this point Roberts is unwilling to concede Ellen's defeat. As she does earlier in the novel, she wavers—when another man looks admiringly at her, Ellen still walks "proudly erect . . . her eye seeing inwardly her slim shadow as it danced," and she can still live "lightly and freely with the passing days" (378).

Richard Gray is one of the few critics who has commented on the tension between the image of a highly idealized, heroic life close to the soil and a more realistic—and even devastating—view of the system of tenant farming and sharecropping that informs *The Time of Man*. He finds its origin in the discrepancy between the reality of the rural South in the 1920s and the continuing impact on the American literary imagination of Thomas Jefferson's famous praise of those "who labor in the earth" and the "rural myth" Jefferson helped to create.[13] The source of this tension may instead be in the more contemporary idealization of the "eternal" farmer that had its origin in a widespread distrust of modern technology and the general cultural pessimism of which Oswald Spengler was the chief exponent. The point is simple: once the farmer was elevated to the status of "the eternal man," a generic figure removed from the flow of history, it was almost impossible to do justice to the social and economic circumstances that determined the life he really led. Therefore, almost all the blood-and-soil literature of the 1920s and 1930s inside and outside of Germany was essentially ahistorical, substituting "myths" of the country for the brand of realism that had prevailed throughout the second half of the nineteenth century. Roberts tried to have it both ways. Although *The Time of Man* is often acutely observant of the lot of the southern poor white, it never ceases in its attempt to elevate the tenant-farmer beyond the ordinary, thereby granting Ellen Chesser's rural existence a heroic stature. Throughout the novel, the high tone Roberts employs counteracts the social picture she draws.

ACCORDING TO SPENGLER, the "true peasant" is terrified at the thought that his family and his name might one day die out. Modern man, however, especially the city dweller, does not think it his duty to continue his bloodline, for to be the last in such a line is no longer felt to be fatal. Children remain unborn, Spengler argues, "not only because [they] have become impossible, but principally because intelligence at the peak of intensity can no longer find reasons for their existence." Dorinda Oakley in Ellen Glasgow's *Barren Ground* seems to prove Spengler's point. Deserted by her lover, she loses her child and from then on finds "the physical aspects of love" repulsive.[14] The man she eventually marries is useful to her but has no real place in her life. Childless and in many ways more like a man than a woman, she has none of the traits of an earth mother. She prides herself in her independence and finds fulfillment in her extraordinary success as an agricultural entrepreneur.

Narrated more conventionally than Roberts's *The Time of Man*, *Barren Ground* nonetheless strikes most readers as the more "modern" of the two. Dorinda relinquishes the traditional ways of farming that have ruined both the soil and the people who depend on it for their living. For her success as a farmer she relies on modern, scientific methods of agriculture she has learned about in the city of New York, on efficient marketing measures and the shrewd investment of borrowed capital. "I wish I knew the science of farming," she says, "the modern ways of getting the best out of the soil" (187). With good reason she later insists that she has put "not the heart, but the head" into the land (362). In Glasgow's novel, then, the ahistorical, elemental figure of the farmer praised by Spengler gives way to a contemporary, individualized person situated "squarely within the agricultural debate" of her time and place.[15]

Dorinda Oakley is the child of "land poor" parents (6) who, despite their hard toil on the thousand acres they have inherited, lead a life of hardship and poverty. Unlike Roberts, Glasgow does not glorify their struggle. Dorinda's father, Joshua Oakley, may have "the humble dignity of one who has kept in close communion with earth and sky," but he is inarticulate and has "no language but the language of toil" (90). At times he reads like a caricature of Spengler's "eternal man." He looks "hairy and earthbound" (74), and "against the murky dawn his figure appeared as rudimentary as some prehistoric image of man. His humble, friendly eyes looked up timidly, like the eyes of a dog that is uncertain whether he is about to receive a pat or a blow" (42f). In the eyes of his daughter, "he had always stood just outside the circle in which they lived, as if he were a member of some affectionate but inarticulate animal kingdom" (206). When he dies, Dorinda feels that although he "had sacrificed his life to the land, his death made as little difference as if a tree had fallen and rotted back into the soil" (231). What ruins him, we are told, is his lack of education and his stubborn clinging to the traditional ways of farming. "I ain't one fur new-fangled ways," he tells his daughter (91), and refuses to change even the location of his tobacco beds, arguing that "they've always been thar" (43).

If the Oakleys are poor, it is their own fault, Glasgow insists, and as Dorinda's success demonstrates, their poverty can be alleviated if the right person comes along. The novel leaves no doubt that her rise from rags to riches is primarily a result of her energy and sense of enterprise. As Jason Greylock declines because of his lack of willpower, Dorinda achieves prosperity because she has stamina, intelligence, and an iron will. Ten years after her return from New York, she muses: "And there was more than hard work in her struggle; there was unflagging enterprise as well. . . . Without borrowed money, without the courage to borrow money, she could never have made the farm even a moderate success. This had required not only perseverance but audacity as well; and it had required audacity again to permeate the methodical science of farming with the spirit of adventure" (269–70).

At the beginning of the novel Glasgow carefully outlines the historical situation into which she places Dorinda's story, almost as if to suggest that we are to see her as a model whose "cool, composed, . . . competent, [and] dignified self-reliance" (201) others might do well to emulate. "Enterprise, industry, and a little capital with which to begin! That was all that one needed!" (190) Dorinda reflects while still in New York, and her success proves her right. As she follows the example of James Ellgood, who owns the only prosperous farm in the neighborhood—she is impressed by "the general air of thrift [that] hovers over the pastures" (225) and, like him, starts her venture on borrowed capital—it is safe to assume that Glasgow believes that if others in turn were to follow her example, the South would be on its way. This is true even for blacks. While Glasgow's tone is usually rather condescending when she refers to Dorinda's black workers who, we are assured, live "contentedly enough as inferiors . . . and instinctively [attach themselves] to the superior powers" (218), she bestows praise on them for being "more diligent" than the "thriftless" poor whites (217). "With intelligence and industry" (60) even a black tenant can manage to acquire his own property. Failure has nothing to do with social or economic systems, but, like success, depends on the individual. It is something "nature abhor[s]" (375).

The issue of poverty in *Barren Ground* is clouded by the fact that Dorinda seeks not only prosperity but revenge. She is a driven woman who has "drilled her energy down into the soil instead of training it upward" (275), because as a young woman she was jilted by the man she loved. The side effects of her success—her pride and arrogance, her possessiveness, her sense of power and superiority—all seem to be rooted in that traumatic experience. As Kathleen Davies has argued, she struggles with the land because of her desire to subdue and finally extinguish Jason Greylock, the lover who betrayed her. On a more abstract level we learn that, giving expression to Glasgow's "poetics of castration," she does not fight against the broom sedge but against "the ever-threatening phallic intrusion." [16] This may well be true. Yet those who focus exclusively on the role of gender may overlook the economic argument the novel makes, namely that rural poverty can be overcome if the right agricultural and marketing methods are used. Dorinda is successful both as a farmer and a businesswoman; the steps she takes to market her dairy products are highly professional ("the products of her dairy, with the name Old Farm stamped under the device of the harp-shaped pine, were bringing the highest prices in the market," 370), and she clearly makes her work pay. As a result of her efforts, the once meager and exhausted soil now yields rich harvests that enable her to lay by money that, like her neighbor, she invests in the newest machinery. Over and over again her affluence is contrasted with the poverty of her parents. While her father felt that he had "the land on [his] back," and that it was "driving" him (96), she finds satisfaction in her property and exults in the "fierce sense of possession" (271): "As far as she could see, east, north, west, the land belonged to her" (280).

The one serious reservation Glasgow makes about Dorinda's success concerns her emotional well-being. Dorinda has studiously avoided "the thriftlessness of the poor" (269), but because after Jason Greylock she has never found another lover she has failed to attain "the spiritual luxury of her parents" (327). Is Glasgow saying that poverty after all is somehow "richer" and more rewarding than prosperity? I do not think so. She does question her heroine's decision not to have children, however—undoubtedly, Dorinda's lack of "inner warmth" (319) of which she so often complains is related to her "distaste for physical love" (366). To argue that "the project of *Barren Ground* is . . . to claim women's authority absolutely—that is, make it phallus-free,"[17] is to overlook Dorinda's deep yearning to satisfy "her diffused maternal instinct" (287). At the end of the novel, Glasgow shows her to be once again close to despair, sensing "that the only thing that made life worth living was the love that she had never known and the happiness that she had missed. . . . Love was the only thing that made life desirable, and love was irrevocably lost to her" (406).

At this point *Barren Ground* reverts to the "rhetoric of the soil" typical of so many other rural novels of the time. As Dorinda feels herself "caught again in the tide of material things" (407), she experiences an almost mystical union with the land:

> The spirit of the land was flowing into her, and her own spirit, strengthened and refreshed, was flowing out again toward life. . . . Again she felt the quickening of that sympathy which was deeper than all other emotions of her heart. . . . —the living communion with the earth under her feet. While the soil endured, while the seasons bloomed and dropped, while the ancient, beneficent ritual of sowing and reaping moved in the fields, she knew that she could never despair of contentment. (408)

All of a sudden, the scientific methods of agriculture, marketing strategies, and plans of capital investment give way to "the ancient, beneficent ritual of sowing and reaping" that "[moves] in the fields" as if by itself. It is as if Glasgow had adopted the language of Knut Hamsun's *Growth of the Soil* and substituted the mythical farmer Isak, "a tiller of the ground . . . a man from the earliest

days of cultivation . . . nine hundred years old, and, withal, a man of the day,"
for the rational modern farming woman bent on the most efficient use of the
land she is cultivating.[18] This passage is foreshadowed in earlier references to
Dorinda's sense of "kinship with the land" that is "filtered through her blood
into her brain" (236) and in her general tendency to see the land in anthro-
pomorphic terms, for example, when she feels that "the land thought and felt,
that it possessed a secret personal life of its own" (211) or that it "contained a
terrible force, whether for good or evil she could not tell" (31). At times she fears
"the relentless tyranny of the soil" (38) and thinks of herself and her parents as
"products of the soil," aware that "the land [had] entered into their souls and
shaped their moods" (98). Such rhetoric permeates the novel, creating a kind
of countereffect to the rational manner in which Dorinda usually approaches
the economic problems she is faced with. Glasgow's reputation as an "agrarian"
writer no doubt emerged from this rhetoric.

The characteristic tension arising from the presence of two conflicting sentiments in *The Time of Man* also informs *Barren Ground*. Whether we consider
the land as "gendered" or not, it is obviously meant to provide some kind of
emotional value in what is otherwise a "barren ground" or spiritual wasteland.[19]
"To the land, [Dorinda] had given her mind and heart with the abandonment
that she had found disastrous in any human relation" (365), and the land in the
end rewards her in material as well as in spiritual terms. The progressive, rational approach to agriculture, it appears, does not suffice; it has to be embedded
in another conceptual mold in which farming and the soil transcend historical
contingencies. Glasgow, too, wants to have it both ways. The "spirit" of the land
and its promise of salvation must be retained, no matter how rationally the
science of agriculture is pursued.

THE IMPULSE TO EXTOL the farmer and his work in the soil affects the representation of poverty in different ways in these two novels. In *The Time of Man*
it keeps the author from going beyond acknowledging the presence of poverty;
the detrimental, paralyzing effects it has on the individual are felt only by implication. Dehistoricizing the action, Roberts barely seems aware of the social and
economic potential her material contains. Nonetheless, the systems of sharecropping and tenant farming that form the background of the novel are at least
partly responsible for the fact that in the end Ellen Chesser falls short of the
self-realization the author has in store for her. In *Barren Ground*, the image of
the timeless, heroic farmer Oswald Spengler envisioned is replaced by that of
an alert and independent woman who energetically responds to the changing
pressures with which her environment confronts her. But her success is bought

at a price. She remains childless, finding personal fulfillment only in a surrender to the soil that contradicts her earlier rationality. Modern farming methods apparently rule out the "spiritual luxury" that, despite their poverty, her parents are said to have possessed.

If neither Roberts nor Glasgow was quite prepared to pursue the economic or social implications of their material, the issue of the rural poor was taken up with a vengeance in the 1930s—no one exposed the brutality of the life of the poor in the South more dramatically than Erskine Caldwell. But Caldwell's fiction has not worn particularly well over the years, either. Is there a middle road between the sort of mythification of the soil typical of Spengler, often accompanied by an almost willful blindness to the conditions of those who work on it, and the kind of caricature Caldwell employed to propagate his message? The current ecocritical debate has not resolved the literary problem of how to write about farmers and farming in a manner that does justice to the social and economic complexity of the subject. Judging from the widely popular writings of Wendell Berry, the urge to find healing power in the soil remains. Berry no doubt would have chastised Ellen Glasgow not only for condoning, but for openly advocating a course that, as he sees it, has led to the ruin of a once healthy and happy way of life. But was the farmer's lot ever a happy one? Annie Proulx, both in her novel *Postcards* and in the collection of short stories *Close Range*, answers the question in the negative, resorting to wit and irony to prove her point. The dilemma Roberts and Glasgow were faced with in the 1920s, then, seems to keep troubling writers; those who can write about rural poverty with the sense of humor and empathy that William Faulkner demonstrates in a novel like *The Hamlet* are few in number. Neither Roberts nor Glasgow was able to shake off the romanticism characteristic of much of the literature about "the soil" at the time. Yet in many ways they were more realistic in their approach to agriculture than the Vanderbilt Agrarians (or, for that matter, than Wendell Berry) who followed them, and they certainly deserve credit for their willingness at least to acknowledge some of the dire traits of a life close to the soil at a time when to do so was the exception rather than the rule.

NOTES

1. Quoted in Lewis P. Simpson, "History and the Will of the Artist: Elizabeth Madox Roberts," *The Fable of the Southern Writer* (Baton Rouge: Louisiana State Univ. Press, 1994), 58. Glasgow commented on her intentions in *Barren Ground* in her *A Certain Measure: An Interpretation of Prose Fiction* (New York: Harcourt, Brace, 1943), 160.

2. Oswald Spengler, *The Decline of the West*, transl. Charles Francis Atkinson (New

York: Alfred A. Knopf, 1926). Atkinson's translation of vol. 2 of *The Decline of the West* was published as *Perspectives of World History* (New York: Alfred A. Knopf, 1928). I am quoting from Spengler, *Decline of the West*, 2:89ff., original emphasis.

3. When she read *I'll Take My Stand*, Roberts wrote to Allen Tate: "Our text books should be rewritten, to foster the true myths and symbols. My own region is rich. We sprang from a race of giants." Quoted in William H. Slavick, "Taken with a Long-handled Spoon: The Roberts Papers and Letters," *Southern Review* 20 (1984): 769. On Spengler's influence on the Southern Agrarians see my article, "The Southern Agrarians and European Agrarianism," *Mississippi Quarterly* 49 (fall 1996): 694.

4. Quoted in Frederick P. W. McDowell, *Ellen Glasgow and the Ironic Art of Fiction* (Madison: Univ. of Wisconsin Press, 1963), 38.

5. Cf. Shields McIlwaine, *The Southern Poor White: From Lubberland to Tobacco Road* (Norman: Univ. of Oklahoma Press, 1939), passim; also Sylvia Jenkins Cook, *From Tobacco Road to Route 66: The Southern Poor White in Fiction* (Chapel Hill: Univ. of North Carolina Press, 1976), esp. 23–26.

6. Elizabeth Madox Roberts, *The Time of Man* (New York: Viking, 1945 [1926]), 333; page citations appear in text.

7. Elizabeth Madox Roberts, *Seit Menschengedenken*, transl. Hans Reisiger (Berlin: S. Fischer, 1928).

8. Richard Gray, *The Literature of Memory: Modern Writers of the American South* (Baltimore: Johns Hopkins Univ. Press, 1977), 108; Margaret Jarman Hagood, *Mothers of the South: Portraiture of the White Tenant Farm Woman* (Charlottesville: Univ. Press of Virginia, 1996 [1939]), especially chapters 8–11.

9. For a different reading of the novel, see Constante González Groba, "Spiritualizing the Domestic Sphere: 'Infinite Affirmation' in the Inward and Outward Journeys of Roberts's *The Time of Man*," *Literature and Belief* 23 (fall 2003): 45–67.

10. Cf. also the passage when Ellen overhears Hep Bodine, the first farmer who hires her father, telling his wife to lock "every last door" against them as "it pays not to take chances with people like that on the place" (19); she feels that even the plants in the garden jeer at her—"You think I'm trash" (31, cf. 99)—and anticipates Mrs. Bodine's accusation when she reassures herself, "I got no lice. . . . I got no more lice'n she's got" (39).

11. Hagood, *Mothers of the South*, 97.

12. On Ellen's sense of language see Victor S. Kramer, "Through Language to Self: Ellen's Journey in *The Time of Man*," *Southern Review* 20 (autumn 1984): 774–784.

13. Gray, *Literature of Memory*, 109.

14. Spengler, *Decline of the West*, 2:95ff.; Ellen Glasgow, *Barren Ground* (New York: Sagamore Press, 1957 [1925]), 192, page citations appear in text.

15. The extent to which Glasgow incorporates agricultural technology considered up-to-date and progressive at her time has recently been shown in an article by William Conlogue, " 'Passion Transfigured': Barren Ground and the New Agriculture", *Mississippi Quarterly* 52 (winter 1998/99): 17–31. According to Conlogue, *Barren Ground* "de-

fines farming as a business [and] champions an urban insistence on the application of industrial techniques to agriculture."

16. Kathleen Davies, "Spinster's Revenge: Creating a Child of One's Own," *Mississippi Quarterly* 49 (spring 1996): 235, 246.

17. Ibid.

18. Knut Hamsun, *Growth of the Soil*, transl. W. W. Worster (New York: Vintage, 1972), 434. In the 1920s, *Growth of the Soil* was highly popular in the United States; see also Richard Ferguson, *Enigma: The Life of Knut Hamsun* (New York: Farrar, Straus & Giroux, 1987), 300.

19. Elizabeth Jane Harrison, *Female Pastoral: Women Writers Re-Visioning the American South* (Knoxville: Univ. of Tennessee Press, 1991), 31.

Trashing Modernism

Erskine Caldwell on the Southern Poor

JOHN T. MATTHEWS

In Erskine Caldwell's once-notorious tales of impoverished farmers in his native Georgia, readers in the early 1930s discovered a world that might have made them rub their eyes in disbelief. Two sensationally popular novels, *Tobacco Road* and *God's Little Acre*, the quick adaptation of the first into a hit Broadway show, as well as several collections of short stories, including the highly regarded *Kneel to the Rising Sun*, helped Caldwell bring the suffering of the South's poor to a nation's attention.[1] Yet where the subject of poverty turned much other fiction about the South fervently political, Caldwell startled readers with grotesque comedy; while others grew sentimental, Caldwell preferred the salacious; when others committed to the social realism of reportage, Caldwell fashioned an indigenous magical realism. Caldwell presented the starkest anomalies of any writer in his era—student of southern sociology yet purveyor of cartoonish Dogpatch pornography; self-described communist yet the most commercially successful author to his time in U.S. history; ardent supporter of leftist causes yet a constant target of skeptical fellow radicals; a writer canonized in the 1930s as one of America's greatest authors, yet hardly read today.

This chapter explores how such contradictions in Caldwell's writing and career reflect the jarring upheavals that marked the South's economic and social modernization during the 1930s, and that led him to reject the dominant modes of literary modernism. Caldwell's grotesquely lascivious yet socially committed fiction has failed to find an interpretation adequate to its profoundly schizophrenic nature. Malcolm Cowley famously gave up and simply decided that there must be two writers in perpetual conflict: the fantasist of wild humor and the social novelist. Reading Caldwell, Cowley complained, was like watching a married couple argue all weekend. But Caldwell's schizoid text may make better sense if we consider it as a manifestation of the powerfully disruptive forces of capitalist modernization on a poorly developed region. By the 1930s, in the moment of belated modernization urged on the South by federal solutions to the Great Depression, we may see the fading of southern peripheralism. The region was to be integrated more fully into a national market capitalism and a culture of consumption. The deeper capitalizing of agricultural modes of production and of labor and social relations caused dislocations for the privileged, as well as new prospects for the disadvantaged—an anxious mix of fear, hope, desire, and confusion troubled the modernizing South.[2]

Gilles Deleuze and Félix Guattari illuminate how the force of such capital on an underdeveloped regional culture tends to deterritorialize desire. Deleuze and Guattari point out that capitalism advances schizophrenically by working toward its own destruction, toward "a threshold of decoding that will destroy the socius . . . and unleash the flows of desire on [the] body as a deterritorialized field." That is, "capitalism[,] through its process of production, produces an awesome schizophrenic accumulation of energy or charge, against which it brings all its vast powers of repression to bear, but which nonetheless continues to act as capitalism's limit." Institutions that offer to code and channel desire through repression—family, church, school, nation, party, market—are authorized but also endangered by capitalism's deterritorialization of desire. The 1920s and 1930s witnessed awkward challenges to the South's long legacy of Oedipalized agencies of social repression. As recent scholarship has shown, economic opportunities not only began to dissolve the southern containment of black laborers, many of whom joined the "great migration" to the industrial cities of the North but also presented blacks and impoverished whites with chances to earn and spend their way toward new personal freedom.[3]

Caldwell develops a kind of realism that conveys the irreality of the modernizing South. His fiction depicts fundamental changes in a primitively capitalist, agrarian, and socially hierarchical world. Caldwell's schizoid text exhibits the disturbance of an emergent modernity: the disorienting intrusion of an economy organized by mass production and consumption; greater social isolation of individuals; the commodification of labor and the decline of land-based sustenance; the satisfaction of social and even somatic hungers by the vicarious experiences of spectacle. Many of the peculiarities of Caldwell's writing derive from his attempts to represent the deformations produced by modernization. The numbing repetitiveness of his style, for example, reflects the stupefaction of mass production; the salacious presentation of female bodies to voyeuristic gaze points to the stimulation and frustration of consumer appetites; the slackness of plot and syntax evoke social lethargy and despair; unstable and depthless characterization strategically identifies the authority of the market logic of exchange and equivalence over individual worth.[4]

Tobacco Road and *God's Little Acre* juxtapose the debasement of the poor before the possessors of capital with the grotesque unleashing of desire caused by the commodification of everything. The former begins with a scene of lust so open and coarse—a farm girl writhes and moans her way across the farmyard to couple with her brother-in-law—that Caldwell's purposes seem unmistakable: the desire making grotesques of his characters arises from capitalism's inadvertent devastation of institutions of socialization. Family, church, land ownership and cultivation, and self-sufficient labor lose their legitimacy in Caldwell's modernized South. The poor suffer the schizophrenia of modern capitalism with magnified clarity: shrinking means, unloosed desire. The flow of pure longing—bundled as a single polymorphous demand for sex, food, money, productive work, possessions—permeates Caldwell's fiction. In *God's Little Acre* he specifies the politically utopian dimension of this desire, as we shall see. The grounds for it have been set repeatedly in the almost unbelievable frank anti-Oedipalism of Caldwell's earlier novels.

Taboo sexual practices are the norm in Caldwell's early fiction, but what makes them remarkable is less their bizarre variety than the way they are practiced without affect, as if human beings are becoming simple desiring organisms, zombies of desire. Lust of the sort Caldwell depicts simply disregards recognized social or moral sanction, and maps a de-Oedipalizing terrain. The title character in *The Bastard* recalls searching for his mother, a prostitute who has abandoned him. He does find her, dancing in a burlesque house, but the reunion ends perversely as mother and son spend the night together in a hotel, presumably as lovers: "she did not know he was her son, or if she did know she didn't care." *Poor Fool* extends Caldwell's vision of a politicized sexual perversity.[5] The novel literalizes the post-Oedipal family by offering the Boxxes—Mr., who has been castrated by moral vigilantes for an earlier sexual indulgence; Mrs., a bordello madam who enjoys the sexual opportunities attendant to her profession and who sees advantages to the castration of all her male lovers; and daughter, who is used to lure men to the household.

By searching out the plight of those who are both exploited but also dangerously activated by modernization—the "trash" of a new order—Caldwell identifies his writing with a dominated sector of the South, itself the dominated sector of the nation. The aesthetic he evolves for such a project, however, deliberately refuses the privilege of the dominant literary fashion of the 1920s and 1930s, high modernism. Later in this chapter I propose that Caldwell situates his writing in the field of cultural production in such a way as to question the facile congeniality of elitist art and a sympathetic disposition toward the socially marginalized. Caldwell rejects the provenance of a high modernism that defends itself against modernity by isolating itself above the fray of market and

social forces. Such autonomy for the artwork, Caldwell sees, may actually reinforce a system that requires the distinction of high and low; cultural hierarchy
buttresses economic and social hierarchies. Instead, for Caldwell, serious writing must scandalize the association of great art with taste and discrimination,
which are sublimated versions of social privilege.

PARADOXICALLY, BY CHANNELING desire toward monetary pursuits, capitalist modernization deterritorializes it. The feature of modernized life that most
sharply captures this situation for Caldwell is the dominance of spectacle. Caldwell's poor represent workers under modern national market capitalism. The
desire that a culture of consumption generates overflows all recognizable forms
of satisfaction, while the essential unreality of a money economy renders action
primarily specular. The decay of community and the economic dislocations of
individuals have begun to turn social relations virtual; the loss of productive
work on the land has heightened the phantasmal practices of speculation and
the monetization of labor and nature; the want of economic means has sapped
individual will and made action a matter of idle visions; the eye has become
the organ of boundless desire in a world of material prohibitions. In *God's Little Acre*, for example, looking has become Ty Ty Walden's whole purpose. The
farmer does nothing for fifteen years but peer into holes he's dug, hoping to
spy gold. *God's Little Acre* assigns gratification to the realm of the imaginary.
Walden's plight, like that of many other small southern planters and their tenants, has so worsened by the early 1930s that the land proves useless except for
speculation. During the present "hard times" (25), one character observes, "cotton ain't worth the raising no longer" (8). The price of cotton had fallen from
16.8¢ per pound in 1929 to a mere 5.6¢ in 1931, creeping back to 6.5¢ in 1932.
With present circumstances clearly in mind (*Tobacco Road* refers to "six- or
seven-cent cotton" [229]), Caldwell wondered if farmers were to "continue a
precarious existence, living from hand to mouth, always in debt, uneducated,
and solemnly waiting for a 'better day.'"[6]

Rather than working the land as an agricultural producer, Ty Ty dreams it
will turn to gold, his fixation an antic commentary on the reach of commodity
fetishism. Ty Ty has transformed his farm into a dreamscape of unreal speculation: "There was very little land remaining under cultivation on the farm
then. Fifteen or twenty acres of the place had been potted with holes. . . . Year
by year the area of cultivated land had diminished as the big holes in the ground
increased" (14). While the novel's earliest readers were entertaining these images
in the months following its publication in February 1933, Roosevelt's first wave
of New Deal measures did in fact begin turning farms across the deep South into
holes in the ground—holes full of cash. With tobacco farmers leading the way,

southern planters overwhelmingly supported crop reduction programs.[7] The haste to raise prices for the 1933 tobacco crop already in the ground led farmers to plow under sown fields. Once the Agricultural Adjustment Act (1933) raised profitability by diminishing production, and paid farmers for what they did not grow, the unreal conditions of state-administered market recovery began to constitute a new reality. In a cruel irony, Ty Ty grotesquely mimes the strategies the New Deal had devised to rescue southern cash crop agriculture, although it was large landowners who found wealth in unplanted land, not small ones like Ty Ty, who more often fell into wage labor.

Ty Ty has internalized the unreality of his prospects so completely that he no longer even demands lived experience. The mere sight of his daughter-in-law's beautiful breasts contents him: "Why, man alive! I spend all my spare time trying to slip up on her when she ain't looking to see them some more. Seen them? Man alive! Just like a rabbit likes clover! And when you've seen them once, that's only the start. You can't sit calm and peaceful and think about nothing else till you see them again" (128). His son's preference for actual sex puzzles him: "What's got into him, anyway? He ought to be satisfied just to sit at home and look at the girls in the house" (6). Ty Ty anticipates a regime that overstimulates desires while confining gratification to compulsive watching.

Caldwell's identification of certain social deformities in the modernizing South with an emergent scopic regime aligns his fiction with later theoretical analyses of the so-called society of spectacle. Guy Debord proposed this term in 1967 for the condition of contemporary life we now recognize as postmodern— a world organized by the domination of market capitalism, the seeming commodification of everything, the circulation and consumption of images. But Debord stipulates that the contemporary society of spectacle began earlier with the adoption of "modern conditions of production," which involve the "generalized separation of worker and product," the transformation of the individual's main economic function from production to consumption, the spread of a benumbing commercial mass culture, and the "shift from *having* to appearing" (original emphasis). The spectacle organizes and authorizes the dislocations by which the "world of the commodity" comes to rule over "all lived experience": "The spectacle is *capital* accumulated to the point where it becomes image" (original emphasis). Caldwell's fiction explores these shifts in economic and social modes as broader perspectives on the particular problem of the South's poverty. The more general impoverishment of the worker's life under the modern conditions of production make the South's farmers and mill workers instances of a more global phenomenon of proletarianization. By grasping the way spectacle constitutes "the very heart of society's real unreality," Caldwell links the distress of the South's poor to fundamental changes in modern ways of life under capitalism.[8]

The spectacle form organizes one of Caldwell's most celebrated short stories about social violence in the South, "Saturday Afternoon."[9] The story describes a "spectacle lynching," that genre of murder practiced in the South as public ritual. The story recounts the slaughter of Will Maxie, an older black farmer whose success makes the townfolk think him "too damn good for a negro" (19). A barbershop rumor races through town that Will has insulted a white girl; a mob hunts him down, subdues him with chains, strings him up, sets fire to a gasoline-soaked pile of brush beneath his suspended body, and then pumps him full of lead before the corpse "go[es] up in smoke" (20). Everyone concedes that Will was a "good negro" who minded his own business and deferred to whites, but Will unsettled racial hierarchy by prospering rather than merely surviving. His accusers report that his crime—patently fabricated—has been to have "said something" to a white girl. For the unreality of this invented crime and its inhuman punishment to be accepted as real, their "naturalness" must be established through a ritual of public assent.

Blacks like Will threatened southern racial hierarchy because market forces in the 1920s and 1930s allowed some enterprising blacks to advance, and some poor whites perceived such advances to be at their expense. White planters preferred black tenants, for example, because they could be intimidated more readily; blacks gained opportunities to buy land when failing white owners needed cash; blacks were even allowed to vote in referenda on New Deal crop policies when they could be counted on to agree with their landlords. Such conditions provoked the more common form of lynching, which was a furtive act of resentment and intimidation. The less common but more socially influential spectacle lynchings took place in town squares before crowds. Besides staging object lessons against black aspiration, they indulged the frenzy of white males desperate to reaffirm declining masculinity—a mood that regularly led to the emasculation of the victim. Grace Elizabeth Hale has recently identified another important motive behind spectacle lynchings; in them surfaced white anxiety about the color blindness of an emergent mass market. Ted Ownby's *American Dreams in Mississippi* points out how national catalogs allowed Mississippi blacks to sidestep the public restrictions of shopping under Jim Crow.[10] Spectacle lynchings recommodified the black body at the very moment blacks sought to leave behind the legacy of slavery by becoming purchasers themselves rather than purchasable goods. Lynchers could try to defend the whiteness of consumption by turning the black victim into an image to be consumed—in the theater of public execution as well as in the grisly market in souvenir body parts and postcards.

Such lynchings worked as spectacle because they mediated the contradictions of modern change. The town whites in "Saturday Afternoon" live in peaceful coexistence with blacks like Will, even though the poorer ones understand they are also competing with him. But the southern ideology of racial animosity helps obscure the common victimization of poor whites and blacks by a system of land ownership and tight capital that has little to do with race. That racial ideology, which substitutes the figment of racialized sexual menace for economic conflict, gets bound to the spectacle form, which mystifies the hidden power of capital that organizes social difference, and reformulates the townspeople less as a community of interests and more as isolated consumers of images. Such estrangement allows the dehumanization of the victim and the impersonality of collective violence. Like the stinging flies around the town butcher shop that "were used to coming in and out and filling up on the fresh blood on the meat-block" (11), the lynchers draw sustenance from bloodletting.

Caldwell devotes a good deal of "Saturday Afternoon" to establishing the lynching as an exercise in consumption.[11] For example, the story painstakingly details the druggist's arrangements for the Coca-Cola concession; a boy sent to the scene hawks cold Cokes while the butcher estimates the house (18–19). We learn how much inventory is required, exactly how the boy will keep the bottles cold, and how sales are progressing throughout the story. In twelve pages there are at least four separate descriptions of the boy's vending, some as long as a paragraph. Odder yet, each instance includes a virtually identical explanation of the drink's popularity:

> Everybody likes to drink a lot of dopes when they are nice and cold. (17)

> He was getting ready to put the other cases in now and give the dopes a chance to get nice and cool. Everybody likes Coca-Cola. (18)

> It was the hot weather that made people have to drink a lot of dopes to stay cool. (18)

> Everybody likes Coca-Cola. There is nothing better to drink on a hot day, if the dopes are nice and cool. (20)

In "Saturday Afternoon" Caldwell's repetitive style formalizes the "doping" rhythms of modern advertisement and consumption. One early ad writer recalled the challenge of saying "the same thing differently three times a week for twenty years." In 1929, Bruce Barton instructed a radio audience that "the American conception of advertising is to arouse desires and stimulate wants . . . [through] constant iteration." Caldwell's prose sways through the field of advertising culture; the refrain "everybody likes Coca-Cola" portends an era of jingles, and the testimonial air—"there is nothing better to drink on a hot day"—interpolates the reader-as-consumer. Caldwell imitates the language of commercial incantation the better to implicate the comfortable consumer of his story in the feverish mindlessness necessary to make a human being an object of consumption. According to Jackson Lears, the early marketing of Coca-Cola emphasized its restorative capacities for the fatigued modern businessman. A 1907 advertisement touted its "invigorating properties," exactly suited for the lost "vim" that comes from "over-working or over-thinking."[12] When Tom awakens to take part in the lynching, he finds that "a big handful of flies had gone to sleep on [his] mouth" and stung him (14). Caldwell disquiets the reader by associating the spectacle of lynching with enflamed organs of consumption. In effect, Caldwell suggests, the modern American culture of consumption depended on the exploitation of the South's cheap labor and raw material, a situation that implicated the readers of his stories in the savagery they depict, and required nothing less than those readers' scandalization to disturb their complacency.

"Saturday Afternoon" concentrates more on the underlying unreality of market practices than on the immediate horror of Will's lynching. For the story suggests that the authority of spectacle, and hence the varieties of brutality it sanctions, rests on the conditions of modern production and consumption that it mystifies. Debord speaks of a regime in which the spectacle rationalizes the abstraction necessary to establish equivalence between commodities in the marketplace, and creates an order in which individuals accept images in place of realities they might confirm experientially, tactilely. Caldwell attends to the "trancelike behavior" exhibited by members of a society given over to spectacle.[13] The unreality of the modern marketplace stupefies the patrons of Tom the butcher in "Saturday Afternoon." No matter what kind of meat the customer asks for, Tom makes his cut from the same chunk of beef: "While you stood around waiting for the chops Tom turned the hunk of beef over two or three times businesslike and hacked off a pound of pork for you" (11). Such illusion, which neither customer nor merchant remarks, betrays "businesslike" logic, in which things sold possess only the reality conferred by the transaction. Such is the magical reality of the commodity.

Caldwell slows and breaks down the act of purchase to the point of defamiliarization. Maddeningly repetitive passages enable Caldwell to dilate critically on the surreality of commerce:

> Everybody ate Tom's meat, and liked it. There was no other butcher-shop in town. You walked in and said, "Hello, Tom. How's everything to-day?" "Everything's slick as a whistle with me, but my old woman's got the chills and fever again." Then after Tom had finished telling how it felt to have chills and fever, you said, "I want a pound of pork chops, Tom." And Tom said, "By gosh, I'll git it for you right away." (11)
>
> . . .
>
> Tom and Jim had to hurry back and open up the meat-market and get to work slicing steaks and chopping soup bones with the cleaver on the meatblock. Tom

was the butcher. He did all the work with the meat. He went out and killed a cow and quartered her. Then he hauled the meat to the butcher-shop and hung it on the hooks in the icehouse. When somebody wanted to buy some meat he took one of the quarters from the hook and threw it on the meatblock and cut what you asked for. You told Tom what you wanted and he gave it to you, no matter what it was you asked for.

Then you stepped over to the counter and paid Jim the money for it. Jim was the cashier. He did all the talking too. Tom had to do the cutting and weighing. Jim's egg-shaped belly was too big for him to work around the meatblock. It got in his way when he tried to slice you a piece of tenderloin steak, so Tom did that and Jim took the money and put it in the cashbox under the counter. (21–22)

This scene compresses the historical passage from a regime of agrarian precapitalist production in which Tom does "all the work with the meat" and people ask for what they want, to one in which the requirements of commercial transaction determine what is being exchanged and the form of gratification. Caldwell reduces the process of commodity production and purchase to the slow motion of incomprehension. It is as if he must describe a store to someone who has never bought anything. The repetitiousness forces the reader to pause over the sorcery that converts goods into commodities—cows into cash, neighbors into service employees, finally even beef into pork. Caldwell captures the strangeness of modern life as Debord describes it: "The world the spectacle holds up to view is at once *here* and *elsewhere*; it is the world of the commodity ruling over all lived experience. The commodity world is thus shown *as it really is*, its logic is one with men's estrangement from one another and from the sum total of what they produce" (26, original emphasis). For Caldwell, it is the spectacle form that mystifies modern life; the work of his fiction is to push the limits of spectacle.[14]

DEBORD ELABORATES THE eye's domination in modern life: "Since the spectacle's job is to cause a world that is no longer directly perceptible to be *seen* via different specialized mediations, it is inevitable that it should elevate the human sense of sight to the special place once occupied by touch; the most abstract of the senses, and the most easily deceived, sight is naturally the most readily adaptable to present-day society's generalized abstraction." Fredric Jameson proposes a link between spectacle and the pornographic gaze: "our society has begun to offer us the world—now mostly a collection of products of our own making—as . . . a body, that you can possess visually, and collect the images of." "The visual is *essentially* pornographic, which is to say that it has its end in rapt, mindless fascination," Jameson continues. "Pornographic films are thus only the potentiation of films in general, which ask us to stare at the world as though it were a naked body."[15] In the 1930s, Caldwell detected how the emergence of commercial mass culture, of scopic desire and consumption, and of commodity capitalism were creating a world on the way to Jameson's postmodern culture of pornography.

In one of Caldwell's most perplexing stories, "A Swell-Looking Girl" (*American Earth*), a sharecropper wishes to show off to his neighbors the charms of his new wife. Boasting that she is no ordinary country girl content to wear mill-end underthings, but one whose fancy lingerie makes her look as swell as someone in a mail-order catalog, Lem places his wife Ozzie on their porch and begins to raise the hem of her skirt before the skeptical assembly. Failing to encounter ocular proof at the expected height, Lem gradually ups the ante, finally reaching the point of desperation: "Now look!" he cries as he jerks Ozzie's dress over the top of her head. The bride's nakedness provokes much eye-rubbing and whistling among the "pop-eyed," grateful neighbors.

Lem inadvertently establishes a connection between the pornographic spectacle and the value that accrues to consumption. His wife's mail-order possessions raise her value to Lem by relating her to national merchandise from the metropolis. As a consumer herself, sadly, Ozzie has been reduced to a mannequin; absurdly, she stands motionless as her husband disrobes her, helpless before the inevitable mutual humiliation. Correspondingly, the farmer's sense of worth involves nothing but the display of acquisitions, phantasmal as they prove to be. Caldwell registers the reduction of the worker to an "inactivity" associated with a new obligation imposed by "the so-called second industrial revolution": that "alienated consumption is added to alienated production as an inescapable duty of the masses."[16] As the sharecropper and his coworkers lose their battle to the idleness enforced by loss of land and federal crop reduction programs, they are reactivated as consumers of spectacle. A community fragments into individual patrons of exhibition.

Many of Caldwell's stories portray the disorientation induced by the emergent culture of image. "Rachel," first published in 1931, presents an enigmatic story of tragic love amid urban poverty.[17] Frank comes from a family of modest means, but Rachel clearly is much poorer, and her home life remains a secret. One day, before leaving to meet Rachel, Frank completes a last chore for his mother: he spreads rat poison around their garbage cans in the alley. As the couple heads toward a restaurant, Rachel suddenly is overcome by desperate thirst; she faints, swells grotesquely, and presumably dies in the ambulance that bears her away.

Like many of Caldwell's Depression-era stories, "Rachel" delivers a fable of economic misery. Reduced to a consumption that poisons, bottom-feeders like Rachel's family invisibly suffer the humiliations of poverty, to the shame and tragic regret of those who unintentionally contribute to their misfortune. Yet Caldwell complicates the reader's relation to this figure of poverty by insisting on its specular dimension. Frank's first-person account closes with a vision: "I could see with a painful clarity the picture of Rachel, in a huge mirror, bending over our garbage can while the reflection of a unique beauty in her sinuous breasts burned in my brain and in my heart" (72). As Rachel leans against him at the drugstore counter, calling for water, Frank glimpses her reflected image. For "the first time I saw in the mirror before us a new and unrevealed charm in the sinuous grace of her breasts" (68). At the instant of Rachel's greatest suffering, Frank can scarcely act for the rapture of gazing: "I strained my eyes once more against the surface of the mirror, and once again I saw there the new sinuous beauty where her breasts began" (69). The repetitive phrasing suggests that Frank has been mesmerized before a spectacle. The mirror commands Rachel's "new, and perhaps unique, beauty" because it transfers it to image. The couple's romance has flourished in the darkened setting at the cinema, and the mirror in the drugstore presents to Frank Rachel's full beauty at the moment she begins to deaden to life, precisely as if she becomes a screen image: "There was some mysterious reflection of light and shadow that had revealed the true loveliness of Rachel. The mirror had revealed in one short moment, like a flash of lightning in a dark room, the sinuous charm that had lain undiscovered and unseen during all the time I had known her" (69). "My head reeled," Frank reports, "when the sensation enveloped me" (69). That sensation binds the pleasure of seeing with the odd deadening of another's suffering.

Because the reader's only relation to the story is through Frank's first-person narration, our position approximates his. Caldwell leaves us with the image of Rachel's hungry foraging in the garbage superimposed by the "reflection" of her "sinuous breasts" (72). Like the dazed and reeling Frank, the reader takes from the story an eroticized image of poverty, one that suggests how the consumption of spectacle refracts the experience of poverty. Rachel's breasts promise the titillating yet poisoned sustenance of images. In movies and magazines, in novels and journalism, in prose and photographs, the 1930s produced a stupefying display of human suffering. For Caldwell and others who struggled against the overly visible invisibility of the poor, this commodification of poverty provided false gratification for even sympathetic cultural consumers. It was this dilemma that tortured James Agee into the fiercely anticommercial measures of *Let Us Now Praise Famous Men*.

The mass media enforce the spectacle form by weakening the capacity of the consumer to initiate communication and by strengthening the administrative totality of the owning class. According to Debord, the emergence of a society of spectacle leads to the neutralization of the proletariat's will to revolt; it reduces the individual to contemplation, interferes with the recognition of the unity of poverty, and finally manufactures "the moment when an *image of the working class* arose in radical opposition to the working class itself."[18] A story like "Rachel" elaborates the spell of the spectacle, although it snags the reader much as Rachel's grasp does Frank: "breaking as one would a mirror, the reflection of my thoughts" (69). The "mirror's eyes" (69) stare back at the reflective reader.

THE WAGER OF CALDWELL'S major writing involves placing the plight of his particular subjects—the South's rural poor—in the context of the dominant social paradigms that organize modern life. I have characterized these in shorthand as the society of spectacle, but in order to understand Caldwell's efforts to disrupt such practices, I return to the notion of anti-Oedipalism. The goal of anti-Oedipalism is to replace the apparatus of hierarchical power—"Oedipus as the figurehead of imperialism"—with a schizophrenic sensibility. The anti-Oedipal schizoid experiences denormalization and deindividualization "through a multiplicity of new, collective arrangements against power." "Against the Oedipal and oedipalized territorialities (Family, Church, School, Nation, Party), and especially the territoriality of the individual, *Anti-Oedipus* seeks to discover the 'deterritorialized' flows of desire, the flows that have not been reduced to the Oedipal codes and the neuroticized territorialities."[19] I can only suggest here this force in Caldwell's writing, but I think the impulse of anti-Oedipalism means to shake the authority of a regime of sight and insight, scopic practices bound to the meaning and authority of Oedipus that constitute a new way to repress desires released by modernization.

Against the background of the unleashed desire evident in Caldwell's first novels, described earlier, his two best-known books zero in on the revolutionary potential of anti-Oedipal desire under modern capitalism. The most explicit example occurs in *God's Little Acre*, a novel loosely based on the well-publicized mill strike of 1929 in Gastonia, North Carolina. Late in the novel, mill worker and strike leader Will Thompson acts on his longstanding lust for his sister-in-law Griselda. After years of looking, Will declares his intentions to "lick" Griselda at last, on the night before the locked-out workers are to storm the factory and restore its power. Will's wife Rosamond and a third sister, Darling Jill, witness much of the scene of orgiastic frenzy, apparently sharing the "surge of savage excitement" that occurs with the realization of unbound desire. It is Darling Jill who embraces Will afterward, hugging him, kissing him, "pushing [his fingers] between her lips and into her mouth" (231). Will's act flouts the codes that territorialize desire in the Oedipal family. In this climactic scene he seems to copulate collectively with all three women, and he and Griselda explicitly perform a sexual act that ignores the male-genital-reproductive requirements of Oedipalized sexuality.

Moreover, as Deleuze and Guattari would lead us to expect, Will experiences

this transgressive libidinal energy as a blow against the political economy op-
pressing him and his fellow mill strikers. Before he consummates his passion,
Will furiously but methodically disrobes Griselda, making her clothes "disinte-
grat[e] in his hands like steam" (225). Will graphically addresses (or redresses,
or dresses down) his labor grievance as he destroys the mills' finished product:

> "I'm going to rip them off and tear them into pieces so small you'll never be able to
> put them together again. I'm going to rip the last damn thread. I'm a loomweaver.
> I've woven cloth all my life, making every kind of fabric in God's world. Now I'm
> going to tear all that to pieces so small nobody will ever know what they were.
> They'll look like lint when I get through. Down there in the mill I've woven ging-
> hams and shirting, denim and sheeting, and all the rest; up here in this yellow
> company house I'm going to tear hell out of the cloth on you. We're going to start
> spinning and weaving again tomorrow, but tonight I'm going to tear that cloth on
> you till it looks like lint out of a gin." (224)

Undoing Griselda's garments lets Will fantasize the unraveling of the entire system of production. Unsurprisingly, this moment feels like his most authentic
labor: "Perspiration covered his face and chest. His breathing was difficult. He
had worked as he had never done before" (225–26). Will's performance negates
the conditions that oppress him by converting work into the production of pure
desire.

CALDWELL INTENDS HIS vulgarity with serious low-mindedness. He attained
maturity as a writer during the period in which high modernism insisted upon
the autonomy of the work of art. Artists of the avant-garde developed aesthetic
means to signal their determination to make art pure, to make it "autonomous
and totally separate from the realms of mass culture and everyday life." The
formal complexity and flight from realism characterizing modern art suggest
that the "major premise of the modernist work is the rejection of all classical
systems of representation, the effacement of 'content,' the erasure of subjectivity
and authorial voice, the repudiation of likeness and verisimilitude, the exorcism
of any demand for realism of whatever kind."[20]

Bourdieu follows the lead of the Frankfurt School's analysis of modernism
by elaborating how the work of art dissents from the dominant mode of economic production. According to Bourdieu's model, modern artists who wish
their work to be appreciated by elite audiences understand they must sacrifice
commercial success to do so: they win by losing. Elite artists play for the future
reward of cultural consecration. As economic "losers," of course, elite artists
occupy a social position inferior to those enjoying wealth and political power.
This may lead many such artists to feel sympathy toward society's lesser classes.

Bourdieu observes that such a situation involves a paradox, however, because cultural producers in general belong to the segment of society that possesses capital, both economic and symbolic. Artists constitute a dominated pole—but of the dominant segment. Thus their identification with economic disadvantage must negotiate the contradiction between the artist's version of impoverishment, on the one hand, and, the advantaged site of their cultural production on the other. According to Bourdieu, elite art must invest in a principle of hierarchy in order to organize the awarding of cultural capital. Symbolic capital may form as the refusal of economic capital, but both depend on a system of competition, discrimination, ranking, winning, and losing. Artists who most want to exempt themselves from market considerations, then, indirectly reinforce the interests of the dominant fraction of the dominant class, who agree with the need for a single principle of hierarchy. Likewise, "pure" art, which shuns mass forms and popularity for the consecration of cultural legitimacy, indirectly countenances the practice of business as business.[21]

In a postscript to *Distinction* Bourdieu traces Kant's efforts to establish artistic purity by ranking "free" art over mercenary art, elevating aesthetic contemplation over the coarseness of bodily sensation, and preferring refined taste to popular enjoyment. In these aesthetic distinctions, Bourdieu argues, one may detect the concealed forms of social difference: "the theory of pure taste is grounded in an empirical social relation."

> *The social categories of aesthetic judgement* can only function, for Kant himself and for his readers, in the form of highly sublimated categories, such as the oppositions between beauty and charm, pleasure and enjoyment or culture and civilization, euphemisms which, without any conscious intention of dissimulating, enable social oppositions to be expressed and experienced in a form conforming to the norms of a specific field.[22]

Caldwell reverses the sublimation of social difference and bodily sensation that allows the illusion of aesthetic purity. By deliberately confusing high and low, spiritual and physical, serious and comic, aesthetic and carnal categories, Caldwell strategically obliterates cultural distinctions that indirectly support social differences. Bourdieu's description of the impulse to transgress a segregated field of cultural production conforms logically with Caldwell's impulse to challenge the ways of his segregated society:

> This barbarous reintegration of aesthetic consumption into the world of ordinary consumption abolishes the opposition, which has been the basis of high aesthetics since Kant, between the "taste of sense" and the "taste of reflection," and between facile pleasure, pleasure reduced to a pleasure of the senses, and pure pleasure, pleasure purified of pleasure, which is predisposed to become a symbol of moral

excellence and a measure of the capacity for sublimation which defines the truly human man.

. . .

The denial of lower, coarse, vulgar, venal, servile—in a word, natural—enjoyment, which constitutes the sacred sphere of culture, implies an affirmation of the superiority of those who can be satisfied with the sublimated, refined, disinterested, gratuitous, distinguished pleasures forever closed to the profane. That is why art and cultural consumption are predisposed, consciously and deliberately or not, to fulfill a social function of legitimating social differences.[23]

By sinking his trashy novels to the level of the social "trash" he cared for, Caldwell boldly flouted not only the social apparatus sanctioning inequity, but the cultural apparatus sustaining it.

NOTES

1. Caldwell, *Tobacco Road* (New York: Grosset & Dunlap, 1932); Caldwell, *God's Little Acre* (New York: Grosset & Dunlap, 1933); Caldwell, *Kneel to the Rising Sun* (New York: Viking, 1935); Caldwell, *We Are the Living* (London: Martin Secker, 1934).

2. Cowley quoted in Scott MacDonald, *Critical Essays on Erskine Caldwell* (Boston: G. K. Hall, 1981), 198; see Jack Temple Kirby, *Rural Worlds Lost: The American South, 1920–1960* (Baton Rouge: Louisiana State Univ. Press, 1987), for an account of the South's modernization during this period.

3. Gilles Deleuze and Félix Guattari, *Anti-Oedipus: Capitalism and Schizophrenia*, transl. Robert Hurley et al. (New York: Viking, 1977 [France, 1972]), 33–34; for recent scholarship, see Grace Elizabeth Hale, *Making Whiteness: The Culture of Segregation in the South, 1890–1940* (New York: Pantheon, 1998), and Ted Ownby, *American Dreams in Mississippi: Consumers, Poverty, and Culture, 1830–1998* (Chapel Hill: Univ. of North Carolina Press, 1999).

4. See Richard L. Godden, "Does Anybody Live in There? Character and Representative, Type and Cartoon in Caldwell's *Trouble in July*," *Pembroke Magazine* 11 (1979): 102–12, for a discussion of the defensive deployment of stereotype amid changing racial relations, and Jay Watson, "The Rhetoric of Exhaustion and the Exhaustion of Rhetoric: Erskine Caldwell in the Thirties," *Mississippi Quarterly* 46 (spring 1993): 215–29, for an analysis of Caldwell's rhetoric of exhaustion as an index of landowners' malaise.

5. Caldwell, *The Bastard* (New York: Heron, 1929), 16; Caldwell, *Poor Fool* (New York: Rariora, 1930).

6. Cotton prices in Bruce J. Schulman, *From Cotton Belt to Sunbelt: Federal Policy, Economic Development, and the Transformation of the South, 1938–1980* (New York: Oxford Univ. Press, 1991), 240 n. 48; Dan B. Miller, *Erskine Caldwell: The Journey from Tobacco Road: A Biography* (New York: Knopf, 1994), 159.

7. See Anthony J. Badger, *Prosperity Road: The New Deal, Tobacco, and North Carolina* (Chapel Hill: Univ. of North Carolina Press, 1980), and Kirby, *Rural Worlds Lost*, 56–79, for accounts of this process.

8. Guy Debord, *Society of the Spectacle* (Detroit: Black & Red, 1983), 12, 16, 26, 24, 13.

9. Caldwell, "Saturday Afternoon," *Nativity* (winter 1930); reprinted in Caldwell, *American Earth* (New York: C. Scribner's Sons, 1931).

10. On blacks voting, see Arthur Franklin Raper, *Preface to Peasantry: A Tale of Two Black Belt Counties* (New York: Atheneum, 1968), and Gavin Wright, *Old South, New South: Revolutions in the Southern Economy Since the Civil War* (New York: Basic, 1986); Hale, *Making Whiteness*, 199–239; Ownby, *American Dreams*, 75–76.

11. Cook notes that Caldwell spends as much prose on the murder as the Coca-Cola, arguing that such a treatment assures Caldwell's "narrative detachment" and suggests "the role of climate, monotony, and sheer randomness in generating the incident." Sylvia Jenkins Cook, *Erskine Caldwell and the Fiction of Poverty: The Flesh and the Spirit* (Baton Rouge: Louisiana State Univ. Press, 1991), 58.

12. Roland Marchand, *Advertising the American Dream: Making Way for Modernity, 1920–1940* (Berkeley: Univ. of California Press, 1985), 43; Barton quoted in T. J. Jackson Lears, *Fables of Abundance: A Cultural History of Advertising in America* (New York: Basic, 1994), 227, advertisement note on 159.

13. Debord, *Society of the Spectacle*, 17.

14. Though I agree with Richard Gray about the importance of the spectacle in Caldwell, I am led to read it contrariwise. Gray understands the spectacular in Caldwell as an effort to recruit the attention and sympathy of indifferent or skeptical audiences: the characters' obsessive "wanting, watching—and witnessing" are meant to stimulate the readers' reciprocal scrutiny, which will ideally allow them to see the "likeness" of these degraded human subjects to themselves. In Gray's reading, the freakish humor and social commentary are complementary. See Richard J. Gray, *Southern Aberrations: Writers of the American South and the Problem of Regionalism* (Baton Rouge: Louisiana State Univ. Press, 2000), 218, 220. I think Caldwell's writing to be more radically schizophrenic, in a way he clearly cannot control, but with the effect of measuring the force of desocialized desire as well as the regime of spectacle that offers to repress it anew. As I read it, spectacle in Caldwell is precisely the problem rather than a means to poverty's solution. When it comes to the purposes of entertainment, I think Caldwell's a lot closer to Disneyland than to Horace.

15. Debord, *Society of the Spectacle*, 17, original emphasis; Frederic Jameson, *Signatures of the Visible* (New York: Routledge, 1992), 1, original emphasis.

16. Debord, *Society of the Spectacle*, 21, 29. Rita Barnard provides a social history of the emergence of a culture of spectacle-consumption in thirties America. She rejects, however, what she takes to be Debord's more negative terminology ("the society of the spectacle") and substitutes her own alternative, a "culture of abundance," in order to emphasize "that this new form of capitalism presented not only dystopian but also distinctly utopian features." The schizoid version of spectacle I derive here from Deleuze

and Guattari accords with this view. Rita Barnard, *The Great Depression and the Culture of Abundance: Kenneth Fearing, Nathanael West, and Mass Culture in the 1930s* (New York: Cambridge Univ. Press, 1995), 14.

17. Anthologized in Caldwell, *We Are the Living*.

18. Debord, *Society of the Spectacle*, 69, original emphasis. Debord's remarks are apropos of the Russian revolution.

19. Deleuze and Guattari, *Anti-Oedipus*, xx, xxi, xvii.

20. Andreas Huyssen, *After the Great Divide: Modernism, Mass Culture, Postmodernism* (Bloomington: Indiana Univ. Press, 1986), 53, 54.

21. Pierre Bourdieu, *The Field of Cultural Production : Essays on Art and Literature*, ed. Randal Johnson (New York: Columbia Univ. Press, 1993), 44, 41, 128.

22. Pierre Bourdieu, *Distinction: A Social Critique of the Judgement of Taste*, transl. Richard Nice (Cambridge: Harvard Univ. Press, 1984), 490, 493–94, original emphasis.

23. Bourdieu, *Distinction*, 6, 7.

Marginalization and Mobility

Segregation and the Representation

of Southern Poor Whites

ROBERT H. BRINKMEYER JR.

In *Southern Folk, Plain and Fancy: Native White Social Types*, John Shelton Reed writes that most stereotypes of white southerners, firmly in place by the mid-nineteenth century, "were developed and imposed by upper-class Southerners, who wished to distinguish themselves from the lower orders of Southern society." While acknowledging how much his statement simplifies many of the complex social dynamics of the South, Reed then argues persuasively that "white Southern social types can be subsumed in a simple, two-class model, reflecting the view from the top: us or them, genteel or common, upper or lower class." If the white upper class typically went to great extremes to distance itself socially and geographically from poor whites, southern elites, as W. J. Cash and others have observed, at the same time encouraged all whites, including the poor, to embrace a racial bond that excluded blacks. This racial allegiance, what Cash called the proto-Dorian bond, of course served the interest of the elites, encouraging economically marginalized whites and blacks to remain not merely separate but antagonistic. In her memoir *Killers of the Dream*, Lillian Smith characterized the deal proposed to the poor whites by the elite as simply: "You boss the nigger, and I'll boss the money."[1] Interrogations of this deal—and other aspects of the dynamics between poor whites and the rest of southern culture—figure prominently in much of southern literature and cultural dialogue during the 1930s through the 1950s.

While the proto-Dorian bond, as Cash underscored, encouraged racial division and antagonism, stressing the differences between poor whites and blacks, the two minority groups actually shared many characteristics in the southern mythology. Indeed, except for the matter of skin color, poor blacks and poor whites are pretty similar in terms of their nature. Just to whom is Jim Goad referring in the opening of *The Redneck Manifesto*?

Don't you just hate 'em? Every gap-toothed, inbred, uncivilized, violent, and hope-
lessly DUMB one of 'em? Jesus, how can you *not* hate 'em? There's no class of people
with less honor. Less dignity. No one more ignorant. More gullible. They're a primitive breed with prehistoric manners, unfit for anything beyond petty crime and
random bloodletting. Their stunted, subhuman minds are mesmerized by cheap
alcohol, Lotto fever, and the asinine superstitions of poor-folks' religion. They stop
beating their wives just long enough to let 'er squeeze out another deformed rug
rat. They scatter their hand-me-down genes in a degenerative spiral of dysfunction.
They breed anencephalic, mouth-breathing children. Vulgarians. All of them.
Bottom feeders. They really bring down their race.

Goad's point here, that poor whites and blacks have shared a similarly constructed racial identity (though it's no longer acceptable to brand blacks along
these lines), points to a conclusion that a number of commentators, including
W. J. Cash and Lillian Smith, have made: that the South's dominant racial ideology masks issues of social justice and economic equality. "Amid all the cream-
puff rhetoric about racial equality, we've entirely lost sight of economic equality," Goad writes, never one to understate his position. "TV talking heads keep
yippie-yi-yo-ing about racial injustice, but the fact that there are rich and poor
people is accepted without question. While all the 'white' and 'colored' drink-
ing fountains may have been removed, there remain thousands of restaurants
and nightclubs and golf courses and gated neighborhoods where working-class
chumps of *any* color wouldn't be welcome. As things stand, it's blasphemous to
exclude someone from your neighborhood based on any color but green." Segregated, marginalized, and scorned, poor whites, according to Goad, are treated
by most Americans as "white niggers."[2]

No doubt few poor whites have ever seen themselves as "white niggers,"
and that's precisely the point made by Cash and Smith: the dictating southern mind is so pervasive and encompassing that economic servitude for whites
has seemed natural—that is, not servitude at all. Cash located the origins of
southern authoritarianism in the plantation system, which he saw as having established permanent frontier conditions in the South, keeping common whites
excluded from the power structure and blind to the social forces that shaped
the system. So powerful was plantation ideology that common whites were im-
prisoned in its system without even knowing it, so that "within the enclosing
walls thrown up by the plantation . . . not one in a thousand of the enclosed
ever even remotely apprehended the existence of such walls."[3] This mindless
servitude continued into the twentieth century as the plantation gave way to
the factory, the South's ideological system adapting to the changing conditions
to keep the mind and culture of the South effectively in a frontier (that is, un-
developed and un-self-critical) condition.

Obsessed by the rise of Hitler and Nazi Germany, Cash came close to describing the South as a totalitarian state in terms of its ideological brainwashing of the populace. Smith flatly called it that, arguing that while southern society didn't have a dictator, it did have a dictating idea—segregation—that effectively controlled all aspects of southerners' lives, white and black alike. For Smith, segregation was not merely the social system structuring southern society but also the psychological fragmentation shaping—or misshaping—the southern mind, and particularly the white southern mind. Southerners, said Smith, were taught from birth what she characterized as the dance of segregation; drilled over and over in the steps, rules, and regulations of segregation, southerners dutifully performed the dance without thinking about it. "What white southerner of my generation ever stops to think consciously where to go or asks himself if it is right for him to go there!" Smith asks. "His muscles know where he can go and take him to the front of the streetcar, to the front of the bus, to the big school, to the hospital, to the library, to hotel and restaurant and picture show, into the best that his town has to offer its citizens. These ceremonials in honor of white supremacy, performed from babyhood, slip from the conscious mind down deep into muscles and glands and become difficult to tear out."[4]

In their analyses of southern authoritarianism, both Smith and Cash point to a crucial element in the ideological construct for controlling the lower orders: the restriction of movement. Rather than movement and motion—metaphors for change and improvement—southern culture has traditionally celebrated a strong sense of place, an ideological choice that, as Lucinda MacKethan has argued, stands opposed to time and progress. "Time and progress belong to the world outside, or so the myth goes," writes MacKethan; "on the plantations or in the small, sleepy Southern towns that are the popular images of the South, time is held back by the places themselves."[5] This is how Robert Penn Warren in *All the King's Men* describes the dynamics of a small southern town: "In a town like Mason City the bench in front of the harness shop is—or was twenty years ago before the concrete slab got laid down—the place where Time gets tangled in its own feet and lies down like an old hound and gives up the struggle. It is a place where you sit down and wait for night to come and arteriosclerosis. . . . Time and motion cease to be. It is like sniffing ether, and everything is sweet and sad and far away."[6]

To celebrate place suggests celebrating stasis and the status quo, perhaps one reason that segregation, with its barriers controlling not only movement in space but also within the social and economic spheres, seemed so natural in the South. Segregation, as Lillian Smith characterized it, not only involved a system of psychological training (Smith's "ceremonials in honor of white supremacy") but also a social order mapped in an intricate maze, both literal and metaphoric, of signs, barriers, doors, and chasms to restrain and direct movement. Smith characterized this system in a chapter of *Killers of the Dream* appropriately titled "The Lessons":

> Few words are needed for there are signs everywhere. *White . . . colored . . . white . . . colored . . .* over doors of railroad and bus stations, over doors of public toilets, over doors of theaters, over drinking fountains. . . . There are the signs without words: big white church on Main Street, little unpainted colored church on the rim of town; big white school, little ramshackly colored school; big white house, little unpainted cabins; white graveyard with marble shafts, colored graveyard with mounds of dirt. And there are the invisible lines that turn and bend and cut the town into segments. Invisible, but electrically charged with taboo. Places you go. Places you don't go. White town, colored town; white streets, colored streets; front door, back door. Places you sit. Places you cannot sit.

For Smith, even morality was best understood in terms of entrances and exits, society's strictures mapped onto the body in order to equate and thereby enforce morality with the most basic human needs and functions. "As you are beginning to see," she imagines a child being told, "what enters and leaves the doors of your body is the essence of morality."[7] Not surprisingly, Smith characterized her efforts to dismantle segregation as opening doors, breaking down walls, and building bridges—in other words, activities promoting unrestricted movement.

Restricting the movement of poor whites and blacks is the underside of southern culture's celebration of place. Celebrating a sense of place, for all its charm to the well-off, has meant for the marginalized being kept "in their place." It's no doubt significant that one of the most visible activities of the civil rights movement was the march, people moving en masse down streets and across bridges and then up to and sometimes through police blockades. For poor whites, the designation "white trash" clearly designates their "place": on the margins of culture, on the outskirts of society where trash is generally dumped, buried, and forgotten. As blacks protested the status quo by marching, so poor whites embarked on what might be understood as marches of their own, immigrating from the countryside to town in search of work and betterment. This migration from the margins to the center of southern society typically generated fear, resentment, and anger in those elites who had once paid poor whites little or no mind. In his memoir, *Lanterns on the Levee*, William Alexander Percy heaps scorn on poor whites who have migrated into the Mississippi Delta, characterizing them as interlopers who had moved in only after all the hard work was done in making the Delta habitable. "We had changed our country attractively for them," Percy writes. "Malaria had been about stamped out; electric fans and ice had lessened the terror of our intolerable summer heat;

we had good roads and drainage and schools, and our lands were the most fertile in the world. We had made the Delta a good place in which to live by our determination and ability to endure hardships, and now other folks were attracted by the results of our efforts." William Faulkner likewise savaged poor white migration, writing in his essay "Mississippi" that "by the beginning of the twentieth century Snopeses [Faulkner's most audacious and on-the-make poor whites] were everywhere: not only behind the counters of grubby little side street stores patronized mostly by Negroes, but behind the presidents' desks of banks and the directors' tables of wholesale grocery corporations and in the deaconries of Baptist churches, buying up the decayed Georgian houses and chopping them into apartments."[8]

Written in 1954, Faulkner's words suggest the intraracial battle Jim Goad would later characterize as "white trash versus white cash," and it's clear that Faulkner believed, at least late in his career, that the traditional South was being dismantled by the influx of poor whites who were progressively gaining control of white cash. In this same essay, Faulkner characterized poor whites as boll weevils overrunning the South, an image manifesting both the economic impact of the poor white surge (resulting in large part from their mobility—like boll weevils) and the traditionalists' view of poor whites as not quite human (poor whites as insects). William Alexander Percy, in his portrayals of traditional southern culture coming undone, typically described poor whites as barbarian hordes overrunning the Delta. In *Lanterns on the Levee*, published thirteen years before Faulkner's "Mississippi," Percy conceded the battle was already lost. "Under the southern Valhalla the torch has been thrust, already the bastions have fallen," Percy writes. "Watching the flames, we, scattered remnant of the old dispensation, smile scornfully, but grieve in our hearts." Years before, the poor whites had begun arriving slowly and without notice, their alien presence camouflaged by the whiteness of their skin. "Unbeknownst, strangers had drifted in since the war—from the hills, from the North, from all sorts of odd places where they hadn't succeeded or hadn't been wanted," Percy writes of the first wave's arrival after World War I. "The town was changing, but so insidiously that the old-timers could feel but not analyze the change. The newcomers weren't foreigners or Jews, they were an alien breed of Anglo-Saxon." Following the lead of a number of social thinkers from the period who characterized the poor as genetic misfits, Percy here suggests that poor white depravity has little to do with class and everything to do with race and eugenics. And it is as genetic misfits that poor whites pose the gravest threat to southern culture, their inferior blood mixing with and permanently polluting superior strains. Percy's fears here echo those of Lothrop Stoddard, who in *The Revolt against Civilization: The Menace of the Under Man*, described the degenerate mixing of "inferior" with "superior" blood as "pacific penetration," the sullying of " 'the thin red line' of rich, untainted blood which stands between us and barbarism or chaos." [9]

Percy represents poor whites, particularly after they had started flexing their muscles by voting and organizing themselves into the Ku Klux Klan, as a manifestation of a new world revolt threatening the entire planet (a representation that also echoes Stoddard's analysis of civilization's struggle to survive under the onslaught of what he calls the "Under-Man"). Describing his feelings after his father's defeat in the 1912 U.S. Senate campaign, Percy writes that "it was my first sight of the rise of the masses, but not my last. Now we have Russia and Germany, we have the insolence of organized labor and the insolence of capital, examples both of the insolence of the parvenu; we have the rise of the masses from Mississippi east, and back again west to Mississippi. The herd is on the march, and when it stampedes, there's blood galore and beauty is china under its hoofs." With one eye on Europe, then in the midst of World War II, Percy characterizes poor whites as "Nazi paratroop jumpers" who have infiltrated the Delta and disguised themselves as everyday people. Their presence has undermined the stability of the Delta. "You never knew if the man you were talking to was a Klansman and a spy," Percy writes, by now identifying poor whites entirely with the Klan, adding that "the most poisonous thing the Klan did to our town was to rob its citizens of their faith and trust in one another. Everyone was under suspicion: from Klansmen you could expect neither frankness nor truth nor honor, and you couldn't tell who was a Klansman. If they were elected judges and law-enforcement officers, we would be cornered into servility or assassination." [10]

Almost all of Percy's portrayals of poor whites point to their transgressive mobility and the powerlessness of southern culture to stop their movement. The Delta falls to the invaders because its borders are porous; the flood of 1927, with the Mississippi River overflowing the levees, becomes for Percy the haunting image of poor white immigration and its destructive power. As *Lanterns* nears its end, so, too, does Percy's world. By the last chapter, with his sacred, unpolluted space having grown progressively smaller, Percy's only refuge is the cemetery. There, he declares: "I am with my own people. With them around me I can seem to read the finished manuscripts of their lives, forever unchangeable, and beautiful in the dim way manuscripts have." [11] Everywhere else is chaos and confusion, pollution and taboo, motion and fluidity; it's only among the dead that Percy can find peace, stability, and stillness.

If Percy's nightmare is the flood of poor whites come to town, for more sympathetic writers the nightmare is the poor whites who never get to town—that is, the poor whites who remain immobilized and marginalized, cut off from civilization and mired in poverty and ignorance. In "Distance and Darkness," a chapter in *Killers of the Dream*, Lillian Smith argues that the isolation of those living deep in the southern countryside keeps them chained to primitive fears and instincts that often erupt in violence and mayhem. "Distance and darkness and starvation and ignorance and malaria ate like vultures on our rural people not for a few Civil War years but for two centuries," Smith writes, explaining that lynchings, the most visible and electrifying manifestation of southern cruelty and violence, are signs "not so much of troubled race relations, as of a troubled way of life that threatens to rise up and destroy all the people who live it." Smith comments further on southern violence and lynchings: "Sex and hate, cohabiting in the darkness of minds too long, pour out their progeny of cruelty on anything that can serve as a symbol of an unnamed relationship that in his heart each man wants to befoul. That, sometimes, the lynchers do cut off genitals of the lynched and divide them into bits to be distributed to participants as souvenirs is no more than a coda to this composition of hate and guilt and sex and fear, created by our way of life."[12]

Smith's analysis of poor whites and their participation in acts of violence and cruelty differs dramatically from Percy's, emphasizing social conditioning rather than genetic pollution. While Percy at times backhandedly acknowledges that social conditions may have had some impact on the plight of poor whites ("the virus of poverty, malnutrition, and interbreeding has done its degenerative work"), poor whites remain for him permanently riddled with poor genetic material, making them beyond improvement and unfit for southern society. "The present breed is probably the most unprepossessing on the broad face of the ill-populated earth," Percy declares forthrightly. Smith, in contrast, saw the degeneracy of poor whites resulting primarily from their social marginalization, and she thus called for a reconstructed southern society that would integrate rather than banish poor whites (along with blacks, of course) into its fold. Always looking hopefully toward a more just and humane future, Smith understood well the tremendous barriers that then separated poor whites from other white southerners. "How can we who were fed so bountifully feel what it means to live with a mind emptied of words, bereft of ideas and facts, unknowing of books and man-made beauty?" Smith writes. "It is as difficult as for our well-fed bodies to know the weakness of one who has never had a full meal."[13] To bridge this divide, Smith believed that people had to live creatively, and by this she meant that southerners had to follow their creative intuition and imagination, rather than the lessons of their upbringing. Only by striving for psychological wholeness could southerners resist and heal the social and psychological ills of segregation.

Erskine Caldwell's fiction illustrates many of Lillian Smith's observations about poor whites, particularly with regard to the damaging effects of "distance and darkness and starvation and ignorance," and also points to the tremendous chasm, in terms of empathy and understanding, separating poor whites from traditional southern culture. The characters in *Tobacco Road*, for instance, have been utterly ground down by their isolation from the social and economic network.[14] Whatever role genetics has played in the Lesters' development, it's clear that the primary reason for their decline is their victimization by a rapacious social and economic system that has condemned them to lives of ignorance and stultification. So far have the Lesters fallen that they seem barely human, rarely thinking about or acting to achieve anything beyond basic survival. This is how Dude describes his sister Ellie May as she attempts to seduce her brother-in-law Lov: "Ellie May's acting like your old hound used to when he got the itch. . . . Look at her scrape her bottom on the sand. That old hound used to make the same kind of sound Ellie May's making, too. It sounds just like a little pig squealing, don't it?" (18).

Scraping around the yard is just about the only action the Lesters can manage; most days, wracked by starvation and poor health, they barely have the energy to move. If Percy and Faulkner characterized the subversive power of poor whites in terms of mobility, the Lesters remain fundamentally powerless. Although Jeeter and his family do occasionally make trips to town, these journeys represent no threat to society because the Lesters only seek to buy, sell, or borrow—that is, to participate in the economic system. However, such trips only further their victimization and marginalization; poorly educated and untrained in the fast-changing social and economic system, the Lesters become easy prey for the town's businessmen, as seen most clearly with Bessie's dealings with the car salesmen and Jeeter's with the loan company. In *Tobacco Road*'s impoverished world, mobility of any significance—that is, movement suggestive of progress and improvement—is thus a mirage. Nothing changes. One day endlessly repeats the day before, a cycle as numbing to the senses as Dude's repeated assault on the house with his baseball. The only motion in this world is downward, a spiral carrying Jeeter and his family further into debt, starvation, and inertia. As the narrator puts it, "Jeeter had sunk each year into a poverty more bitter than that of the year before" (65); and as the narrator further suggests, without the help of an economic system that is willing to make a place for him (and other poor white farmers), Jeeter and those like him will continue to sink:

There was no longer any profit raising cotton under the Captain's antiquated system, and he abandoned the farm and moved to Augusta. Rather than to attempt to show his tenants how to conform to the newer and more economical methods of modern agriculture, which he thought would have been an impossible task from the start, he sold the stock and implements and moved away. An intelligent employment of his land, stocks, and implements would have enabled Jeeter, and scores of others who had become dependent upon Captain John, to raise crops for food, and crops to be sold at a profit. Co-operative and corporate farming would have saved them all. (63)

Captain John moves when things go bad; Jeeter remains stuck in place.

Perhaps if Jeeter weren't such a good southerner, one who has completely internalized the southern ideology of place, he would have moved to town in order to better his family's situation. Though clearly Jeeter would never have heard of the Vanderbilt, or Nashville, Agrarians, his fierce loyalty to the land and to farming nevertheless echoes many of their ideas as expressed in *I'll Take My Stand*.[15] In defending southern traditionalism against the threat of industrial capitalism, the Agrarians typically characterized the conflict in terms of rootedness versus mobility. Southern traditionalism was for the Agrarians provincialist, extolling the values of place; the provincialist, writes John Crowe Ransom, "identifies himself with a spot of ground, and this ground carries a good deal of meaning; it defines itself for him as nature." Industrial capitalism, on the other hand, was progressivist, caring nothing about place and everything about moving forward, with no goal other than movement itself. "It is only too easy to define the malignant meaning of industrialism," Ransom writes. "It is the contemporary form of pioneering; yet since it never consents to define its goal, it is pioneering on principle, and with an accelerating speed." Speed, flux, change, motion: these are the characteristics of the modernity that the Agrarians believed threatened to overrun the South—and these are the characteristics given to poor whites on the make, those who leave the country for the city, no longer perceived as country bumpkins but as subversive agents of modernity. "It is the character of our urbanized, anti-provincial, progressive, and mobile American life that it is in a condition of eternal flux," Ransom adds. "Affections, and long memories, attach to the ancient bowers of life in the provinces; but they will not attach to what is always changing."[16]

Precisely this attachment to the land—Jeeter's thoughts, memories, and identity firmly located in the Georgia countryside—makes him appear close to being a full-fledged agrarian, despite his crushing impoverishment.[17] Sounding like a commentary out of *I'll Take My Stand*, the narrator in *Tobacco Road* says of Jeeter: "There was an inherited love of the land in Jeeter that all his disastrous experiences with farming had failed to take away. He had lived his whole life there on a small remnant of the Lester plantation, and while he realized it was not his legally, he felt that he would die if he had to move away from it" (68). While other tenants have begun to abandon the land and drift into towns to work in the mills (movement that traditionalists like the Agrarians saw as undermining traditional southern culture), Jeeter never considers leaving, despite the fact that he and his family are starving and that they have no means to support themselves. "I can't move off to the cotton mills like the rest of them do," Jeeter says. "The land has got a powerful hold on me" (16). Enmeshed in the ideology of agrarianism, Jeeter ultimately poses no threat to anyone but himself and his family. He won't move and can't move. He's in place. And ironically it's his rootedness, his failure to move, that makes him so hard for readers to come to terms with, as he appears at one and the same time agrarian hero, mindless primitive, and victimized tenant farmer—a grotesque combination that never fully comes to interpretative resolution.

Quite different from Jeeter is Will Thompson from Caldwell's *God's Little Acre*, a poor white who has rejected any notion of place (manifesting what John T. Matthews in the previous chapter identifies as the deterritorialization of desire arising from the social and economic upheaval caused by modern capitalism) and whose mobility represents, to southern traditionalists, the poor white threat to southern culture.[18] If Jeeter is a grotesque version of the Agrarians' hero, Will is a frightening manifestation of the Agrarians' nightmare of the poor white as agent of modernity. Having moved off the farm to work in the mills, Will knows that movement and placement define his power. "Back there in Georgia, out there in the middle of all those damn holes and piles of dirt, you think I'm nothing but a dead sapling sticking up in the ground," he says. "Well, maybe I am, over there. But over here in the Valley, I'm Will Thompson. You come over here and look at me in this yellow company house and think that I'm nothing but a piece of company property. And you're wrong about that, too. I'm Will Thompson. I'm as strong as God Almighty Himself now, and I can show you how strong I am" (221). A poor white *Übermensch*, Will threatens to undo the economic system; rather than being a piece of property, Will seizes property, leading the strikers to take over a shut-down factory so they can run it themselves. This revolutionary act threatens the town's economic order, the workers becoming the bosses, the dispossessed the possessors. Significantly, the insurrection begins with a border crossing, the men uprooting the fence surrounding the factory ("The fence was raised into the air—iron posts, concrete holes, and the barb-wire and steel mesh," 240) and then swarming inside.

Will's power threatens not only the economic order but also the social. Rather than living by rule and custom, Will flouts all social restrictions, single-mindedly following his own desires. Besides a manifestation of the deterritorialization of desire, Will here also embodies, again with reference to the previous essay by Matthews, forces of revolutionary anti-Oedipal desire (as described by Gilles Deleuze and Félix Guattari) standing opposed to the structures of modern capitalism. He electrifies similar desire in those around him; customary relationships of kinship and propriety dissolve before his compelling presence. People revolve around Will almost in drunk infatuation; they eventually realize through his example the emptiness of their lives, their allegiances having been bound by the mandates of accepted manners and mores rather than responding to their inner needs and desires. Ty Ty describes the restrictive and deadening life that Will directly challenges:

> "The trouble with people is that they try to fool themselves into believing that they're different from the way God made them. You go to church and a preacher tells you things that deep down in your heart you know ain't so. But most people are so dead inside that they believe it and try to make everybody else live that way. People ought to live like God made us to live. When you sit down by yourself and feel what's in you, that's the real way to live. It's feeling. Some people talk about your head being the thing to go by, but it ain't so. Your head gives you sense to show you how to deal with people when it comes to striking a bargain and things like that, but it can't feel for you. People have got to feel for themselves as God made them to feel. It's folks who let their head run them who make all the mess of living. Your head can't make you love a man, if you don't feel like loving him. It's got to be a feeling down inside of you like you and Will had." (262–63)

Darling Jill, gaining insight through her relationship with Will, underscores the subversive power he embodies when she says that "there's no particular spot in the world where real men live. . . . You can find just as many in Horse Creek Valley as you can on the Hill in Augusta, or on farms around Marion" (264). Her words here turn southern ideology on its head, denying that place, the foundation of class identification and segregation in southern culture, has any significance in determining worth.

While Will and Darling Jill move freely across both geographic and social boundaries meant to constrain them, most of the rural poor in Caldwell's world are closer to Jeeter Lester in *Tobacco Road*—stuck in place, moving beyond their little patches of earth (when they are able) submissively (if not fearfully) rather than subversively. Pluto in *God's Little Acre*, for instance, recoils from what he finds when he comes to town with Darling Jill. "He knew then he was out of place in the cotton mill town," the narrator reports him thinking. "The country, back at home in Marion, was the place for him to go as quickly as possible. He promised himself he would never again leave if only he could get back safely this time" (252).

Pluto's words here echo the ending of Flannery O'Connor's "The Artificial Nigger," a 1955 story about two poor whites and their journey to the big city.[19] "The Artificial Nigger" illustrates many of the issues discussed here, particularly those regarding the subversive power of mobility to break down the rigid boundaries marking the segregated South. In Caldwell's *God's Little Acre*, poor whites moving from farm to mill town make visible the flimsy construction of class and social boundaries; in O'Connor's story, that same movement from country to city reveals the tenuousness of an even more fundamental southern divide—that separating poor whites and blacks, W. J. Cash's proto-Dorian bond.

In "The Artificial Nigger," Mr. Head takes Nelson to the city to teach him a lesson to keep him in his place; he wants him to know that he's not as smart as he thinks he is and that he has no reason to be proud that he was born in the city. He hopes that the trip will make Nelson "content to stay at home for the rest of his life" (251). Mr. Head in this way wants to use mobility to stifle mobility; he wants one journey to restrict future journeys, knowledge gained from a journey beyond cultural borders to cement rather than to interrogate those borders. Central to Mr. Head's authority and to the cultural system he both represents and wants Nelson to follow is the barrier between whites and blacks. To Mr. Head's way of thinking, blacks and whites share nothing and live entirely separately; and more specifically, the lives of blacks have nothing to do with his and Nelson's lives. "They rope them off," Mr. Head says to Nelson, referring specifically to the segregated dining car and more generally to the entire segregated southern cultural system (256).

But rather than confirming the racial divide, Mr. Head and Nelson's trip to the city increasingly calls that divide into question. As hard as they try to distinguish themselves from blacks on the trip, they find themselves time and again in situations in which their lives are integrally bound up with blacks. At one point, having crossed over into and become lost in the black section of town, Nelson approaches a black woman for directions. He knows he should scowl at her (he's learned that much from Mr. Head), but he's paralyzed by her overwhelming maternal presence, a presence clearly lacking in Nelson's life and one that on a somatic level has nothing to do with skin color. Here's his reaction:

> He stood drinking in every detail of her. His eyes traveled up from her great knees to her forehead and then made a triangular path from the glistening sweat on her neck down and across her tremendous bosom and over her bare arm back to where her fingers lay hidden in her hair. He suddenly wanted her to reach down and pick him up and draw him against her and then he wanted to feel her breath on his face. He wanted to look down and down into her eyes while she held him tighter and tighter. He had never had such a feeling before. He felt as if he were reeling down through a pitchblack tunnel. (262)

Beyond its obvious references to sexuality and the female body, the representation of Nelson's attraction to the black woman in terms of movement through a tunnel suggests a perilous journey away from the known and the secure, a displacement both geographic and psychological. Earlier, Mr. Head, in an effort to squelch Nelson's pride at being from the city, had used the same threatening image to explain the city's sewer system, emphasizing not sanitation but degradation and danger. He tells Nelson that the sewers "contained all the drainage and was full of rats and how a man could slide into it and be sucked along down endless pitchblack tunnels. At any minute any man in the city might be sucked into the sewer and never heard from again." Nelson recoils in terror, equating the sewer with the entrance to hell and reaching a new understanding about "how the world was put together in its lower parts" (259). Falling in the tunnel voices the logic of southern racism: blacks live in and are associated with a dangerous underground world of waste and defilement. It's to save Nelson from this world that Mr. Head pulls Nelson from the black woman by whom he's entranced, admonishing him, "You act like you don't have any sense!"—that is, he's not acting by the logic of southern racial ideology (262).

If Nelson's attraction to the black woman suggests a shared humanity between whites and blacks, a fundamental connection overwhelming the socially-constructed barriers of segregation, a similar overpowering connection comes in Mr. Head's and Nelson's epiphany when they see the deteriorating yard statue. The damaged statue, its once cheerful face now exhibiting "a wild look of misery" (268), becomes for Mr. Head and Nelson a manifestation not only of their own shared misery but of the misery they share with black people. It's a stunning moment, the two frozen in postures resembling that of the yard statue itself:

> The two of them stood there with their necks forward at almost the same angle and their shoulders curved in almost exactly the same way and their hands trembling identically in their pockets. Mr. Head looked like an ancient child and Nelson like a miniature old man. They stood gazing at the artificial Negro as if they were faced with some great mystery, some monument to another's victory that brought them together in their common defeat. They could both feel it dissolving their differences like an action of mercy. (268–69)

Put another way (a way that Mr. Head and Nelson no doubt could never bring themselves fully to accept): in their blinding visionary moment of connection with blacks, Mr. Head and Nelson become in a sense exactly what they are looking at—artificial niggers, or in Jim Goad's term, "white niggers."[20]

While "the common defeat" Mr. Head and Nelson feel they share with blacks could (and should) be read in terms of the fall of humanity (O'Connor's stories, and this one is no exception, always push toward the divine), "the common defeat" also points to the sufferings that poor whites and blacks share in southern society—sufferings that poor whites, blinded by their victimization and allegiance to whiteness, typically don't acknowledge. This subversive if not revolutionary knowledge, similar to that which Lillian Smith and W. J. Cash called for southerners to embrace, in the end proves too much for Mr. Head and Nelson to accept. Like Pluto in *God's Little Acre*, who is more comfortable in the familiar world of the back country, they return home to reground themselves in the way of life they have always lived. The story ends with Nelson declaring, "I'm glad I've went once, but I'll never go back again!" (270).

"The Artificial Nigger" demonstrates that mobility and border crossings can expose the flimsy construction of the southern racial divide. But it also shows how deep-seated is the acceptance of that divide in the southern mind even when the system is seriously challenged. While Mr. Head and Nelson come to see the wrongheadedness of their interactions with each other and with black people, in the end they only reconfigure the dynamics of their personal relationship, leaving the dynamics of their relationship with black people unchanged. They are too trained in what Lillian Smith called the *dance of segregation* to step free from southern racial ideology; their return home reasserts their southernness, rejecting the subversive freedom of mobility for the restrictive security of place. As they stand by the rail line at the end of the story, the train from which they've just gotten off "glided past them and disappeared like a frightened serpent into the woods" (270). Defeating Satan? Maybe. Spurning knowledge, and specifically the knowledge to remake southern society (the creative imagination called for by Lillian Smith and the critical intelligence called for by W. J. Cash)— definitely. These poor whites aren't going anywhere, and for most southerners of their day that was just fine.

NOTES

1. John Shelton Reed, *Southern Folk, Plain and Fancy: Native White Social Types* (Athens: Univ. of Georgia Press, 1986), 23; Lillian Smith, *Killers of the Dream*, rev. ed. (New York: Norton, 1961 [1949]), 176.

2. Jim Goad, *The Redneck Manifesto* (New York: Simon & Schuster, 1997), 15, 105.

3. W. J. Cash, *The Mind of the South* (New York: Vintage, 1991 [1941]), 39.

4. Smith, *Killers of the Dream*, 96.

5. Lucinda MacKethan, *The Dream of Arcady: Place and Time in Southern Literature* (Baton Rouge: Louisiana State Univ. Press, 1980), 181.

6. Robert Penn Warren, *All the King's Men* (New York: Harcourt Brace Jovanovich, 1982 [1946]), 52–53.

7. Smith, *Killers of the Dream*, 95–96, 88. Smith's analysis of morality calls to mind many of the ideas on pollution and taboo in the work of Mary Douglas, particularly *Purity and Danger: An Analysis of the Concepts of Pollution and Taboo*.

8. William Alexander Percy, *Lanterns on the Levee: Recollections of a Planter's Son* (Baton Rouge: Louisiana State Univ. Press, 1988 [1941]), 230; William Faulkner, "Mississippi," in *Essays, Speeches, and Public Letters*, ed. James B. Meriwether (New York: Random House, 1965), 12.

9. Goad, *Redneck Manifesto*, 34; Percy, *Lanterns on the Levee*, 63, 230; Lothrop Stoddard, *The Revolt against Civilization: The Menace of the Under Man* (New York: Charles Scribner's Sons, 1923), 5, 106.

10. I do not know if Percy knew Stoddard's *The Revolt against Civilization*, but the parallels between his thoughts and Stoddard's are striking; Percy, *Lanterns on the Levee*, 153, 237.

11. Percy, *Lanterns on the Levee*, 345.

12. Smith, *Killers of the Dream*, 163–64, 163, 162–63.

13. Percy, *Lanterns on the Levee*, 20; Smith, *Killers of the Dream*, 163.

14. Erskine Caldwell, *Tobacco Road* (Athens: Univ. of Georgia Press, 1995 [1932]). Page numbers for quotations appear in the text.

15. While the twelve writers of *I'll Take My Stand: The South and the Agrarian Tradition* varied in their specific views and emphases, all no doubt would have endorsed the general analysis expressed in the book's first chapter, "Introduction: A Statement of Principles." Although unsigned, this chapter was apparently written by John Crowe Ransom.

16. John Crowe Ransom, "Reconstructed but Unregenerate," in Twelve Southerners, *I'll Take My Stand: The South and the Agrarian Tradition* (Baton Rouge: Louisiana State Univ. Press, 1977 [1930]), 19, 15, 5.

17. Jeeter and the degradation inflicted upon him by his poverty can be understood as a telling commentary on the idealism of *I'll Take My Stand*, which presents a portrait of the rural South essentially free of the poor.

18. Erskine Caldwell, *God's Little Acre* (New York: Grosset & Dunlap, 1933). Page numbers for quotations appear in the text.

19. Flannery O'Connor, "The Artificial Nigger," in *The Complete Stories of Flannery O'Connor* (New York: Farrar, Straus & Giroux, 1971). Page numbers for quotations appear in the text.

20. Goad, *Redneck Manifesto*, 105.

ABOUT THE CONTRIBUTORS

Robert H. Brinkmeyer Jr. is professor and chair of the English Department at the University of Arkansas.

Martin Crawford is professor of Anglo-American history at Keele University (Staffordshire, U.K.).

Siobhan Davis is RPS former curatorial assistant at the National Museum of Photography, Film, and Television, Bradford, West Yorkshire, U.K.

James C. Giesen earned a Ph.D. in history from the University of Georgia in 2004.

Richard Godden is professor of American Literature at the University of Sussex (Brighton, U.K.).

Richard Gray is professor of American literature at the University of Essex (Colchester, U.K.).

John C. Inscoe is professor of history at the University of Georgia.

Stuart Kidd was lecturer in twentieth-century American history at Reading University (Berkshire, U.K.). He died in September 2005.

John T. Matthews is professor of English at Boston University.

Vivien M. L. Miller is principal lecturer in American studies at Middlesex University (London).

Peter Nicolaisen formerly taught English and American literature at Flensburg University, Germany. He is now retired.

Ted Ownby is professor of history and southern studies at the University of Mississippi.

Andrew Warnes is lecturer in American literature at Leeds University (Yorkshire, U.K.).

Clive Webb is reader in American history at the University of Sussex (Brighton, U.K.).

INDEX